RW.Dox.1.85

CASEBOOK SERIES

Shakespeare: *King Lear*

D1025940

Shakespeare
King Lear

A CASEBOOK
EDITED BY

FRANK KERMODE

MACMILLAN

Selection and editorial matter © Frank Kermode 1969

All rights reserved. No part of this publication
may be reproduced or transmitted, in any form
or by any means, without permission.

First edition 1969
Reprinted 1973

Published by
THE MACMILLAN PRESS LTD
London and Basingstoke
Associated companies in New York Dublin
Melbourne Johannesburg and Madras

SBN 333 06003 2 (hard cover)

333 03441 4 (paper cover)

Printed in Great Britain by
THE ANCHOR PRESS LTD
Tiptree, Essex

The paperback edition of this book is sold subject to the condition
that it shall not, by way of trade or otherwise, be lent, re-sold,
hired out, or otherwise circulated without the publisher's prior
consent in any form of binding or cover other than that in which
it is published and without a similar condition including this
condition being imposed on the subsequent purchaser.

CONTENTS

ACKNOWLEDGEMENTS

Maynard Mack, 'Actors and Redactors', from *King Lear in Our Time* (University of California Press); A. C. Bradley, *Shakespearean Tragedy* (the representatives of the late A. C. Bradley); G. Wilson Knight, *The Wheel of Fire* (Methuen & Co. Ltd); Enid Welsford, *The Fool* (Curtis Brown Ltd); George Orwell, 'Lear, Tolstoy and the Fool', from *Shooting an Elephant* (Miss Sonia Brownell, Secker & Warburg and Harcourt, Brace & World Inc.; © Sonia Brownell Orwell 1945, 1946, 1950); Robert B. Heilman, 'The Unity of *King Lear*', from *Sewanee Review*, LVI i (Winter 1948); Terence Hawkes, ' "Love" in *King Lear*', from *Review of English Studies*, May 1959 (The Clarendon Press); Barbara Everett, 'The New *King Lear*', from *Critical Quarterly*, Winter 1960 (Mrs Barbara Jones); John Holloway, *The Story of the Night* (University of Nebraska Press); Charles Jasper Sisson, *Shakespeare's Tragic Justice* (W. J. Gage Ltd); William R. Elton, 'Double Plot', chapter 9 of *King Lear and the Gods* (Henry E. Huntington Library and Art Gallery, San Marino); Northrop Frye, *Fools of Time* (Oxford University Press and University of Toronto Press); Jan Kott, *Shakespeare our Contemporary* (Methuen & Co. Ltd and Geisenheyner & Crone, Stuttgart).

GENERAL EDITOR'S PREFACE

EACH of this series of Casebooks concerns either one well-known and influential work of literature or two or three closely linked works. The main section consists of critical readings, mostly modern, brought together from journals and books. A selection of reviews and comments by the author's contemporaries is also included, and sometimes comments from the author himself. The Editor's Introduction charts the reputation of the work from its first appearance until the present time.

What is the purpose of such a collection? Chiefly, to assist reading. Our first response to literature may be, or seem to be, 'personal'. Certain qualities of vigour, profundity, beauty or 'truth to experience' strike us, and the work gains a foothold in our mind. Later, an isolated phrase or passage may return to haunt or illuminate. Where did we hear that? we wonder – it could scarcely be better put.

In these and similar ways appreciation begins, but major literature prompts to very much more. There are certain facts we need to know if we are to understand properly. Who were the author's original readers, and what assumptions did he share with them? What was his theory of literature? Was he committed to a particular historical situation, or a set of beliefs? We need historians as well as critics to help us with this. But there are also more purely literary factors to take account of: the work's structure and rhetoric; its symbols and archetypes; its tone, genre and texture; its use of language; the words on the page. In all these matters critics can inform and enrich our individual responses by offering imaginative recreations of their own.

For the life of a book is not, after all, merely 'personal'; it is more like a tripartite dialogue, between a writer living 'then', a reader living 'now', and whatever forces of survival and honour link the two. Criticism is the public manifestation of this dialogue, a witness to the continuing power of literature to arouse and excite. It illuminates the possibilities and rewards of the dialogue, pushing 'interpretation' as far forward as it can go.

And here, indeed, is the rub: how far can it go? Where does 'interpretation' end, and nonsense begin? Why is one interpretation superior to another, and why does each age need to interpret for itself? The critic knows that his insights have value only in so far as they serve the text, and that he must take account of views differing sharply from his own. He knows that his own writing will be judged as well as the work he writes about, so that he cannot simply assert inner illumination or a differing taste.

The critical forum is a place of vigorous conflict and disagreement, but there is nothing in this to cause dismay. What is attested is the complexity of human experience and the richness of literature, not any chaos or relativity of taste. A critic is better seen, no doubt, as an explorer than as an 'authority', but explorers ought to be, and usually are, well equipped. The effect of good criticism is to convince us of what C. S. Lewis called 'the enormous extension of our being which we owe to authors'. This Casebook will be justified only if it helps to promote the same end.

A single volume can represent no more than a small selection of critical opinions. Some critics have been excluded for reasons of space, and it is hoped that readers will follow up the further suggestions in the Select Bibliography. Other contributions have been severed from their original context, to which some readers may wish to return. Indeed, if they take a hint from the critics represented here, they certainly will.

                                             A. E. DYSON

INTRODUCTION

THE entry for *King Lear* in the Stationer's Register is dated 26 November 1607, and it mentions that the play had been performed 'uppon S. Stephans night at Christmas last', that is, 26 December 1606. This is the upper limit for the play's date; the lower is March 1603, the date of the publication of Samuel Harsnett's *Declaration of Egregious Popish Impostures*, a work from which Shakespeare borrowed several elements, including the names of Edgar's devils. The old *King Leir*, which he also used, was published on 8 May 1605; this was probably an attempt to deceive the customer into believing that he was buying, not a long-disused chronicle, but Shakespeare's new play. Anyway, it claims on its title-page to have been 'sundry times lately acted'. It therefore appears that Shakespeare's play was in production early in 1605, or even in 1604; a sonnet by William Strachey, published with Jonson's *Sejanus* in November 1604, seems to have some echoes of Shakespeare's play. Some scholars still think that Gloucester's words on 'these late eclipses' (I ii 112) allude to lunar and solar eclipses in September and October 1605, but the prevailing view is that *Lear* belongs to late 1604.

Publication as a Quarto followed in 1608. This was the Pied Bull Quarto (so called because it was printed by Nathaniel Butter at the sign of the Pied Bull). This is an inaccurate and messy text, and unfortunately the Folio text of 1623 to some extent depends on it. The Folio text has some things omitted from the Quarto, but leaves out others which the Quarto contains.

There is no direct evidence as to the reception of Shakespeare's play whether on the stage or as a book, in his own day. Like *Hamlet*, it took an existing work on the same theme and transformed it, in such a manner that, like *Hamlet*, it seems to have presupposed a high degree of sophistication in its audience. But that audience, though fit for great tragedy, lacked the desire, or perhaps the terminology, to record its reactions. And by the time the desire was felt and the terminology current, the whole situation had altered. The issue now was not whether the audience was fit, but whether the play was; it had to fit the rules. And the rules of tragedy were not deduced from such plays as *King Lear*. Restoration playwrights, conscious of their own knowledge of *art*, and crediting their Jacobean predecessors, Jonson apart, only with *nature*, saw no reason why they should not 'improve' Shakespeare, introduce regularity into his chaos, polish his rough stones into jewels. Nahum Tate's version of *Lear*, of which the prefatory matter is printed in this collection, is only one of many such. Published in 1681, it was the basis of all stage performances for almost a century and a half until Macready restored Shakespeare's text in 1838.

Maynard Mack, whose essay gives the gist of Tate's highly adulterate version, rightly insists on the extraordinary resilience of Shakespeare's play – upon what I think of as its *patience*, its power to suffer interpretation, to speak, through veils of prejudice and distortion, to the predominant interests of various persons and periods. Though Tate seems absurd to us, it was possible to condone his version and still think nobly of Shakespeare. Dr Johnson, who believed that there was always an appeal open from the rules to nature, accepted 'Tatification' not because he found Shakespeare too irregular but because he found him too painful. In particular, he thought the conclusion of the play 'contrary to the natural ideas of justice'.

This is no superficial judgement. We know that Johnson dreaded the task of re-reading *Lear* for his edition. He saw that Shakespeare, whose sources provide a happy ending, brought Lear to an apparent end of his torment and then, with the death of Cordelia, denied him the restoration afforded his prototype Job and made him suffer beyond the limit of pain. Johnson rightly believed that Shakespeare had done this with deliberation; and, holding a higher view than we perhaps can of the ultimate justice of providence, he found this as much in conflict with a truth to which he desperately held as those jaunty explanations of pain and evil he condemned in Jenyns and Pope. Lear is like a felon, hanged and then cut down and revived for further torment; and to Johnson, behind whose criticism is the force of a venerable intellect and a temperament subject to strong agitation at the idea of punishment without mercy, this was intolerable. For him to prefer Tate to Shakespeare is not a failure of attention or taste but a great critic's despairing choice.

As time went by, the discrepancy between what could be seen on the stage, and what Shakespeare himself wrote, grew more troublesome, and gave rise to the opinion that the play was unactable, or anyway ought not to be acted. This view is, of course, consistent with a very high opinion of its merits, as may be gathered from Lamb's essay, and also from Bradley's. Since Bradley's day the stage has regained some of the flexibility it had when Shakespeare was writing, and it no longer seems sensible to call a play 'too great for the stage'; the modern praise of *King Lear* is not subject to such conditions. Nor are we likely to think of it as violating some established faith in order and justice. For these reasons we tend to think of ourselves as understanding the play better than the generations between Shakespeare's and our own.

We should not be too confident of this. As Mr Mack implies, *King Lear* has many 'subtexts', is patient of many interpretations. It suffers Mr Kott's apocalyptic Absurdity, it sustains Mr Peter Brook's cruel production. In choosing the Absurd or the Cruel one asks the play to complement one's own interests, and it patiently does so, for us as it did for Tate. In Shakespeare's Quarto text the servants of Cornwall are horrified by the putting out of Gloucester's eyes, and one undertakes to 'fetch some flax and whites of eggs / To apply to his bleeding face' (III vii); but in Mr Brook's production they pushed the old man off the stage. And in explaining this change Mr Brook, who might have defended it (however unconvincingly) by arguing that the lines were cut in the Folio text, simply says that he wished 'to remove the taint of sympathy usually found in this place'. *Lear* was too cruel to fit Johnson's world-view, too soft for Mr Brook's. In either case it is distorted into compliance.

There is, it must be admitted, a major difference between our attitudes to the play and those of the eighteenth century. Then there was, in aesthetic judgements as well as in ethical and scientific, a uniformity relatively little disturbed by vagaries of individual taste or theory. This could not, on the longest view, be said of us. In these matters ours is an age of plurality. More, and more various, opinions have been expressed about the play in this century than in the whole period of its life before 1900. We shall come to this matter of plurality of opinion in a moment. But it would be folly to allow it to deflect our attention from what is equally striking – that the play remains what it has been for at least a century and a half, part of our canon of master-pieces, essential to our very notion of literary value. It is thus a testimony of a certain continuity in our culture. Our plural and dissenting opinions are not of a kind that destroys that con-tinuity of valuation; to attempt that would be to attack cultural assumptions far wider than one play can represent.

There has been such an assault; but I suppose we nowadays pay as little attention to Tolstoy's strictures on *Lear* as we do to Bradley's systematic exposure of its defects and improbabilities. This is in some ways unfortunate, for Tolstoy's is, as it has to be, an attack not only on Shakespeare but upon the whole culture which receives *King Lear* as a central classic. He understands that the character of a culture, and its choice of central classics, are related, and holds that neither is exempt from the enquiries of the moralist. Most of us think of the late Tolstoy as a crank – it is the culture's judgement on him. But this does not in itself invalidate all his judgements on the culture. For example, the view that our often uncritical veneration of Shakespeare looks like the result of some form of 'mass hypnosis' is one that students have a real duty to consider. Tolstoy is often wrong as to facts, often simply intemperate or silly, but he is nonetheless talking about something important, which is why Orwell thought it worth the trouble to dig out his essay and refute it.

Orwell's essay has always seemed to me a very good one, but it is once more a duty of the reader to reflect that one can be on the right side and yet make some of the mistakes Tolstoy made.

Consider, for example, Orwell on the defects of the play: 'One wicked daughter would have been quite enough, and Edgar is a superfluous character.' There are other remarks of the same kind, and Orwell is candid about what he 'sees' when he closes his eyes and thinks about *Lear*. It is a play, evidently, without the great scene in which Goneril and Regan turn upon their father and show him what it means to value love in terms of possessions. It is a play lacking the moment, which others take to be central, where Lear, inspired by Poor Tom, tears off his 'lendings'. There is no scene on the cliff at Dover, none of Edgar's comment on the depth of human suffering (so much more profound, he discovers, than anybody can actually *say*). Edgar is called superfluous. He is not essential to what Orwell thinks *King Lear* should be, or really is, *about*. In other words, Orwell, too, chooses a 'subtext'. And because we can all do that, and have the terms, inherited or invented, to describe and defend our choice, our cultural unanimity on the value of *King Lear* is expressed in a great variety of ways.

This doesn't mean that we are always fully conscious of the partial and tentative character of our appraisals. In fact, we are more likely to represent them as striving towards an ideal of wholeness, the restoration of integrity which we know must always be partial. Commentators – Mr Hawkes here represents them – illuminate some particular word or allusion, restore some sense that we had lost of the whole effect. Armed with the vast range of interpretative instruments devised in our century, critics indicate lost patterns of theme and image. Scholars will plunder the past, as Mr Elton does, for evidence of an historical integrity, a lost Renaissance context; and Mr Kott will, as it were, counter him by emphasising the propriety of Shakespeare's tragic grotesquerie to a modern world he finds to be Absurd. All honour the integrity of the central document; all are selective, partial.

The situation of modern criticism in respect of this play is therefore a matter of aspects. It is there, worth the most concentrated attention from any point of view. Its integrity is what the plurality of views tends to establish. What is said may be the product of a more or less systematic study of literature as a whole,

as in Frye, and Knight; or the product of an historical technique, as in Elton; or a specimen of 'holist' New Criticism, as
in Heilman. One could easily multiply instances of this diversity.

However, it is not the purpose of this collection to make the
play subserve an investigation into the problems and the variety
of critical techniques (something that has been done, very use-
fully, in Morris Weitz's *Hamlet and the Philosophy of Literary
Criticism*, 1964). Here the critics ought to be servants of the play
and its readers; their business is to freshen the medium in which
the work survives, and to provide us with insights and explanations that will strengthen our own apprehension of it. This is not
a function we can be systematic about, since every reader will
absorb from the criticism what blends best with his own mind.
Nevertheless it may be useful to isolate two aspects of the criticism that follows. In so far as the play has a continuous cultural
effect we should expect some continuity of topic in the criticism; and in so far as we test its patience by varying our reading
by period and person we should be able to differentiate between
types of modern criticism.

As to the first of these, it seems clear that although the limitations of Bradley's approach are now commonplace we continue
to meditate upon some of his central problems – for example,
upon the meanings and implications of Lear's last words over
Cordelia's body. And these are essentially the crux also of Dr
Johnson's difficulties. The problems, then, are perennial; but the
solutions vary. It may seem strange, but one characteristically
modern solution to the problem of justice in the play is Christian,
or as Professor Empson would say neo-Christian. This crops up
with many different emphases, including the candidly allegorical.
Some critics consider and qualify this interpretation, others throw
it out altogether. But the topic continues to seem important, for
reasons which doubtless should be sought outside the play, in
the texture of our civilisation. Even critics who are fully in the
Romantic tradition, and seek in a work of this kind a whole self-
sufficient world, with no ethical or religious elements directly
derived from the world outside, are nevertheless unable to evade

this issue. At least this proves we are still talking about the same play.

To Swinburne there was no justice in *King Lear*, which has so much to say on the subject; there was no 'twilight of atonement', only a night of tragic fatalism. Therefore he made Gloucester's

> As flies to wanton boys are we to the gods,
> They kill us for their sport –

a central text. Bradley dissented, feeling that no work could be called great that was so totally pessimistic, and that the truth lies no more in Gloucester's attitude (which in any case he changes) than in Edgar's 'The gods are just', with its confidence in a rigidly vengeful god; rather we feel pity and terror blend with 'a sense of law and beauty' to form a quasi-religious mystery. Evil exists, and must be renounced, but the soul may be untouched by evil, and in the long run good survives; evil is self-limiting.

The merit of Bradley's approach, though we may sometimes find his terms too vague, is that he persistently treats the play as a very complex whole, containing many apparent contradictions which cannot be resolved on the ethical level. He thought of Lear as in some sense purified and redeemed, as dying in joy, though he allows our pain at knowing the joy to be baseless. Later critics are not content with this formulation; if there is mysterious suffering they want to show that it cannot be without reference to the religion of mysterious suffering. So Lear is a Christ-figure and the play alludes constantly to Christian doctrines of patience and redemption, heaven and hell. Sometimes Cordelia too is a Christ-figure, going about her father's business, harrowing hell.[1]

Clearly there are enormous cultural differences between a critic who reads the play thus, and one who refuses to do so; but they still share a problem. This was originally posed by Shakespeare himself, as we have seen. In his source neither the King

---

[1] For a summary account of Christian interpretations, see W. R. Elton, *King Lear and the Gods* (1966), ch. 1.

nor Cordelia died. There was no Edmund, no madness. The
storm was the wrath of a Christian god meting out justice.
Shakespeare offers intimations of Christian apocalypse but frus-
trates them; he makes Lear like Job, but denies him divine com-
pensations; Lear's sufferings seem to end and are then renewed.
Job curses the day he was born but Job has a Redeemer; Lear
speaks of life as beginning in misery only to continue and end in
it. Edgar teaches his father that we have to seek the strength to
bear all, and then bear more. Sunk, as he thinks, to the lowest
possible point, Edgar is at once confronted by his father blind
and miserable (IV i). In one of the most extraordinary scenes in
the whole of Shakespeare (V ii) he leaves his father to go to
battle, hoping to return with the comfort of a victory for the
right. The battle proceeds offstage, and we are left with the
sightless Gloucester to guess at its outcome. Then Edgar returns
with news of defeat, and one more rough lesson in patience:

> What, in ill thoughts again? Men must endure
> Their going hence, even as their coming hither:
> Ripeness is all. Come on.
> *Glo.*   And that's true too.

How often does one hear 'Ripeness is all' without the rest of that
line? Yet the need to carry on, the need to accept, are essential to
its meaning. The eleven lines of this scene prepare us for the
dreadful end. It is wrong to select meanings from them, especially,
I think, Christian meanings.

Perhaps, as Mr J. C. Maxwell has suggested – and it is an
insight which Mr Elton does much to confirm in his big book –
perhaps Shakespeare was always thinking of a situation in which
he would place his pagan world before the eyes of an audience
which would make its own religious corrections, knowing themselves better instructed than the ancient men on the stage. Or
perhaps we should think of the whole thing as a fictive experiment in human misery, saying, 'This is what it could, or will, be
like, when kings are reduced to mere mortality, when men's
lives are as cheap as beasts; when reason is reduced to madness,

and virtue to destruction.' But having rejected the partial interpretation we find our own explanations even more partial and generalised. We return to the basic dilemma.

The present collection includes a thoughtful study of the Christian interpretation by Barbara Everett, whose view is that the play is a product of a naturally Christian world-view, but that it lacks doctrinal and allegorical Christian dimensions. Here, as in Mr Elton's more historical survey of Renaissance attitudes to providence (not all of them by any means 'Christian'), we have necessary correctives, and as Mr Elton remarks, 'the obstacles to an orthodox theological reading of *King Lear*, in which the protagonist moves from sin and suffering to redemption are . . . formidable . . .' (*King Lear and the Gods*, p. 263). In *Hamlet*, a few years earlier, Shakespeare had christianised, to some extent, a pagan story; here he de-christianises the old *Leir*; and in both plays he is asking for, counting on, a strong response from the audience to a series of implicit questions. This is where we have to cope with the plurality of modern interpretations. If the play is of this kind, how should we expect the critics to fare who seek global explanations, or who say, 'This play is a world of its own, and we are trying to find out its physics'?

Some take the physics to be accessible to historical method, as when Mr Elton tells us about Renaissance scepticism, or Miss Welsford about the background of the Fool. But some of it requires new ways of looking, new techniques. 'Holist' approaches, of rather different kinds, are represented by the essays of G. Wilson Knight and R. B. Heilman. Each of these critics has written more about the play than is included here. Knight's famous essay here reprinted is followed, in *The Wheel of Fire*, by an equally impressive study of 'The *Lear* Universe', a work of revolutionary importance which nevertheless finally rejoins the 'redemptive' view of the play; and Heilman wrote a long book, *This Great Stage* (1948), developing the thematic approach of the present essay. Readers of Knight's essay should reflect that it preceded Kott's 'absurdist' approach by a generation, and appeared before Beckett was heard of; and it exposes to our view an authentic dimension of the work which Dr Johnson, say, never suspected. As Heilman observes, 'the unity of *King Lear* lies very little on the surface' – he himself seeks it in 'the ramifications of dramatic and imagistic constructs', and in this brief essay adumbrates a concept of that unity which he required a whole book to work out. Nevertheless, that concept is very different from Northrop Frye's, which depends more upon aspects of social and natural man than upon emanations of moral being; and other critics, hostile to Heilman's 'spatial' approach, would reject his insights with his method. The question of what the play *means* – whether it is 'pessimistic' or whatever, is inseparably related to the question of how one apprehends its wholeness, for example whether spatially or sequentially. We see only what is visible from where we stand, and what we have trained our eye to observe.

That criticism, even of a work whose value is unchallenged, should be incorrigibly plural, is a justification for a book of this kind. There are continuities of topic, but the handling must vary with the needs of periods and individuals. Kott's *Lear* is still concerned with the matter of Justice, yet it is modern *à outrance*. And this Absurd *Lear* is just as selective as the happy-ending *Lear* or the redemptive *Lear*. In our minds as readers these critical propositions dissolve like sugar into some new and also imperfect whole, from which in turn, perhaps, another soluble proposition will derive.

It may well seem too facile for an editor to take so grandly judicial an attitude to his contributors, and I agree that I have an obligation, in the last page or two available, to offer a hint of my own partial *Lear*. In this play, not for the first time, Shakespeare concerns himself with the contrast between the two bodies of the king: one lives by ceremony, administers justice in a furred gown, distinguished by regalia which set him above nature. The other is born naked, subject to disease and pain, and protected only by the artifices of ceremony from natural suffering and nakedness. So Lear is stripped, and moves from the ceremonies of the first scene to the company of a naked 'natural', the thing itself. The play deals with what intervenes between our natural and our artificially comfortable conditions: ceremony, justice, love, evil. Since our defences against nature are fallible we need to learn the patience to do without them. On the heath any shelter is a grace, and there too the ceremonious folly of the Court Fool yields to the authentic natural madness of Poor Tom. Robbed of the contrivances which make life tolerable, we are like men at the end of the world, when no hope can exist except of an end and a divine judgement; but the pain, though terrible, is never at an end, the trial can be protracted beyond our worst imagining.

Lear does not *say* such things, it only presents them. It forces us to contemplate what, day in and day out, we prefer to forget: this is what it can be like, this is what it can mean to be human. Its characters jump, as we do, to their premature conclusions: Gloucester sees men as a game for the gods, but later he calls the gods 'ever gentle'; Albany sees the operation of justice in the death of Cornwall; Cordelia says the gods are 'kind'. As in life there are indications of providence, demands upon fortitude, occasions of despair. The end is woe and nakedness. But the play is not committed; it only shows us humanity at the cliff-edge of its own imaginings. It allows Lear his beautiful delusions of a life with Cordelia. It gives to the encounter of Lear and Glouces-ter at Dover, which I take to be the highest point in the history of tragedy, the blaze of human imagination, the full power of human speech. And however we may dwell upon the detail – the fusion of such themes as nature, clothing, nothingness, sight – we shall only possess the play by a living submission to it, and by a readiness to accept that each of us, in the course of a life-time, may well – as if we too were a succession of different persons and different periods – know many different versions of *King Lear*.

FRANK KERMODE

PART ONE

Early Comments and Critiques

NAHUM TATE

T o my Esteemed Friend *Thomas Boteler*, Esq; Sir, You have a natural Right to this Piece, since by your Advice I attempted the Revival of it with Alterations. Nothing but the Pow'r of your Persuasions, and my Zeal for all the Remains of *Shakespear* cou'd have wrought me to so bold an Undertaking. I found that the New-modelling of this Story wou'd force me sometimes on the difficult Task of making the chiefest Persons speak something like their Character, on Matter whereof I had no Ground in my Author. *Lear's* real and *Edgar's* pretended Madness have so much of *extravagant Nature* (I know not how else to express it), as cou'd never have started but from our *Shakespear's* Creating Fancy. The Images and Language are so odd and surprizing, and yet so agreeable and proper, that whilst we grant that none but *Shakespear* could have form'd such Conceptions; yet we are satisfied that they were the only Things in the World that ought to be said on those Occasions. I found the whole to answer your account of it, a Heap of Jewels, unstrung, and unpolisht; yet so dazling in their Disorder, that I soon perceiv'd I had seiz'd a Treasure. 'Twas my good Fortune to light on one Expedient to rectify what was wanting in the Regularity and Probability of the Tale, which was to run through the whole, as *Love* betwixt *Edgar* and *Cordelia*; that never chang'd a Word with each other in the Original. This renders *Cordelia's* Indifference, and her Father's Passion in the first Scene, probable. It likewise gives Countenance to *Edgar's* Disguise, making that a generous Design that was before a poor Shift to save his Life. The Distress of the Story is evidently heightened by it; and it particularly gave Occasion of a New Scene or Two, of more Success (perhaps) than Merit. This method necessarily threw me on making the Tale conclude in a Success to the innocent distrest Persons: Otherwise I must have incumbred the Stage with dead Bodies, which Conduct makes many Tragedies conclude with unseasonable Jests. Yet was I wract with no small Fears for so bold a

Change, till I found it well receiv'd by my Audience; and if this will not satisfy the Reader, I can produce an Authority that questionless will. *Neither is it of so Trivial an Undertaking to make a Tragedy end happily, for 'tis more difficult to save than 'tis to Kill: The Dagger and Cup of Poison are always in Readiness; but to bring the Action to the last Extremity, and then by probable means to recover All, will require the Art and Judgment of a Writer, and cost him many a Pang in the Performance.*

I have one thing more to apologize for, which is that I have us'd less Quaintness of Expression even in the Newest Parts of this Play. I confess, 'twas Design in me, partly to comply with my Author's Style, to make the Scenes of a Piece, and partly to give it some Resemblance of the Time and Persons here Represented. This, Sir, I submit wholly to you, who are both a Judg and Master of Style. Nature had exempted you before you went Abroad from the Morose Saturnine Humour of our Country, and you brought home the Refinedness of Travel without the Affectation. Many faults I see in the following Pages, and question not but you will discover more; yet I will presume so far on your Friendship as to make the whole a Present to you, and Subscribe myself *Your obliged Friend and humble Servant*, N. TATE.

PROLOGUE

Since by Mistakes your best delights are made
(For e'en your Wives can please in Masquerade),
'Twere worth our while, to have drawn you in this Day
By a new Name to our old honest Play;
But he that did this Evenings Treat prepare
Bluntly resolv'd before hand to declare
Your Entertainment should be most old Fare.
Yet hopes since in rich *Shakespear's* soil it grew
'Twill relish yet, with those whose tasts are true,
And his Ambition is to please a Few.
If then this Heap of Flow'rs shall chance to wear
Fresh beauty in the Order they now bear,
Even this *Shakespear's* Praise; each rustick knows
'Mongst plenteous Flow'rs a Garland to Compose

Which strung by this Course Hand may fairer show
But 'twas a Power Divine first made 'em grow,
Why should these Scenes lie hid, in which we find
What may at once divert and teach the Mind;
Morals were always proper for the Stage,
But are ev'n necessary in this Age.
Poets must take the Churches Teaching Trade,
Since Priests their Province of Intrigue invade;
But we the worst in this Exchange have got,
In vain our Poets Preach, whilst Churchmen Plot.

(Dedication and Prologue to his version of *King Lear*, 1681)

SAMUEL JOHNSON

To the end of most plays I have added short strictures, containing a general censure of faults or praise of excellence; in which I know not how much I have concurred with the current opinion; but I have not, by any affectation of singularity, deviated from it. Nothing is minutely and particularly examined, and therefore it is to be supposed that in the plays which are condemned there is much to be praised, and in those which are praised much to be condemned.

General Observation. The tragedy of *Lear* is deservedly celebrated among the dramas of Shakespeare. There is perhaps no play which keeps the attention so strongly fixed; which so much agitates our passions and interests our curiosity. The artful involutions of distinct interests, the striking opposition of contrary characters, the sudden changes of fortune, and the quick succession of events, fill the mind with a perpetual tumult of indignation, pity, and hope. There is no scene which does not contribute to the aggravation of the distress or conduct of the action, and scarce a line which does not conduce to the progress of the scene. So powerful is the current of the poet's imagination that the mind which once ventures within it is hurried irresistibly along.

On the seeming improbability of Lear's conduct it may be observed that he is represented according to the histories at that time vulgarly received as true. And perhaps if we turn our thoughts upon the barbarity and ignorance of the age to which this story is referred, it will appear not so unlikely as while we estimate Lear's manners by our own. Such preference of one daughter to another, or resignation of dominion on such conditions, would be yet credible if told of a petty prince of Guinea or Madagascar. Shakespeare, indeed, by the mention of his earls and dukes, has given us the idea of times more civilized and of life regulated by softer manners; and the truth is that though he so nicely discriminates and so minutely describes the characters of men, he commonly neglects and confounds the characters of ages, by mingling customs ancient and modern, English and foreign.

My learned friend Mr Warton, who has in the *Adventurer* very minutely criticized this play, remarks that the instances of cruelty are too savage and shocking, and that the intervention of Edmund destroys the simplicity of the story. These objections may, I think, be answered by repeating that the cruelty of the daughters is an historical fact, to which the poet has added little, having only drawn it into a series by dialogue and action. But I am not able to apologize with equal plausibility for the extrusion of Gloucester's eyes, which seems an act too horrid to be endured in dramatic exhibition, and such as must always compel the mind to relieve its distress by incredulity. Yet let it be remembered that our author well knew what would please the audience for which he wrote.

The injury done by Edmund to the simplicity of the action is abundantly recompensed by the addition of variety, by the art with which he is made to co-operate with the chief design, and the opportunity which he gives the poet of combining perfidy with perfidy and connecting the wicked son with the wicked daughters, to impress this important moral, that villainy is never at a stop, that crimes lead to crimes and at last terminate in ruin.

But though this moral be incidentally enforced, Shakespeare

has suffered the virtue of Cordelia to perish in a just cause, contrary to the natural ideas of justice, to the hope of the reader, and, what is yet more strange, to the faith of chronicles. Yet this conduct is justified by the Spectator, who blames Tate for giving Cordelia success and happiness in his alteration and declares that, in his opinion, *the tragedy has lost half its beauty*. Dennis has remarked, whether justly or not, that to secure the favorable reception of *Cato, the town was poisoned with much false and abominable criticism*, and that endeavors had been used to discredit and decry poetical justice. A play in which the wicked prosper and the virtuous miscarry may doubtless be good, because it is a just representation of the common events of human life; but since all reasonable beings naturally love justice, I cannot easily be persuaded that the observation of justice makes a play worse; or that, if other excellencies are equal, the audience will not always rise better pleased from the final triumph of persecuted virtue.

In the present case the public has decided. Cordelia, from the time of Tate, has always retired with victory and felicity. And, if my sensations could add anything to the general suffrage, I might relate, I was many years ago so shocked by Cordelia's death that I know not whether I ever endured to read again the last scenes of the play till I undertook to revise them as an editor.

There is another controversy among the critics concerning this play. It is disputed whether the predominant image in Lear's disordered mind be the loss of his kingdom or the cruelty of his daughters. Mr Murphy, a very judicious critic, has evinced by induction of particular passages that the cruelty of his daughters is the primary source of his distress, and that the loss of royalty affects him only as a secondary and subordinate evil. He observes with great justness that Lear would move our compassion but little, did we not rather consider the injured father than the degraded king.

The story of this play, except the episode of Edmund, which is derived, I think, from Sidney, is taken originally from Geoffrey of Monmouth, whom Holinshed generally copied; but perhaps

immediately from an old historical ballad, of which I shall insert
the greater part. My reason for believing that the play was
posterior to the ballad, rather than the ballad to the play, is that
the ballad has nothing of Shakespeare's nocturnal tempest, which
is too striking to have been omitted, and that it follows the
chronicle; it has the rudiments of the play but none of its ampli-
fications; it first hinted Lear's madness but did not array it in
circumstances. The writer of the ballad added something to the
history, which is a proof that he would have added more if more
had occurred to his mind, and more must have occurred if he
had seen Shakespeare.

(from the Preface and Notes of his edition, 1765)

A. W. SCHLEGEL

As in *Macbeth* terror reaches its utmost height, in *King Lear* the
science of compassion is exhausted. The principal characters here
are not those who act, but those who suffer. We have not in this,
as in most tragedies, the picture of a calamity in which the sudden blows of fate seem still to honour the head which they strike,
and where the loss is always accompanied by some flattering
consolation in the memory of the former possession; but a fall
from the highest elevation into the deepest abyss of misery,
where humanity is stripped of all external and internal advantages
and given up a prey to naked helplessness. The threefold dignity
of a king, an old man, and a father, is dishonoured by the cruel
ingratitude of his unnatural daughters; the old Lear, who out of a
foolish tenderness has given away every thing, is driven out to
the world a wandering beggar; the childish imbecility to which
he was fast advancing changes into the wildest insanity, and
when he is rescued from the disgraceful destitution to which he
was abandoned, it is too late: the kind consolations of filial care
and attention and of true friendship are now lost to him; his
bodily and mental powers are destroyed beyond all hope of
recovery, and all that now remains to him of life is the capability

of loving and suffering beyond measure. What a picture we have
in the meeting of Lear and Edgar in a tempestuous night and in
a wretched hovel! The youthful Edgar has, by the wicked arts
of his brother, and through his father's blindness, fallen, as the
old Lear, from the rank to which his birth entitled him; and, as
the only means of escaping further persecution, is reduced to
assume the disguise of a beggar tormented by evil spirits. The
King's fool, notwithstanding the voluntary degradation which
is implied in his situation, is, after Kent, Lear's most faithful
associate, his wisest counsellor. This good-hearted fool clothes
reason with the livery of his motley garb; the high-born beggar
acts the part of insanity; and both, were they even in reality
what they seem, would still be enviable in comparison with the
King, who feels that the violence of his grief threatens to overpower his reason. The meeting of Edgar with the blinded
Gloster is equally heart-rending; nothing can be more affecting
than to see the ejected son become the father's guide, and the
good angel, who under the disguise of insanity, saves him by an
ingenious and pious fraud from the horror and despair of self-
murder. But who can possibly enumerate all the different com-
binations and situations by which our minds are here as it were
stormed by the poet? Respecting the structure of the whole I will
only make one observation. The story of Lear and his daughters
was left by Shakespeare exactly as he found it in a fabulous
tradition, with all the features characteristical of the simplicity of
old times. But in that tradition there is not the slightest trace of
the story of Gloster and his sons, which was derived by Shakespeare from another source. The incorporation of the two stories
has been censured as destructive of the unity of action. But whatever contributes to the intrigue or the *dénouement* must always
possess unity. And with what ingenuity and skill are the two
main parts of the composition dovetailed into one another! The
pity felt by Gloster for the fate of Lear becomes the means which
enables his son Edmund to effect his complete destruction, and
affords the outcast Edgar an opportunity of being the saviour of
his father. On the other hand, Edmund is active in the cause of
Regan and Goneril; and the criminal passion which they both

entertain for him induces them to execute justice on each other
and on themselves. The laws of the drama have therefore been
sufficiently complied with; but that is the least: it is the very
combination which constitutes the sublime beauty of the work.
The two cases resemble each other in the main: an infatuated
father is blind towards his well-disposed child, and the unnatural children, whom he prefers, requite him by the ruin of all
his happiness. But all the circumstances are so different, that
these stories, while they each make a correspondent impression
on the heart, form a complete contrast for the imagination. Were
Lear alone to suffer from his daughters, the impression would be
limited to the powerful compassion felt by us for his private
misfortune. But two such unheard-of examples taking place at
the same time have the appearance of a great commotion in the
moral world: the picture becomes gigantic, and fills us with such
alarm as we should entertain at the idea that the heavenly bodies
might one day fall from their appointed orbits. To save in some
degree the honour of human nature, Shakspeare never wishes his
spectators to forget that the story takes place in a dreary and barbarous age: he lays particular stress on the circumstance that the
Britons of that day were still heathens, although he has not made
all the remaining circumstances to coincide learnedly with the
time which he has chosen. From this point of view we must judge
of many coarsenesses in expression and manners; for instance, the
immodest manner in which Gloster acknowledges his bastard,
Kent's quarrel with the Steward, and more especially the cruelty
personally inflicted on Gloster by the Duke of Cornwall. Even
the virtue of the honest Kent bears the stamp of an iron age,
in which the good and the bad display the same uncontrollable
energy. Great qualities have not been superfluously assigned to
the King; the poet could command our sympathy for his situation, without concealing what he had done to bring himself into
it. Lear is choleric, overbearing, and almost childish from age,
when he drives out his youngest daughter because she will not
join in the hypocritical exaggerations of her sisters. But he has a
warm and affectionate heart, which is susceptible of the most
fervent gratitude; and even rays of a high and kingly disposition

burst forth from the eclipse of his understanding. Of Cordelia's heavenly beauty of soul, painted in so few words, I will not venture to speak; she can only be named in the same breath with Antigone. Her death has been thought too cruel; and in England the piece is in acting so far altered that she remains victorious and happy. I must own, I cannot conceive what ideas of art and dramatic connexion those persons have who suppose that we can at pleasure tack a double conclusion to a tragedy; a melancholy one for hard-hearted spectators, and a happy one for souls of a softer mould. After surviving so many sufferings, Lear can only die; and what more truly tragic end for him than to die from grief for the death of Cordelia? and if he is also to be saved and to pass the remainder of his days in happiness, the whole loses its signification. According to Shakspeare's plan the guilty, it is true, are all punished, for wickedness destroys itself; but the virtues that would bring help and succour are everywhere too late, or overmatched by the cunning activity of malice. The persons of this drama have only such a faint belief in Providence as heathens may be supposed to have; and the poet here wishes to show us that this belief requires a wider range than the dark pilgrimage on earth to be established in full extent.

(from *Lectures on Dramatic Art and Literature*, 1811)

S. T. COLERIDGE

OF all Shakespeare's plays *Macbeth* is the most rapid, *Hamlet* the slowest, in movement. *Lear* combines length with rapidity – like the hurricane and the whirlpool, absorbing while it advances. It begins as a stormy day in summer, with brightness; but that brightness is lurid, and anticipates the tempest.

I i 1–6

> *Kent.* I thought the king had more affected the Duke of
> Albany than Cornwall.
> *Glou.* It did always seem so to us: but now, in the division of

the kingdom, it appears not which of the dukes he values most; for equalities are so weighed that curiosity in neither can make choice of either's moiety.

It was not without forethought, and it is not without its due significance, that the triple division is stated here as already determined and in all its particulars, previously to the trial of professions, as the relative rewards of which the daughters were to be made to consider their several portions. The strange, yet by no means unnatural, mixture of selfishness, sensibility, and habit of feeling derived from and fostered by the particular rank and usages of the individual; the intense desire to be intensely beloved, selfish, and yet characteristic of the selfishness of a loving and kindly nature – a feeble selfishness, self-supportless and leaning for all pleasure on another's breast; the selfish craving after a sympathy with a prodigal disinterestedness, contradicted by its own ostentation and the mode and nature of its claims; the anxiety, the distrust, the jealousy, which more or less accompany all selfish affections, and are among the surest contradistinctions of mere fondness from love, and which originate Lear's eager wish to enjoy his daughter's violent professions, while the inveterate habits of sovereignty convert the wish into claim and positive right, and the incompliance with it into crime and treason; these facts, these passions, these moral verities, on which the whole tragedy is founded, are all prepared for, and will to the retrospect be found implied in, these first four or five lines of the play. They let us know that the trial is but a trick; and that the grossness of the old king's rage is in part the natural result of a silly trick suddenly and most unexpectedly baffled and disappointed. This having been provided in the fewest words, in a natural reply to as natural a question, which yet answers a secondary purpose of attracting our attention to the difference or diversity between the characters of Cornwall and Albany; the premises and data, as it were, having been thus afforded for our after-insight into the mind and mood of the person whose character, passions, and sufferings are the main *subject-matter* of the play; from Lear, the *persona patiens* of his drama, Shakespeare passes without delay to the second in importance, to the main *agent* and prime mover – introduces Edmund to our acquaintance, and with the same felicity of judgement, in the same easy, natural way, prepares us for his character in the seemingly casual communication of its origin and occasion. From the first drawing up of the curtain he has stood before us in the united strength and beauty of earliest manhood. Our eyes have been questioning him. Gifted thus with high advantages of *person*, and further endowed by nature with a powerful intellect and a strong energetic will, even without any concurrence of circumstances and accident, pride will be the sin that most easily besets him. But he is the known and acknowledged son of the princely Gloster. Edmund, therefore, has both the germ of pride and the conditions best fitted to evolve and ripen it into a predominant feeling. Yet hitherto no reason appears why it should be other than the not unusual pride of person, talent, and birth, a pride auxiliary if not akin to many virtues, and the natural ally of honorable impulses. But alas! in his own presence his own father takes shame to himself for the frank avowal that he is his father – has 'blushed so often to acknowledge him that he is now braz'd to it'. He hears his mother and the circumstances of his birth spoken of with a most degrading and licentious levity – described as a wanton by her own paramour, and the remembrance of the animal sting, the low criminal gratifications connected with her wantonness and prostituted beauty assigned as the reason why 'the whoreson must be acknowledged'. This, and the consciousness of its notoriety – the gnawing conviction that every shew of respect is an effort of courtesy which recalls while it represses a contrary feeling – this is the ever-trickling flow of wormwood and gall into the wounds of pride, the corrosive virus which inoculates pride with a venom not its own, with envy, hatred, a lust of that power which in its blaze of radiance would hide the dark spots on his disk, with pangs of shame, personally undeserved and therefore felt as wrongs, and a blind ferment of vindictive workings towards the occasions and causes, especially towards a brother whose stainless birth and lawful honors were the constant remembrancers of *his* debasement, and were ever in the way to prevent all chance of its being unknown or overlooked and forgotten. Add to this that with excellent judgement, and provident for the claims of the moral sense, for that which relatively to the drama is called poetic justice; and as the fittest means for reconciling the feelings of the spectators to the horrors of Gloster's after sufferings – at least, of rendering them somewhat less unendurable (for I will not disguise my conviction that in this one point the tragic has been urged beyond the outermost mark and *ne plus ultra* of the dramatic) – Shakespeare has precluded all excuse and palliation of the guilt incurred by both the parents of the base-born Edmund by Gloster's confession that he was at the time a married man and already blest with a lawful heir of his fortunes. The mournful alienation of brotherly love occasioned by primogeniture in noble families, or rather by the unnecessary distinctions engrafted thereon, and this in children of the same stock, is still almost proverbial on the continent – especially, as I know from my own observation, in the south of Europe – and appears to have been scarcely less common in our own island before the Revolution of 1688, if we may judge from the characters and sentiments so frequent in our elder comedies – the younger brother, for instance, in Beaumont and Fletcher's *Scornful Lady*, on one side, and the Oliver in Shakespeare's own *As You Like It*, on the other. Need it be said how heavy an aggravation the stain of bastardy must have been, were it only that the younger brother was liable to hear his own dishonor and his mother's infamy related by his father with an excusing shrug of the shoulders, and in a tone betwixt waggery and shame.

By the circumstances here enumerated as so many predisposing causes, Edmund's character might well be deem'd already sufficiently explained and prepared for. But in this tragedy the story or fable constrained Shakespeare to introduce wickedness in an outrageous form, in Regan and Goneril. He had read nature too heedfully not to know that courage, intellect, and strength of character were the most impressive forms of power, and that to power in itself, without reference to any moral end, an inevitable admiration and complacency appertains, whether it be displayed in the conquests of a Napoleon or Tamerlane, or in the foam and thunder of a cataract. But in the display of such a character it was of the highest importance to prevent the guilt from passing into utter *monstrosity* – which again depends on the presence or absence of causes and temptations sufficient to *account* for the wickedness, without the necessity of recurring to a thorough fiendishness of nature for its origination. For such are the appointed relations of intellectual power to truth, and of truth to goodness, that it becomes both morally and poetically unsafe to present what is admirable – what our nature compels us to admire – in the mind, and what is most detestable in the heart, as co-existing in the same individual without any apparent connection, or any modification of the one by the other. That Shakespeare has in one instance, that of Iago, approached to this, and that he has done it successfully, is perhaps the most astonishing proof of his genius, and the opulence of its resources. But in the present tragedy, in which he was compelled to present a Goneril and Regan, it was most carefully to be avoided; and, therefore, the one only conceivable addition to the inauspicious influences on the preformation of Edmund's character is given in the information that all the kindly counteractions to the mischievous feelings of shame that might have been derived from co-domestication with Edgar and their common father, had been cut off by an absence from home and a foreign education from boyhood to the present time, and the prospect of its continuance as if to preclude all risk of his interference with the father's views for the elder and legitimate son:

He hath been out nine years, and away he shall again.

It is well worthy notice, that *Lear* is the only serious performance of Shakespeare the interest and situations of which are derived from the assumption of a gross improbability; whereas Beaumont and Fletcher's tragedies are, almost all, founded on some out-of-the-way accident or exception to the general experience of mankind. But observe the matchless judgement of Shakespeare! First, improbable as the conduct of Lear is, in the first scene, yet it was an old story, rooted in the popular faith – a thing taken for granted already, and consequently without any of the *effects* of improbability. Secondly, it is merely the canvas to the characters and passions, a mere *occasion* – not (as in Beaumont and Fletcher) perpetually recurring, as the cause and *sine qua non* of the incidents and emotions. Let the first scene of *Lear* have been lost, and let it be only understood that a fond father had been duped by hypocritical professions of love and duty on the part of two daughters to disinherit a third, previously, and deservedly, more dear to him, and all the rest of the tragedy would retain its interest undiminished, and be perfectly intelligible. The *accidental* is nowhere the groundwork of the passions, but the κάθογον, that which in all ages has been and ever will be close and native to the heart of man – parental anguish from filial ingratitude, the genuineness of worth, tho' coffered in bluntness, the vileness of smooth iniquity. Perhaps I ought to have added the *Merchant of Venice*; but here too the same remarks apply. It was an old tale; and substitute any other danger than that of the pound of flesh (the circumstance in which the improbability lies), yet all the situations and the emotions appertaining to them remain equally excellent and appropriate.

1 i 84–92

> *Lear.* . . . what can you say to draw
>   A third more opulent than your sisters? Speak.
> *Cor.* Nothing, my lord.
> *Lear.* Nothing!
> *Cor.* Nothing.
> *Lear.* Nothing will come of nothing: speak again.
> *Cor.* Unhappy that I am, I cannot heave
>   My heart into my mouth: I love your majesty
>   According to my bond; nor more nor less.

Something of disgust at the ruthless hypocrisy of her sisters, some little faulty admixture of pride and sullenness in Cordelia's 'Nothing'. It is well contrived to lessen the glaring absurdity of Lear; but the surest plan is that of forcing away the attention from the nursery-tale the moment it has answered its purpose, that of supplying the canvas to paint on. This is done by Kent –

his punishment displaying Lear's *moral* incapability of resigning the sovereign power in the very moment of disposing of it.

Kent is the nearest to perfect goodness of all Shakespeare's characters, and yet the most *individualized*. His passionate affection and fidelity to Lear acts on our feelings in Lear's own favor; virtue itself seems to be in company with him.

I ii 9–14
> *Edm.*   ... Why brand they us
> With base? with baseness? bastardy? base, base?
> Who in the lusty stealth of nature take
> More composition and fierce quality
> Than doth, within a dull, stale, tired bed,
> Go to the creating a whole tribe of fops.

In this speech of Edmund you see, as soon as a man cannot reconcile himself to reason, how his conscience flies off by way of appeal to nature, who is sure upon such occasions never to find fault, and also how shame sharpens a predisposition in the heart to evil. For it is a profound moral, that shame will naturally generate guilt; the oppressed will be vindictive, like Shylock, and in the anguish of undeserved ignominy the delusion secretly springs up, of getting over the moral quality of an action by fixing the mind on the mere physical act alone.

I iii 13–22. *Goneril authorizes the Steward to be rude to Lear*
The Steward (as a contrast to Kent) is the only character of utter unredeemable *baseness* in Shakespeare. Observe even in this the judgement and invention. What could the willing tool of a Goneril be? Not a vice but this of baseness was left open for him.

I iv. Old age, like infancy, is itself a character. In Lear the natural imperfections are increased by life-long habits of being promptly obeyed. Any addition of individuality would be unnecessary and painful. The relations of others to him, of wondrous fidelity and frightful ingratitude, sufficiently distinguish him. Thus he is the open and ample play-room of *nature's* passions.

The Fool is no comic buffoon to make the groundlings laugh, no forced condescension of Shakespeare's genius to the taste of his audiences. Accordingly, he is *prepared* for – brought into living connection with the pathos of the play, with the sufferings.

> Since my young lady's going into France, sir, the fool hath
> much pined away.

The Fool is as wonderful a creation as the Caliban – an inspired idiot.

The monster Goneril prepares what is *necessary*, while the character of Albany renders a still more maddening grievance possible; viz. Regan and Cornwall in perfect sympathy of monstrosity. Not a sentiment, not an image that can give pleasure on its own account is admitted. Pure horror when they are introduced, and they are brought forward as little as possible.

I v 43
> *Lear.* O, let me not be mad, not mad ...

The mind's own anticipation of madness.

The deepest tragic notes are often struck by a half sense of an impending blow. The Fool's conclusion of this act by a grotesque prattling seems to indicate the dislocation of feeling that has begun and is to be continued.

II i 66–7
> *Edm.*   ... he replied,
>   'Thou unpossessing bastard ...'

'*Thou unpossessing bastard*' – the secret poison in Edmund's heart – and then poor Gloster's 'Loyal and *natural* boy', as if praising the *crime* of his birth!

II i 91–2
> *Reg.* What, did my father's godson seek your life?
>   He whom my father named? Your Edgar?

Incomparable! 'What, did *my father's*', etc., compared with the unfeminine violence of the 'all vengeance comes too short' – and yet no reference to the guilt but to the accident.

II ii 90–2
> *Corn.*   This is some fellow,
> Who, having been praised for bluntness, doth affect
> A saucy roughness.

In thus placing these profound general truths in such mouths as Cornwall's, Edmund's, Iago's, etc., Shakespeare at once gives them and yet shews how indefinite their application.

II iii. Edgar's false madness taking off part of the shock from the true, as well as displaying the profound difference. Modern attempts at representing madness lightheadedness, as Otway's, etc.

In Edgar's ravings Shakespeare all the while lets you see a fixed purpose, a practical end in view; in Lear's, there is only the brooding of the one anguish, an eddy without progression.

III iv. What a world's *convention* of agonies! Surely, never was such a scene conceived before or since. Take it but as a picture for the eye only, it is more terrific than any a Michael Angelo inspired by a Dante could have conceived, and which none but a Michael Angelo could have executed. Or let it have been uttered to the blind, the howlings of convulsed nature would seem converted into the voice of conscious humanity.

The scene ends with the first symptoms of positive derangement – here how judiciously interrupted by the fifth scene in order to allow an interval for Lear in full madness to appear.

III vii. What can I say of this scene? My reluctance to think Shakespeare wrong, and yet –

Later. Necessary to harmonise their cruelty to their father.

(from Notes on *King Lear*)

.   .   .   .   .

If indeed *King Lear* were to be tried by the laws which Aristotle established, and Sophocles obeyed, it must be at once admitted to be outrageously irregular; and supposing the rules regarding the unities to be founded on man and nature, Shakespeare must be condemned for arraying his works in charms with which they ought never to have been decorated. I have no doubt, however, that both were right in their divergent courses, and that they arrived at the same conclusion by a different process.

Without entering into matters which must be generally known to persons of education, respecting the origin of tragedy and comedy among the Greeks, it may be observed, that the unities grew mainly out of the size and construction of the ancient theatres: the plays represented were made to include within a short space of time events which it is impossible should have occurred in that short space. This fact alone establishes, that all dramatic performances were then looked upon merely as ideal. It is the same with us: nobody supposes that a tragedian suffers real pain when he is stabbed or tortured; or that a comedian is in fact transported with delight when successful in pretended love.

If we want to witness mere pain, we can visit the hospitals: if we seek the exhibition of mere pleasure, we can find it in ball-rooms. It is the representation of it, not the reality, that we require, the imitation, and not the thing itself; and we pronounce it good or bad in proportion as the representation is an incorrect, or a correct imitation. The true pleasure we derive from theatrical performances arises from the fact that they are unreal and fictitious. If dying agonies were unfeigned, who, in these days of civilisation, could derive gratification from beholding them?

Performances in a large theatre made it necessary that the human voice should be unnaturally and unmusically stretched, and hence the introduction of recitative, for the purpose of rendering pleasantly artificial the distortion of the face, and straining of the voice, occasioned by the magnitude of the building. The fact that the ancient choruses were always on the stage made it impossible that any change of place should be represented, or even supposed.

The origin of the English stage is less boastful than that of the Greek stage: like the constitution under which we live, though more barbarous in its derivation, it gives more genuine and more diffused liberty, than Athens in the zenith of her political glory ever possessed. Our earliest dramatic performances were religious, founded chiefly upon Scripture history; and, although countenanced by the clergy, they were filled with blasphemies and ribaldry, such as the most hardened and desperate of the present day would not dare to utter. In these representations vice and the principle of evil were personified; and hence the introduction of fools and clowns in dramas of a more advanced period.

While Shakespeare accommodated himself to the taste and spirit of the times in which he lived, his genius and his judgment taught him to use these characters with terrible effect, in aggravating the misery and agony of some of his most distressing scenes. This result is especially obvious in *King Lear*: the contrast of the Fool wonderfully heightens the colouring of some of the most painful situations, where the old monarch in the depth and fury of his despair, complains to the warring elements of the ingratitude of his daughters.

> ... Spit, fire! spout, rain!
> Nor rain, wind, thunder, fire, are my daughters:
> I tax not you, you elements, with unkindness,
> I never gave you kingdom, call'd you children;
> You owe me no subscription: then, let fall
> Your horrible pleasure; here I stand, your slave,
> A poor, infirm, weak, and despis'd old man.   (III ii)

Just afterwards, the Fool interposes, to heighten and inflame the passion of the scene.

In other dramas, though perhaps in a less degree, our great poet has evinced the same skill and felicity of treatment; and in no instance can it be justly alleged of him, as it may be of some of the ablest of his contemporaries, that he introduced his fool, or his clown, merely for the sake of exciting the laughter of his audiences. Shakespeare had a loftier and a better purpose, and in this respect availed himself of resources, which, it would almost seem, he alone possessed.

(from his second lecture in the series *Shakespeare and Milton*, 1811–12)

CHARLES LAMB

To see Lear acted, to see an old man tottering about the stage with a walking-stick, turned out of doors by his daughters in a rainy night, has nothing in it but what is painful and disgusting. We want to take him into shelter and relieve him. That is all the feeling which the acting of Lear ever produced in me. But the Lear of Shakspeare cannot be acted. The contemptible machinery by which they mimic the storm which he goes out in, is not more inadequate to represent the horrors of the real elements, than any actor can be to represent Lear: they might more easily propose to personate the Satan of Milton upon a stage, or one of Michael Angelo's terrible figures. The greatness of Lear is not in corporal dimension, but in intellectual: the explosions of his passion are terrible as a volcano: they are storms turning up and disclosing to the bottom that sea, his mind, with all its vast riches. It is his mind which is laid bare. This case of flesh and blood seems too insignificant to be thought on; even as he himself neglects it. On the stage we see nothing but corporal infirmities and weakness, the impotence of rage; while we read it, we see not Lear, but we are Lear, we are in his mind, we are sustained by a grandeur which baffles the malice of daughters and storms; in the aberrations of his reason, we discover a mighty irregular power of reasoning, immethodized from the ordinary purposes of life, but exerting its powers, as the wind blows where it listeth, at will upon the corruptions and abuses of mankind. What have looks, or tones, to do with that sublime identification of his age with that of the *heavens themselves*, when in his reproaches to them for conniving at the injustice of his children, he reminds them that 'they themselves are old'. What gesture shall we appropriate to this? What has the voice or the eye to do with such things? But the play is beyond all art, as the tamperings with it shew: it is too hard and stony; it must have love-scenes and a happy ending. It is not enough that Cordelia is a daughter, she must shine as a lover too. Tate has put his hook in the nostrils of this Leviathan, for Garrick and his followers, the showmen of the scene, to draw the mighty beast about more easily. A happy ending! as if the living martyrdom that Lear had gone through, the flaying of his feelings alive, did not make a fair dismissal from the stage of life the only decorous thing for him. If he is to live and be happy after, if he could sustain this world's burden after, why all this pudder and preparation, why torment us with all this unnecessary sympathy? As if the childish pleasure of getting his gilt robes and sceptre again could tempt him to act over again his misused station, as if at his years, and with his experience, any thing was left but to die.

Lear is essentially impossible to be represented on a stage.

(from 'On the Tragedies of Shakespeare', in *The Reflector*, 1810–11)

JOHN KEATS

O golden-tongued Romance, with serene lute!
    Fair plumed Siren, Queen of far-away!
    Leave melodizing on this wintry day,
Shut up thine olden pages, and be mute:
Adieu! for, once again, the fierce dispute
    Betwixt damnation and impassioned clay
    Must I burn through; once more humbly assay
The bittersweet of this Shakespearian fruit:
Chief poet! and ye clouds of Albion,
    Begetters of our deep eternal theme!
When through the old oak forest I am gone,
    Let me not wander in a barren dream,
But, when I am consumèd in the fire
Give me new phoenix wings to fly at my desire.

('On Sitting Down to Read *King Lear* Once Again', 1818)

P. B. SHELLEY

THE Athenians employed language, action, music, painting, the dance, and religious institutions, to produce a common effect in the representation of the highest idealisms of passion and of power; each division in the art was made perfect in its kind by artists of the most consummate skill, and was disciplined into a beautiful proportion and unity one towards the other. On the modern stage a few only of the elements capable of expressing the image of the poet's conception are employed at once. We have tragedy without music and dancing; and music and dancing without the highest impersonations of which they are the fit accompaniment, and both without religion and solemnity. Religious institution has indeed been usually banished from the stage. Our system of divesting the actor's face of a mask, on which the many expressions appropriated to his dramatic character might be moulded into one permanent and unchanging expression, is favourable only to a partial and inharmonious effect; it is fit for nothing but a monologue, where all the attention may be directed to some great master of ideal mimicry. The modern practice of blending comedy with tragedy, though liable to great abuse in point of practice, is undoubtedly an extension of the dramatic circle; but the comedy should be as in *King Lear*, universal, ideal, and sublime. It is perhaps the intervention of this principle which determines the balance in favour of *King Lear* against the *Oedipus Tyrannus* or the *Agamemnon*, or, if you will, the trilogies with which they are connected; unless the intense power of the choral poetry, especially that of the latter, should be considered as restoring the equilibrium. *King Lear*, if it can sustain this comparison, may be judged to be the most perfect specimen of the dramatic art existing in the world; in spite of the narrow conditions to which the poet was subjected by the ignorance of the philosophy of the drama which has prevailed in modern Europe. Calderon, in his religious *Autos*, has attempted to fulfil some of the high conditions of dramatic representation neglected by Shakespeare; such as the establishing a relation between the drama and religion, and the accommodating them to music and dancing; but he omits the observation of conditions still more important, and more is lost than gained by the substitution of the rigidly-defined and ever-repeated idealisms of a distorted superstition for the living impersonations of the truth of human passion.

(from *A Defence of Poetry*, 1821)

PART TWO

Twentieth-century Studies

Maynard Mack

ACTORS AND REDACTORS (1965)

I

King Lear is a problem. Lamb, as everyone knows, judged the role of the king unactable.[1] Thackeray found the play in performance 'a bore', despite his feeling that 'it is almost blasphemy to say that a play of Shakespear's is bad'.[2] Tolstoy deplored 'the completely false "effects" of Lear running about the heath, his conversation with the Fool and all these impossible disguises, failures to recognize and accumulated deaths'.[3] And Bradley, who regarded the play as Shakespeare's greatest work but 'too huge for the stage', drew up a long list of gross 'improbabilities' that no one has succeeded in arguing away.[4]

Among the grosser improbabilities that Bradley points out are Edgar's and Kent's continuing in disguise well after the purposes of disguise have been served; Gloucester's willingness to believe when Edmund shows him the forged letter, that one son would write to another when both are living in the same house, and specifically would put in writing such patricidal meditations as these; Gloucester's failure to show surprise when suddenly, during the fight with Oswald, his escort drops into peasant dialect; Gloucester's determination to go to Dover to commit suicide, as if there were no other way or place of dying; and finally, Edmund's long delay in telling of his order on the lives of Lear and Cordelia after he himself is mortally wounded and has nothing to gain. One could add considerably to the list. Probably we should add to it at least the unlikely nature of Edgar's disguise, the implausibility that neither his disguise nor Kent's is seen through, the fact that Gloucester is blinded for his treason instead of being killed, and the 'almost babyish' goings on, as one reviewer describes them, of the play's first scenes:

The old man who parcels out his kingdom by the map; the daughters who overdo their thanks with a fulsome excess that any child would see through; the simple, obvious contrast of the daughter who cannot say 'thank you' at all; the absurd wrath of the old man over a situation that any father with any daughter could not fail to understand. Then follow undignified things, acts of schoolboy rudeness, pushings and kickings and trippings up.... How, you ask, are these primitive, rather absurd, folks going to excite in you the proper tragic emotions?[5]

It will not do to say that these things go unnoticed in performance. What we notice in performance is whatever we bring with us a capacity to notice, and this includes all we have learned from reading and discussion. Moreover, anyone who goes to a performance of *King Lear* with his eyes open will soon be aware that what he watches onstage deviates markedly from the ordinary Shakespearean norms of probability in tragedy. In this play alone among the tragedies we are asked to take seriously literal disguises that deceive. Romeo's appearing masked at the Capulet ball and Iago's advising Roderigo to 'defeat thy favor with a false beard' in following Desdemona to Cyprus (a circumstance we never hear of again) obviously put no similar strain on credulity. This is the only Shakespearean tragedy, too, in which a number of the characters are conceived in terms of unmitigated goodness and badness, and the only one, apart from the early *Titus*, where the plot is made up of incidents each more incredible – naturalistically – than the last: from the old king's love test and Kent's return to serve him as Caius, through Edmund's successful rise, Edgar's implausible disguise, Lear's mad frolic in the storm with beggar and fool, to Gloucester's leap and Edmund's duel with a nameless challenger who subsequently proves to be his brother. This is the heady brew of romance, not tragedy. If Polonius had seen a performance of *King Lear*, we can be sure he would have invented a suitable compound name for its kind: something like 'tragical-comical-historical-pastoral-romantical', each of which terms might be defended as suiting one aspect of the play.

Neither will it do to pretend that the problematic *King Lear* is an invention of the scholar and literary critic. Quite the reverse. All that is necessary to appreciate the puzzles the play poses on-stage is to think seriously about producing it. Mr Peter Brook, we are told, described it, while readying it for his recent production with Paul Scofield in the title role, as 'a mountain whose summit had never been reached', the way up strewn with the shattered bodies of earlier visitors – 'Olivier here, Laughton there: it's frightening.'[6] Miss Margaret Webster, whose experience in directing Shakespeare for all sorts of actors and audiences is formidable, has called *King Lear* 'the least actable of the four plays' (i.e. *Hamlet, Othello, King Lear,* and *Macbeth*), adding that '*Macbeth* whatever the spiritual or abstract significance with which it has been variously endowed, has always been played for its tremendous dramatic impact', and that '*Othello* insures a sweep of movement which, in the theatre, over-whelms all theoretical debate as to the motivation of its principal characters' – whereas in *Lear* 'the lack of this fundamental theatre economy' makes difficulty.[7] Reviewers and theatre critics have many times voiced similar reservations. When friendly to the play, they have questioned at the very least whether it is possible to perform the first storm scene (III ii) 'so that it looks and sounds like an intelligible piece of theatre'.[8] When un-friendly, they have been more pungent:

You like Shakespeare?
Maybe this is an unfair question, because there is an awful lot of Shakespeare, and you could be pardoned for liking some but not all.
Frankly, that's the way I feel. I have never liked *King Lear*, the excessively wordy and expensive bijou which opened at the National Theatre last night with Louis Calhern in the lead role . . .
Mr Calhern munches on most of the scenery and, at one juncture, nearly gnaws the occupants of the first row center, but that is the requirement of the title part and he plays it to what used to be called the hilt.
If you will harken back to the days of your childhood when somebody made you read it, you will recall that the story

concerns the mad convolutions of this King and the deceitful behavior of his three daughters and their separate swains. Things
get so tough, as you'll remember, that the monarch flips his
skimmer.[9]

Give or take a Broadway cliché or two, this approximates many
a theatregoer's impression of *King Lear* today, onstage as well as
off, and (if the truth were told) many a student reader's.

If *King Lear* as a work of literature is either Shakespeare's
greatest achievement, freely compared by its devotees to the
sublimest inventions of the artistic imagination, or else a work of
childish absurdity inspiring 'aversion and weariness'[10] in others
besides Tolstoy; if as a play it is either unsuited to actual stage
performing, or on the contrary is only understood when performance has tied together the 'series of intellectual strands'
which compose it[11] and drawn our attention 'away from what
otherwise might seem puzzling, distasteful, or foolish',[12] clearly
we have a problem. . . .

II

The stage history of *King Lear* has been haunted, possibly from
its very beginnings, by practical problems of communication
with the audience. We do not know why the mad scene in the
'farmhouse', where Lear stages a mock trial of his hard-hearted
elder daughters with joint stools to represent them (III vi), is
missing from the folio text, printed seventeen years after the
play was first acted. The excision may have been made only to
shorten the playing time; but it may also have been made, as
Professor Kenneth Muir acknowledges in his Arden edition
(Introduction, p. xlviii), because the original audiences laughed.
If we may judge from the asides that Edgar utters to guide the
spectators' response to Lear's antics whenever he is on the stage
with him, this possibility was a matter of real concern to the
playwright, who knew, as the creator of Malvolio and Hamlet
well might, that for the most part contemporary audiences
expected madness to be entertaining. One other complete scene
missing from the folio text is that in which Kent and a Gentleman

discuss Cordelia's reception of the news of her father's sufferings (IV iii). Here they wrap Cordelia in a mantle of emblematic speech that is usually lost on a modern audience's ear and difficult for a modern actor to speak with conviction. We cannot assume that the Elizabethan actor and audience had our kinds of difficulty with the scene, but what kind did they have – or was this omission too intended merely to shorten the performance?

During the first seventy-five years of its existence, we can make only guesses like these about the history of *King Lear* onstage. We know that on the reopening of the theatres after the Restoration it continued to be played for a time 'as Mr Shakespeare wrote it, before it was altered by Mr Tate' – so John Downes assures us in his *Roscius Anglicanus* (1708), p. 26 – but we do not know what interpretation it was given or what success it met. There may, however, be an answer to the latter question in the fact that the play was before long wholly rewritten by Nahum Tate, so that between 1681, the date of Tate's redaction, and 1838, the year in which Macready restored almost the whole of Shakespeare's original text in a historic production at Covent Garden, Shakespeare's *King Lear* was never, as far as is known, seen in performance. Tate's *King Lear* occupied the stage and throve.

Tate's *King Lear* invites ridicule and deserves it, but is nonetheless illuminating. A line in its verse prologue may be taken to mean (what would not be at all surprising) that Shakespeare's version had ceased to appeal to Restoration playgoers, whose favored diet, apart from comedy, consisted mainly of heroic plays and other subspecies of epic romance. 'Why should', Tate writes,

> These Scenes lie hid, in which we find
> What may at once divert and teach the Mind?

From his dedicatory letter it is clear that he regards his bringing of Shakespeare's scenes before the Restoration public as a pious tribute. He has been emboldened to it by a persuasive friend (a certain Thomas Boteler) and by his own 'Zeal for all the Remains of Shakespeare'. When we open to the text, we discover that his

zeal for these remains has carried him to invent a love affair
between Cordelia and Edgar, to omit France and Lear's Fool, to
give Cordelia a waiting woman named Arante, to supply a happy
ending, and to omit, conflate, and rearrange Shakespeare's scenes
while rewriting (and reassigning) a good deal of his blank verse.
Tate's own description of these efforts, in his letter to Boteler,
suggests that, like 'art' in Aristotelian aesthetics, his function
has been to help extravagant 'Nature' – 'a Heap of Jewels, unstrung, and unpolisht . . . dazling in their Disorder' – realize its
implicit goals. And in a curious literal-minded way, that is
exactly what he has done. He has seized on the romance characteristics of Shakespeare's play and restored it to what must have
seemed to him its intended genre.

In his version Cordelia is abducted by ruffians at the command
of Edmund, who intends to rape her. The ruffians are driven off
by Edgar in his Poor Tom disguise – upon which, he reveals
himself and receives avowal of his beloved's affection. They
exeunt together with a convenient flint and steel ('the Implements
Of Wand'ring Lunaticks') to light a fire at which she can dry her
'Storm drench'd Garments'. In similar vein, we have a scene in
'*A Grotto*' with 'Edmund *and* Regan *amorously seated, listening to
Musick*'; a scene in which Edmund receives and reads a billet-
doux from each of Cordelia's sisters; an episode in which
Gloucester repines at his incapacity to take part in the battle,
comparing himself (in a reminiscence of Job) to a 'disabled
Courser' who snuffs the fighting from afar and foams 'with
Rage'; and another episode in which King Lear, asleep in prison
with his head in Cordelia's lap, rouses as Edmund's soldiers enter
to hang Cordelia, and holds them at bay, killing two of them, till
Edgar and Albany come to his rescue. Tate had an unerring eye
for romantic melodrama, and his handling of his original points
up very clearly for all who are willing to see them the melodramatic potentialities of the plot from which Shakespeare began.

The other goal of Tate's changes was to clarify motivations.
He notes in his dedicatory letter that the virtue of the love affair
he has invented for Edgar and Cordelia lies in rendering 'Cordelia's Indifference, and her Father's Passion in the first Scene,

probable', and in giving 'Countenance to Edgar's Disguise, making that a generous Design that was before a poor Shift to save his life'. What this means, in detail, is that Tate's Cordelia consciously tempts her father to leave her dowerless in order that Burgundy may refuse her (Tate's play, as noted, omits the King of France altogether), and that Tate's Edgar, whom after her own rejection Cordelia unexpectedly rejects that she may test his devotion, determines to disguise himself (rather than make away with himself in his lover's despair) on the chance that he may yet be of service to her. With the same end in view, Tate firms up the appearances of plausibility throughout. His play opens with Edmund's soliloquy, in order that Edmund may inform us that he has incensed his father against his brother, with

> A Tale so plausible, so boldly utter'd,
> And heightned by such lucky Accident,
> That now the slightest Circumstance confirms him,
> And base-born *Edmund* spight of Law inherits.

Here Edmund is credited with an initial deception of his father offstage and earlier, details remaining unspecified, in order to render more credible the scene in which Gloucester accepts the forged letter. Lear's scene of folly is also prepared for. Immediately following Edmund's soliloquy, Gloucester and Kent enter to him, and when he has been introduced by Gloucester as the 'generous Boy' whose loyalty he means to reward, both men deplore the forthcoming division of the kingdom, bearing witness in advance to Lear's 'Infirmity' of age, his customary 'wild Starts of Passion', and his 'Temper . . . ever . . . unfixt, chol'rick and sudden'.

Other difficulties are met with similar expedients. Edmund's deception of his brother takes place while Edgar is in a brown study induced by Cordelia's rejection of his love and hardly follows what his brother says. Cornwall's speech marking Edmund for his own – 'Natures of such deep trust we shall much need' – is given by Tate to Regan and extended by a comment which prepares the audience for their subsequent liaison.

Gloucester's incriminating letter 'guessingly set down' and sent by 'one that's of a neutral heart And not from one oppos'd' becomes in Tate some despatches Gloucester has himself addressed to the Duke of Cambrai urging help against the sisters, and thus gives Cornwall a more acceptable motive for his cruelty to the old man. When Edgar is seen with his blind father, he tells us immediately why he does not reveal himself: it is for fear the old man's heart will break of extremes of grief and joy. Such is Tate's method throughout. The upshot of his reworking is that there is no longer question but that the play is indeed tragi-cal-comical-historical-pastoral romance and, in a sad, shriveled way, effective 'theatre'. And so it proved for one hundred and fifty-seven years.

III

I have dwelt on Tate's *King Lear* because its stage history is actually longer than any other continuous stage history the play has yet had, and because it established, I think, for a very long time (even after the text had been restored) the performer's approach to the play. Tate's text was the vehicle for all the actors who tried Lear during Pope's and Johnson's century: Betterton, George Powell, Robert Wilkes, Barton Booth, Anthony Boheme, James Quin, Garrick, Spranger Barry, John Kemble, and several more. We know very little about any of them before Garrick. Lear was widely reputed to be Garrick's finest role. His interpretation of the part, as well as the sensibility of his period, may be seen in Edward Tighe's account of his effect on the Montgomery sisters:

The expression of the eldest was wonderful and such as the mighty master would have smiled to see. She gazed, she panted, she grew pale, then again the blood rose in her cheeks, she was elevated, she almost started out of her seat, and *tears began to flow*.[13]

Garrick played the king as an 'honest, well-meaning, ill-used old man',[14] partly perhaps because his own stature was unsuited to a more majestic mien, but largely, one suspects, because that was the one genuine human thing that Tate's *King Lear* had left in it. A contemporary describes him in the role as a 'little old white-haired man . . . with spindle-shanks, a tottering gait, and great shoes upon the little feet';[15] and though this was intended to ridicule him, there is no reason to doubt its substantial accuracy. We know from other sources that great age was emphasized in his make-up, that his performance colored 'all the Passions, with a certain Feebleness suitable to the Age of the King',[16] and that in his own view, expressed in a letter to his friend Tighe, '*Lear* is certainly a *Weak* man, it is part of his Character – violent, old and *weakly* fond of his Daughters'.[17] What Garrick saw in the play as a whole, according to Professor G. W. Stone, who had studied Garrick productions of *King Lear* more carefully than any man alive, was a 'Shakespearean play which could surpass competition from all writers of pathetic tragedy and could command the emotional pleasure of tears more successfully than sentimental comedy'.[18]

Garrick was a very great actor and played the play that he saw in *King Lear* with a kind of absolute distinction, if we may judge from the lyrical responses of his contemporaries. But he was the prisoner of the Tate text and perhaps of his audience's expectations. After toying at one point with the idea of restoring the Fool, he abandoned the idea as too 'bold an attempt',[19] and though urged early in his career to put away Tate and give '*Lear* in the *Original, Fool* and all',[20] he never got further than restoring part of the original Shakespearean verse: the story remained 'Tatefied', including love affair, happy ending, and all. With respect to his audience's expectations, Garrick's caution was well advised. We know how Samuel Johnson felt about the death of Cordelia ('I was many years ago so shocked by Cordelia's death that I know not whether I ever endured to read again the last scenes of the play till I undertook to revise them as an editor'),[21] and when George Colman produced a version of the play in 1768 with the love story omitted and (it would seem) the catastrophe restored, it received short shrift. One review observed: '[Colman having] considerably heightened the distress of the catastrophe, we doubt very much whether humanity will give him her voice in preference to Tate';[22] and another:

We have only to observe here, that Mr *Colman* has made several very judicious alterations, at the same time that we think his having restored the original distressed catastrophe is a circumstance not greatly in favour of humanity or delicacy of feeling, since it is now rather too shocking to be borne; and the rejecting the Episode of the loves of Edgar and Cordelia, so happily conceived by Tate, has beyond all doubt, greatly weakened the Piece, both in the perusal and representation . . .[23]

Even Colman had not ventured so far as to restore the Fool. 'After the most serious consideration,' he tells us in his Advertisement to the published copy, 'I was convinced that such a scene "would sink into burlesque" in the representation and would not be endured on the modern stage.'[24]

For all the talent of the eighteenth-century actors, there was nothing in their representations of Lear to give the lie to Lamb's penetrating summary: 'Tate has put his hook in the nostrils of this Leviathan, for Garrick and his followers, the showmen of the scene, to draw the mighty beast about more easily.'[25]

IV

The qualities in *King Lear* which impressed the eighteenth century, when it confronted Shakespeare's play instead of Tate's, may be gathered from Samuel Johnson:

The tragedy of *Lear* is deservedly celebrated among the dramas of Shakespeare. There is perhaps no play which keeps the attention so strongly fixed; which so much agitates our passions and interests our curiosity. The artful involutions of distinct interests, the striking opposition of contrary characters, the sudden changes of fortune, and the quick succession of events, fill the mind with a perpetual tumult of indignation, pity, and hope. There is no scene which does not contribute to the aggravation of the distress or conduct of the action, and scarce a line which does not conduce to the progress of the scene. So powerful is the current of the poet's imagination that the mind which once ventures within it is hurried irresistibly along.[26]

When we place beside this a passage from Hazlitt's review of Edmund Kean's production of 1820, we realize at once that the critical emphasis has significantly changed:

There is something ... in the gigantic, outspread sorrows of Lear, that seems to elude his grasp, and baffle his attempts at comprehension. ... [The passion in Lear is] like a sea, swelling, chafing, raging, without bound, without hope, without beacon, or anchor. Torn from the hold of his affections and fixed purposes, he floats a mighty wreck in the wide world of sorrows. ... Abandoned of fortune, of nature, of reason, and without any energy of purpose, or power of action left – with the grounds of all hope and comfort failing under it – but sustained, reared to a majestic height out of the yawning abyss ... [the character of Lear] stands a proud monument, in the gap of nature, over barbarous cruelty and filial ingratitude. ... There are pieces of ancient granite that turn the edge of any modern chisel: so perhaps the genius of no living actor can be expected to cope with Lear. Mr Kean chipped off a bit of the character here and there: but he did not pierce the solid substance, nor move the entire mass.[27]

'Gigantic, outspread', 'like a sea', 'a mighty wreck', 'reared to a majestic height out of the yawning abyss', 'ancient granite', 'mass' – all this is a new world, and it does not stem exclusively from Hazlitt's characteristic intellectual abandon and hyperbole of style. Lamb's testimony, we recall, is essentially the same: 'they might more easily propose to personate the Satan of Milton upon a stage, or one of Michael Angelo's terrible figures'.[28] And the note continues to be heard right down the century to Bradley, whose lectures bring the Romantic expansionist interpretation of Shakespeare to a noble close:

the immense scope of the work; the mass and variety of intense experience which it contains; the interpenetration of sublime imagination ... the vastness of the convulsion both of nature and

of human passion ... the strange atmosphere, cold and dark,
[enfolding the play's figures] and magnifying their dim outlines
like a winter mist; the half-realized suggestions of vast universal
powers working in the world of individual fates and passions.[29]

The theatre, however, is more conservative than are literary
critics. There is very little evidence to show that any of the great
nineteenth-century productions of *King Lear* departed essentially
from the lines laid down by Garrick's feeble and downtrodden
king. Edmund Kean played for passion rather than pathos, and
was scolded by the *Examiner* for doing so: '[Lear's] ebullitions
of rage cannot be more freely given than by Mr Kean, but there
is something in that gifted Actor, which is at war with a delineation of corporeal and mental weakness; and consequently of the
pathos which may spring out of them.'[30] Yet even Kean missed
the grandeur of the part sadly, as Hazlitt testifies. His madness
was 'imbecility instead of phrenzy';[31] 'he drivelled and looked
vacant'.[32]

Macready also played *King Lear* for passion, but not to the
exclusion of pathos, especially in his relations with the Fool. In
Macready's production of 1838 the part of the Fool was restored
to the play for the first time since the seventeenth century,
together with a text that was now entirely Shakespearean apart
from some cuts and rearrangements.[33] Macready had even graver
doubts than Garrick's and Colman's about how the Fool would
go down with a contemporary audience, and considered omitting
the part till after rehearsals were under way. But on describing
to a colleague his notion of 'the sort of fragile, hectic, beautiful-
faced, half-idiot-looking boy that he should be', it was observed
to him that the part should be played by a woman, and this suggestion won him over.[34] We can see here very clearly that the
processes of sentimentalizing set in motion by Tate did not
come to a halt when Tate's text was replaced. The Restoration
and eighteenth century had excluded the Fool as coarse and
grotesque; the Victorian period readmitted him, but not as a
cracked brain guarding 'incommunicable secrets' – this is
Robert Speaight's fine phrase;[35] rather, as a sort of feverish

Peter Pan, or a Burne-Jones rendering of Matthew Arnold on Shelley.

Macready's conception of the role of Lear suggests that possibly he had encountered Lamb's strictures on the usual Lear of the theatre ('an old man tottering about the stage with a walking-stick'), or Hazlitt's on Kean. 'The towering range of thought with which [Lear's] mind dilates, identifying the heavens themselves with his griefs,' Macready noted, 'and the power of conceiving such vast imaginings, would seem incompatible with a tottering trembling frame.'[36] But as with Macready's Fool, so with his King. He was moving in his tragic kingliness and paternity; he spoke the first curse with a terrifying 'still intensity',[37] the second with a 'screaming vehemence' that 'greatly exceeded in power the first',[38] and, like all his predecessors, drew 'sighs and tears which shook the audience' when he woke to recognize Cordelia.[39] But nothing in the reviews suggests that he brought to life, or was in any way aware of, the brooding, mythic, almost apocalyptic hints and intimations that for most of us today lie just beyond the story of domestic pathos and seem already to be glimpsed fitfully in the sentences of Hazlitt and Lamb, quoted earlier, and in Coleridge's superb outburst on III iv:

O what a world's convention of agonies is here! All external nature in a storm, all moral nature convulsed – the real madness of Lear, the feigned madness of Edgar, the babbling of the Fool, the desperate fidelity of Kent. Surely such a scene was never conceived before or since! Take it but as a picture for the eye only, it is more terrific than any which a Michel Angelo, inspired by a Dante, could have conceived, and which none but a Michel Angelo could have executed.[40]

Though Macready was an exceptionally fine actor, like Garrick, and like Garrick one of very few of the older actors who could feel his way to a total conception of a role rather than play a pastiche of electrifying moments in the manner of Kean, he remained the prisoner of conceptions that had got their start

with Tate. So did the remainder of the nineteenth century. The
role of Lear was altogether sentimentalized by Phelps; played
by Booth, according to one review, like 'an angry, conventional
Polonius',[41] and according to Tennyson, in a way 'most interesting, most touching and powerful, but not a bit like Lear';[42]
and then 'degraded' by Irving ('to the level of a doddering
lunatic')[43] in a performance after which one drama critic is
reported to have said to his colleagues: 'Now who's going to tell
the truth about this?'[44] To sum up with the verdict of a witty
student of mine,[45] himself a promising actor, the Lears of the
nineteenth century after Macready may 'best be pictured as a
halting procession of senile old men, trudging at various rates
of speed toward the sacred grove of Bathos'.

v

Two changes by Kean's and Macready's time 'revised' the impression of *King Lear* onstage almost as thoroughly as Tate had
done. One was the use of stage machines. Already in Kean's
production of 1820 there had been provided for the heath scenes
a river overflowing its banks and 'scenic trees . . . composed of
distinct boughs which undulated in the wind, each leaf . . . a
separate pendant rustling with the expressive sound of nature
itself'.[46] When Macready produced his wholly Shakespearean
King Lear in 1838, such effects were continued and improved.
'From beginning to end', said the reviewer for *John Bull*:

the scenery of the piece . . . corresponds with the period, and
with the circumstances of the text. The castles are heavy, sombre,
solid; their halls adorned with trophies of the chase and instruments of war; druid circles rise in spectral loneliness out of the
heath, and the 'dreadful pother' of the elements is kept up with
a verisimilitude which beggars all that we have hitherto seen
attempted. Forked lightnings, now vividly illumine the broad
horizon, now faintly coruscating in small and serpent folds, play
in the distance; the sheeted element sweeps over the foreground,
and then leaves it in pitchy darkness; and wind and rain howl
and rush in 'tyranny of the open night'.[47]

The persistence of this taste in staging *Lear* through the rest of the century may be best gauged from the comment of G. C. D. Odell, to whose pioneering *Shakespeare from Betterton to Irving* all studies of Shakespeare in performance are necessarily in debt. It was the opinion of Odell, writing as late as 1920, that this passage from *John Bull* describes an ideal performance – 'a nobly conceived and ably executed revival of a great tragedy; in intention nothing could surpass it even to-day'.[48]

The other theatrical change that shielded nineteenth-century audiences from the savage impact of the play as Shakespeare wrote it was localization in time. Those who have *King Lear* fresh in mind will recall that the primitivism of its atmosphere and the folk-tale cast of the 'choosing' episode in the first scene are offset continually by a vivid contemporaneous Elizabethanism, giving the effect, as so often in Shakespeare, of no single time and therefore all time. No member of Shakespeare's original audience, hearing Edgar's chatter on the life of farm communities (III iv) or Lear's on urban knavery (IV vi), or looking at the symbolic hierarchies of state and family in their 'robes and furr'd gowns' (I i), could doubt for a moment that the play was about a world with which he was deeply and centrally engaged. Such engagement by Victoria's time was a commodity not easily to be enjoyed.

We must be careful not to exaggerate the impairments suffered by Shakespearean drama when replacement of the apron stage by curtain and proscenium increased the imaginative distance between spectator and action; or when elaboration of scenery and scene changing and stage machines impinged on the role that Shakespeare had assigned to poetry, sometimes rendering it superfluous, sometimes swallowing it up in noise (as happened invariably with the storm scene in *Lear*), and always so far extending the playing time as to require cutting the poetic text severely. We must not exaggerate the losses, but some loss there certainly was, increased in the case of *Lear* by the sentimentalization which was a legacy from Tate. When to these factors was added the archaeological impulse of the nineteenth-century stage to convert poetry and myth into history, something like a dead

end was in sight for all plays like *King Lear* in which poetry and
myth contribute most of what rises above the level of *drame
bourgeois*.

It made little difference which historical epoch was chosen:
Macready played the play with druid circles, Charles Kean as
belonging to 'the Anglo-Saxon era of the eighth century',[49]
Irving as of 'a time, shortly after the departure of the Romans,
when the Britons would naturally inhabit the houses [that the
Romans had] left vacant'.[50] The result was to mask the play's
archetypal character, distancing its cruelties as the errors of a
barbarous age with no compelling relation to oneself. This
attitude the abrupt opening scene too easily encourages in any
case. It so encouraged it in Samuel Johnson that he temporarily
lost his usual sensitivity to what is *semper, ubique, et ab omnibus*:

Perhaps if we turn our thoughts upon the barbarity and ignorance
of the age to which this story is referred, it will appear not so
unlikely as while we estimate Lear's manners by our own. Such
preference of one daughter to another, or resignation of dominion
on such conditions, would be yet credible if told of a petty prince
of Guinea or Madagascar.[51]

And it continued to encourage opinion of this kind for a century
and a half. Here is the reaction of a London theatre critic in 1909:

The people remind you of some simple South Sea Islanders in
some 18th century traveller's narrative – peering through the
wrong end of a telescope, expressing their emotions by uncouth
dances, and filled with delight by the present of some coloured
beads.[52]

VI

The eighteenth-century *King Lear*s with their benign ending
were perhaps the natural product of an age which held that under
the appearances of things lay an order of justice which it was the
job of literature to imitate, not to hide. Those of the nineteenth
century, in which Shakespeare's text had been increasingly
restored but was trammeled in stage effects and historical place

and time, gave equally natural expression to the principles of a period whose best poet (happily he did not often practice his own preachment) said that poetry was made of the real language of real men, and whose most systematic critic imagined he had engaged what was important about literature when he talked of *race, milieu, moment*.

In a number of ways, our own century seems better qualified to communicate and respond to the full range of experience in *King Lear* than any previous time, save possibly Shakespeare's own. We are familiar with the virtues of the bare unlocalized Elizabethan platform stage, and can recover them at will, with the immense added resource of modern lighting. After two world wars and Auschwitz, our sensibility is significantly more in touch than our grandparents' was with the play's jagged violence, its sadism, madness, and processional of deaths, its wild blends of levity and horror, selfishness and selflessness, and the anguish of its closing scene. We have not the Victorians' difficulty, today, in discerning behind its foreground story of a family quarrel intimations of mortality on a far grander scale: we know that we go to see in Lear one who is as much a portent as a man[53] – 'a great oak struck by lightning',[54] 'a stricken Colossus',[55] a 'broken column at whose feet others bewail their lesser woes',[56] a figure out of 'Blake, with a suggestion of Dürer'[57] – and that the play as a whole, with its kings, beggars, fools, blindness, madness, and storm, casts shadows of unearthly grandeur on any twentieth-century imagination that will submit itself to it. Its fascination for us is plain from the statistics of performance. During the eighteenth century there were nineteen distinct productions on the London stage, five by Garrick; during the nineteenth century, twenty-one, fourteen by 1845, but only six in the sixty-two years from 1858 to 1920. Already (to 1962) in this century there have been twenty-three London (and I include Stratford-on-Avon) productions, nineteen beginning with 1931, or better than one each biennium through the past three decades. As a critic for the London *Times* wrote in reviewing Olivier's performance in 1946, it has been 'a period rich in notable Lears'.[58]

Rich indeed. Without going outside the English stage or the

period since 1930, one may name John Gielgud, William Devlin, Randall Ayrton, Donald Wolfit, Laurence Olivier, Stephen Murray, Michael Redgrave, Charles Laughton, Paul Scofield. Some of these have taken the part in as many as four separate productions,[59] and all have played it with gratifying and instructive differences. Interpretations have ranged from Gielgud's monarch of 'Olympian grandeur'[60] in 1940 (from all accounts the greatest performance of our time) – through Olivier's 'Swell-head the Tyrant' of 1946, an interpretation containing, we are told, 'an illuminating remnant of the fussy, feeble, Justice Shallow'[61] – through Redgrave's towering ruin of 1953, who even in the opening scene was 'almost too decrepit to draw his huge sword'[62] – to Laughton's uncompromising repudiation of the 'grand' Lear in 1959, in favor of an intense portrayal of a smaller, more immediately sympathetic figure, less king than father, less father than 'representative of the common man',[63] whose physical appearance is said to have reminded spectators of 'Father Christmas' and 'Old King Cole'.[64]

Interpretations of the play as a whole have also run the gamut. The stress of Byam Shaw's production in 1959 for Laughton was 'modern', 'realistic', 'human' – calculated 'to put the play within the scope and comprehension of a mass Shakespearean audience'.[65] The Lewis Casson–Granville-Barker production of 1940 for Gielgud appears to have been largely based on Barker's intuition of 'megalithic grandeur' in the play as in the monarch.[66] Gielgud's 1955 production, with contributions by the Japanese designer Isamu Noguchi, sought a setting and costumes which 'would be free of historical and decorative conventions, so that the timeless, universal, and mythical quality of the story may be clear'[67] – though the effect proved at odds with the intent and, as Gielgud recalled later, 'little short of disastrous'.[68] In 1962, Peter Brook tried for a 'frame of reference' as 'Beckettian' as possible, and a 'world . . . like Beckett's . . . in a constant state of decomposition', even down to costumes of leather 'textured to suggest long and hard wear' and furniture 'once sturdy, but now decaying back into its hard, brown grain'.[69] A year earlier (to cross abruptly an ocean and a continent) Herbert Blau of the San

Francisco Actors' Workshop had mounted the play with a group of Method actors by relating it for them to Beckett and Genet.[70]

All this is healthy, no doubt, and shows the vitality of the play as well as of the twentieth-century theatre. But the question as to whether it is Shakespeare's play that is communicated by these means is not settled by the presence of enthusiastic audiences and rave reviews (even supposing, which is far from the truth, that most of these productions drew such audiences and reviews): Garrick's Tatefied and sentimentalized text also drew them, and so did Macready's coruscating lightning and leaves. If I may consult my own experience during the same three decades, I am obliged to register the suspicion that our stage, for all its advantages, and with a few honorable exceptions, has worked out ways of altering the effect of Shakespeare's text which are quite as misleading as any our ancestors used, and seem to spring, at least in large part, from the same determination to rationalize, or generalize, or unify according to a particular plan what is not regular, not rational, or not really unifiable on that plan.

VII

The siren's rock on which efforts to bring *King Lear* to the stage (as well as, in some quarters, critical efforts to interpret it) oftenest split is the desire to motivate the bizarre actions that Shakespeare's play calls for in some 'reasonable' way. This desire lay behind many of Tate's alterations, as we saw. It helped influence the nineteenth century to rationalize absurdity and barbarity by attributing them (in the manner exemplified by Dr Johnson's allusion to petty princes of Madagascar) to some appropriately remote and barbarous time or place. It prompted Bradley to regard his considerable list of inconsistencies and implausibilities as serious 'dramatic defects'. And it seems to have misled Mr Empson, usually an astute critic, into seeing in Lear's speeches to Gloucester in Dover fields a sex interest that is 'ridiculous and sordid' in so elderly a man[71] – as indeed it may have to be considered if we assume that the relation of Lear to his speeches is the same as that of (say) Hedda Gabler to hers.

Such expectancies have disposed most directors and actors in our period to ignore Shakespeare's clear signposts (informing us that psychological structure is not what we are to look for) in favor of rationalistic expedients of varying absurdity. Laughton's 'funny old Father Christmas in a white nightgown, mild and chubby, looking forward to a party where he is to give away the presents',[72] was, among other things, a way of supplying character-motivation to Lear's perplexing behavior in the opening scene, as was Gielgud's senile mandarin of 1955, 'all mutterings, shakings, graspings, and palsied twitchings'.[73] But these solutions were purchased at high cost to the 'great image of authority' – inviolable, charismatic, a kind of *primum mobile* (as the monarch always is in the Renaissance) of the political and social macrocosm, and properly too its chief stay against anarchy. This is the Lear which Shakespeare's opening scene calls for and without which both the subsequent collapse of the image and the anarchy generated by its removal lose force. Something like a climax in this rationalizing mode was reached in Peter Brook's production for Paul Scofield in 1962. There in I iv, evidently to justify Goneril's complaints about her father's retinue and thus motivate her insolence to him, Lear's knights literally demolished the set, throwing plates and tankards, upending the heavy table on which presumably the king's dinner was soon to be served, and behaving in general like boors[74] – as if the visible courtesy of their spokesman earlier (I iv 54–78), Albany's significant unawareness of what Goneril is complaining about, and Lear's explicit description of his knights:

> My train are men of choice and rarest parts,
> That all particulars of duty know,
> And in the most exact regard support
> The worships of their name –

had no existence in the play.

Lear is not an easy domestic guest: this we know from his conduct in the first scene, and from however much we may choose to believe of the list of grievances his daughter catalogues to Oswald in I iii. But to justify Goneril is to obscure from the audience the relentless movement by which the man who is cynically humored so long as (in the Fool's words) he bears bags is maneuvered into surrender by two daughters whom Kent calls 'dog-hearted', Albany calls 'Tigers, not daughters', and the gentlest voice in the play calls 'Shame of ladies!' This movement begins to take shape in I i ('We must do something and i' th' heat'); is implemented, with Oswald as tool, in I iii ('Put on what weary negligence you please . . . I'd have it come to question'); is reported on and perhaps expanded in the letters Goneril sends Regan, which decide the latter to be absent from her house when Lear arrives there; and is finally revealed, in II iv, as a visible trap, between whose ponderous jaws, whether by studied plan or opportunism, Lear is first squeezed dry of all his remaining dignities and illusions and then spat away.

The destruction of Goneril's dining hall by Lear and his knights was so vivid an act of aggression in the Brook production that it fixed Lear in the mind as not only a vindictive but a powerfully supported figure, who might easily take back his gift of the kingdom at any time and was silly not to. It also obscured the fact that in the play's terms, Lear being her father, nothing can possibly justify Goneril. As Lear feels that Cordelia in scene i 'wrench'd' his 'frame of nature From the fix'd place' – an image which invites us to see beyond it the ruining of a great building or even a rupture in the cosmic frame itself – so Goneril's actions are eventually seen by Albany to be violences striking at the very foundation of the natural order. On the one hand, she is like the flood which 'cannot be border'd certain in itself', and will, given the opportunity, as Ulysses says in *Troilus and Cressida*, 'make a sop of all this solid globe'; on the other hand, she is like the branch that tears itself from the fostering tree. Throughout the play, Shakespeare brilliantly humanizes both Goneril and Regan by the shifting passions and appetites he traces in their speech, but this is a different matter from 'motivation'. The motivation of the sisters lies not in what Lear has done to them, but in what they are. The fact that they are paradigms of evil rather than (or as well as) exasperated spoilt children whose patience has been exhausted gives them their stature and dramatic force.

The 'subtext' an excuse for distortion of meaning over the text

VIII

The newest and most unpromising form that efforts to rationalize *King Lear* have taken is that of playing what is called in today's theatrical jargon the 'subtext'. A play's subtext, according to the views of those who favor this approach, is the underlying 'reality' to which its verbal text points: 'language is gesture, there is a life to which the words give life, and it is to that life we [are] finally responsible' (see below, p. 73). As a device for training actors, I am willing to believe that this conception has merit. It derives from but extends familiar Stanislavsky techniques which seek to help the actor transform the disjunct speeches and gestures of an acting part as written into some sort of organic and, as it were, psychosomatic continuum. But in the hands of many directors in today's theatre, where the director is a small god, subtext easily becomes a substitute for text and a license for total directorial subjectivity – in ways that may readily be illustrated from the recent productions of Peter Brook and Herbert Blau.

The most obvious result of subtextualizing is that director and (possibly) actor are encouraged to assume the same level of authority as the author. The sound notion that there is a life to which the words give life can with very little stretching be made to mean that the words the author set down are themselves simply a search for the true play, which the director must intuit in, through, and under them. Once he has done so, the words become to a degree expendable. This view of a text probably does no harm when applied to plays whose destiny is to be consumed this season and forgotten next. In these, directors and actors often collaborate throughout rehearsals and trial run, and the resulting 'vehicle', as it is so rightly called, conveys the talents of both.

Directing a classical text might, one supposes, be conducted on more modest principles. And in theory it is. Modern directors of Shakespeare, no less than Garrick, profess to love him. As Blau points out in his interesting and sensitive account of his San Francisco production, 'We have done some plays in which we have thrown a text to the winds of our own psychological behavior – but who is going to feel superior to *King Lear?*'[75] A page earlier, in a description of Blau's management of the heath scene, we meet with this:

Let me say this: we lost words. To do what we tried to do, especially on the heath, and make every word absolutely intelligible is almost impossible. There was an incredible amount of detailed activity, incessant motion – what we were after was the muscular projection of the interior nature of madness. I am not saying that every word shouldn't be intelligible; but I don't think it was the fault of the actors' methodology ... so much as what was required of them. Nor am I saying that the scenes were unintelligible. Far from that. Whatever they didn't have, one felt the storm as a nightmare; one saw the descent to absolute dispossession on the part of the King; one felt the visceral dominance of lunacy in that lucid trial of the daughters. To the extent that the words are the life of the design, we did everything we could to respect them. Even our improvisations were not improvisations emancipated from the text; but language is gesture, there is a life to which the words give life, and it is to that life we were finally responsible. But let me emphasize again: we relinquished clarity only in those marginal cases where what was being done couldn't be done without relinquishing it – given those circumstances and those actors.

In short, even in *King Lear*, when the chips are down for the sub-textualist, rather than relinquish 'what we were after', or 'what was being done' by directorial inspiration, he will relinquish the author's text.

And what *was* being done on this occasion? How marginal were the situations in which clarity had to be relinquished? We may gather an answer from Blau's description of the staging of the storm. It is worth attention because it shows the often very fine creative imagination by which, in the modern directorial theatre, Shakespeare's own imaginative effort, his text, is swallowed up. 'The unifying factor' in the storm scene, says Mr Blau, 'was the music, chaos dazzled by its own coherence'. The phrase alone might give us pause: how will a mere actor make out where chaos itself is dazzled? But we hasten on to discover how the bedazzlement was achieved:

It was an electronic score. . . . The basic sound was a kind of drone of vast amplitude . . . composed . . . of three elements: the sound of Lear's voice saying the word 'I' into an open piano; a single pure pitch; and a cello note – which was a subliminal factor, buried in the storm, but which emerged as the storm progressed as an impulse of healing. That cello note later emerged in the sleep music of Lear, in the reunion with Cordelia. Exquisite, lovely then. But in the storm it was part of the swell of derangement. The three elemental sounds were impacted on tape, improvised upon, made dense until the drone appeared, like the troubled breathing of the earth projected by Lear upon the universe. Over this was imposed another sound track of accidental electronic sounds; during the whole sequence, perhaps about thirty-five minutes, during which the sound never stopped, these occurred at unpredictable moments. Thus, the scene could never be the same. They came whirling or hissing or singing out of the atmosphere, and the actors had to play with them. Then there was still another sequence of sounds, orchestrated explicitly with Lear's 'Blow winds' speech – in which the synchronization of language, sound, and action was meant to establish a perfect harmony of derangement, Lear and the storm locked by sound in a kind of cosmic embrace. Some of the sounds were fierce, indescribably active; and the Fool danced half-witted in their ambience, like an hallucinated lightning bug.

. . . Tom screamed. The Fool screamed. Lear screamed. Adding the unison of their derangement to the sound and fury of the storm. This unison was what we worked for. In the body. They moved like animals, improvising on each other's gestures and sounds, borrowing them from each other, virtually changing identities. A metamorphosis. A sound would screech down from above; Tom would seem to pluck it out of the air; Lear would move as if he had created it. The Fool would slither between them, recovering the cloak which Lear had given Tom, jealous that his function was being preëmpted. Synesthesia. We worked for a precise disorder of sense impressions. . . .[76]

Some of the ideas here are fascinating. They would be superbly at home in *King Lear* rewritten as a tragic ballet. But the homely circumstance that the reader of this hypnotic account must not lose sight of is that, onstage for thirty-five minutes during the heath scenes, three sequences of electronic sounds – some 'fierce, indescribably active', one sequence a complete variable occurring 'at unpredictable moments', all the sequences overlaid by wild screams and accompanied by 'incessant motion . . . the muscular projection of the interior nature of madness' – competed for the spectator's attention with Shakespeare's words. We may safely guess which factor won. But this, I suspect, was not the only or perhaps the chief damage. Shakespeare's words were intended, with the help of a few rumblings of cannon balls in the Elizabethan theatre's upper storey, to produce a storm in the audience's imagination. When instead the storm is produced *for* the audience with such brilliance of detail by nontextual means, Shakespeare's text is left without a function, and so is the audience's imagination. The spectator understands the storm in the sense or senses the director has attached to it; he is not compelled, as he is by Shakespeare's poetry, to grope for meanings and relations and to compound them for himself.

IX

This point becomes clear if we consider a further aspect of the Brook and Blau productions. Mr Blau's subtext was, he tells us, based on Nothing – that is to say on the 'nothing' uttered by Cordelia in her first answer to her father's question, and in his reply: 'Nothing will come of nothing.' Following this lead, the San Francisco production presented in Edgar's disguising an effort to feel 'what it is like *to become nothing*', in Lear's madness the upsurge of 'Nothing', in Goneril's and Regan's stripping away of Lear's knights a 'rhythm of reduction, back to Nothing'; in Cordelia's 'no cause, no cause' the mystery of what issues from Nothing – her *acte gratuit* of I i, and later her gratuitous charity. Even the exit of the three madmen from the heath was contrived on a 'movement . . . with a regressive motion, as if Lear were thinking back to that elusive Nothing'.[77]

One is impelled again to pay tribute to the subtlety of the director's imagination. Once more, however, to the extent that any of his intention managed to cross the footlights as meaning, directorial imagination has run away with the play. Shakespeare's text unquestionably includes the arabesque on Nothing that Blau notes, together with many cognate allusions of the same character; but in the play itself all these must struggle for *lebensraum* with other allusions and patterns of widely different colorings and contrasting implications. They are not extrapolated out, as here, to suffuse the whole with one hue. How subjective and simplistic the view of *King Lear* is that finally emerges from this kind of reading may be assessed from Blau's comment on suicide, 'In this world', he writes, 'we are back, as the Bishop says in [Genet's] *The Balcony*, in the sacred clearing where suicide at last becomes possible. In fact, the subtext constantly brings the characters to that question which Gloucester makes explicit and which Camus thought the major philosophical question of our time: why not suicide?'[78]

This is intoxicating stuff – but what resemblance does it bear to the play that Shakespeare wrote? One casts about in vain to name the characters that the play 'constantly brings' to the question of suicide. Gloucester? Yes, but only once. Lear? Not a trace of it. Edgar? Only to thwart his father's intent, and in his mad speeches as the unjust serving-man on the heath. Cordelia, Kent, Albany, the Fool? Unimaginable. Not really imaginable for Edmund or Cornwall either. Only Goneril in the play actually commits suicide, and her act, undertaken to avoid retribution for her poisoning of Regan and her plot on her husband's life, is hardly what Genet and Camus had in mind.

According to Charles Marowitz's 'log' of the Brook production, for which he was assistant director, the search for the subtext of *King Lear* in London yielded equally exhilarating results. 'Everywhere one looks', he notes, summarizing Brook's conception of the play and presumably his own,

one sees only the facade and emblems of a world, and, ironically, as characters acquire sight, it enables them to see only into a void. . . . It is not so much Shakespeare in the style of Beckett as it is Beckett in the style of Shakespeare, for Brook believes that the cue for Beckett's bleakness was given by the merciless *King Lear*.[79]

Merciless, it may be. Yet Marowitz confesses that it took tinkering to give the play the bleakness that Beckett is supposed to have derived from it. 'One problem with *Lear*', he notes, in a sentence that seems to contemplate the problem as the driver of a bulldozer contemplates a tree, 'is that like all great tragedies it produces a catharsis. The audience leaves the play shaken but assured.' Clearly this would not do in a production of *King Lear* describable as 'Beckett in the style of Shakespeare'. Something had to be done, 'and i' th' heat'.

Accordingly, 'to remove the tint of sympathy usually found at the end of the Blinding Scene',

Brook cut Cornwall's servants and their commiseration of Gloucester's fate. Once the second 'vile jelly' had been thumbed out of his head, Gloucester is covered with a tattered rag and shoved off in the direction of Dover. Servants clearing the stage collide with the confused blind man and rudely shove him aside. As he is groping about pathetically, the house-lights come up – the action continuing in full light for several seconds afterwards. If this works, it should jar the audience into a new kind of adjustment to Gloucester and his tragedy. The house-lights remove all possibility of aesthetic shelter, and the act of blinding is seen in a colder light than would be possible otherwise.[80]

At the end of the play, where 'the threat of a reassuring catharsis is even greater', Marowitz suggested that

instead of silence and repose, which follows the last couplet, it might be disturbing to suggest another storm – a greater storm – was on the way. Once the final lines have been spoken, the thunder could clamour greater than ever before, implying that the worst was yet to come. Brook seconded the idea, but instead of an overpowering storm, preferred a faint, dull rumbling which would suggest something more ominous and less explicit.[81]

x

After such knowledge, what forgiveness – for those who would be content to see *King Lear* as Shakespeare wrote it? To censure virtuosity and experiment seems ungenerous: no one good

custom must be allowed to corrupt the world. To insist on fidelity to ancient texts may be pedantic: it is the scholar's habit at
his least endearing. Yet the question that inevitably arises in the
mind after studying either of these recent treatments of *King
Lear* (or indeed, most we have been given in my lifetime) is
Robert Frost's question: what to make of a diminished thing?
However liberating the conception of subtext may be in theory,
it is reductive in practice, as has been the directorial theatre
generally.[82] Both are too likely to persuade to 'nameless some-
things' (as Pope calls unformed creative impulses in his great
lines on literary distortion in the *Dunciad*) in preference to the
author's text; both encourage emphasizing a part of the text in
lieu of the whole and amplifying that part so as to unmake the
intricacies and overset the balance of the original; even in the
most sensitive hands, their effect is to do the work that in poetic
drama is properly the work of the audience's imagination, and
thus make 'entertainment' out of what should be participation in
a ritual enactment of one's own deepest experience; and this is
to say nothing of the cuttings, rearrangements, and reapportion-
ings which are also justified in their name.

It is true that Shakespeare's play, with a little adjusting, can be
made to yield Brook, Blau, and Beckett as it was formerly made
to yield Tate and Garrick. Like the spokesman of *Leaves of
Grass* it is large, it contains multitudes; and it is inexhaustibly
patient of the images of ourselves we thrust upon it . . . What is
also true is that our extrapolations from it in order to get a hook
into the nostrils of Leviathan do no permanent harm. The mountain remains, as Brook says, long after those who seek to climb
it have been decently interred. Does this mean that nothing like
the whole play is actable, that the best we can do in the theatre, as
so often in our criticism, is to capture one dimension of it at a time?
Or does it mean that something like the whole play might be actable and knowable if we were to come to it with other ends in view
than rationalizing the irrational, regularizing the irregular, and unifying on a particular plan what cannot be unified on such a plan?

Source: *King Lear in Our Time* (1965).

NOTES

1. 'On the Tragedies of Shakespeare' (1808) in *The Life, Letters, and Writings of Charles Lamb*, ed. Percy Fitzgerald (n.d.) IV 205.

2. *The Letters and Private Papers of William Makepeace Thackeray*, ed. Gordon Ray (1945) II 292.

3. L. N. Tolstoy, 'On Shakespeare and the Drama', tr. V. Tchertkoff, in *Fortnightly Review*, NS, LXXXVII (1907) 66.

4. A. C. Bradley, *Lectures on Shakespearean Tragedy* (1904) pp. 247, 256 ff.

5. A. B. Walkley in *The Times*, 1909; reprinted in *The English Dramatic Critics*, ed. James Agate (1932) p. 270.

6. As quoted by Charles Marowitz, Brook's associate in the production, in '*Lear* Log', in *Encore*, X (1963) 22.

7. *Shakespeare Today* (1957) p. 214.

8. Brooks Atkinson in *New York Times*, 26 Dec 1950, reviewing the Louis Calhern–John Housman production.

9. John McLain, *New York Journal-American*, 26 Dec 1950.

10. Tolstoy, op. cit. in *Fortnightly Review*, NS, LXXXVI (1906) 981.

11. Brook's opinion, as quoted by Marowitz, op. cit. p. 21.

12. Arnold Szyfman, '*King Lear* on the Stage: a producer's reflections', in *Shakespeare Survey*, XIII (1960) 71.

13. *Private Correspondence of David Garrick*, ed. James Boaden (1831) I 157.

14. Thomas Wilkes, *A General View of the Stage* (1759) p. 241.

15. Sir John Hill, *The Actor, or A Treatise on the Art of Playing* (1755) p. 151.

16. [Samuel Foote], *A Treatise of the Passions* (1747) p. 22.

17. *Letters of David Garrick*, ed. D. M. Little and G. M. Kahrl (1963) II 682.

18. See his 'Garrick's Production of *King Lear*: a study in the temper of the eighteenth-century mind', in *Studies in Philology*, XLV (1948) 91. See also A. C. Sprague, *Shakespearean Players and Performances* (1953) pp. 21–40, and *Shakespeare and the Actors* (1944) pp. 281–97, and K. A. Burnim, *David Garrick, Director* (1961) pp. 141–51.

19. Thomas Davies, *Dramatic Miscellanies* (1783) II 267.

20. *An Examen of the New Comedy, Call'd The Suspicious Husband, With Some Observations upon Our Dramatick Poetry and Authors, To Which Is Added, a Word of Advice to Mr G-rr-ck* (1747) p. 35.

21. 'General Observations' on *King Lear* in his edition of Shakespeare (1765), reprinted in *Samuel Johnson on Shakespeare*, ed. W. K. Wimsatt, Jr (1960) p. 98.

22. *The Theatrical Review, or The New Companion to the Playhouse* (1772) I 213.

23. Ibid. p. 334. In his *Shakespeare from Betterton to Irving* (1920) G. C. D. Odell assigns this quotation – I believe erroneously – to *The Theatrical Register, or A Complete List of Every Performance at the Different Theatres, for the year 1769*, a publication I have not been able to identify.

24. *The History of King Lear, As It Is Performed at the Theatre Royal in Covent Garden* (1768) p. v. This published version retains Tate's ending.

25. Op. cit. IV 206.

26. Op. cit. p. 96.

27. *London Magazine*, I (1820) 687.

28. Op. cit. IV 205.

29. Op. cit. p. 247.

30. *Examiner* (London), 2 Mar 1823.

31. *Courier* (London), 25 Apr 1820.

32. *London Magazine*, I 689.

33. Kean, in 1823, had replaced much of Tate's fifth Act, including the happy ending, and had been criticized by reviewers for not extending his restorations to the whole.

34. *Diaries of William Charles Macready*, ed. William Toynbee (1912) I 438.

35. 'The Actability of *King Lear*: reminiscences of thirty years of performances', in *Drama Survey*, II (1962) 51.

36. *Macready's Reminiscences and Selections from His Diaries and Letters*, ed. Sir Frederick Pollock (1875) I 207.

37. *Examiner*, 4 Feb 1838.

38. William Winter, *Shakespeare on the Stage* (1915) p. 401. See also Lady Juliet Pollock, *Macready as I Knew Him* (1884) p. 104.

39. Winter, op. cit. p. 402.

40. *Lectures and Notes on Shakespeare . . . Now First Collected by T. Ashe* (1908) p. 341.

41. *Bell's Life in London, and Sporting Chronicle*, 19 Feb 1881.

42. Reported by Winter, op. cit. p. 449.

43. H. B. Baker, *A History of the London Stage and Its Famous Players, 1576–1903* (1904) p. 305.

44. See Laurence Irving, *Henry Irving, the Actor and His World* (1951) p. 551.

45. Donald D. Knight, formerly of the Yale School of Drama.

46. George Raymond, *Memoirs of Robert William Elliston, Comedian* (Concluding Series, 1845) pp. 232–3.

47. *John Bull*, 28 Jan 1838, XVIII 45.

48. *Shakespeare from Betterton to Irving*, II 211.

49. Charles Kean's preface to his acting edition, quoted by Odell, op. cit. II 352. Garrick had introduced historical costuming – 'Old English Dresses' – in his last production of the play, 21 May 1776 (*London Chronicle*, 21–3 May 1776).

50. *The Times* (London) 11 Nov 1892.

51. In his 'General Observation', op. cit. p. 96.

52. A. B. Walkley, *The Times*, 4 Sept 1909. (Walkley goes on to show, however, that the play gets 'hold of you' in spite of this.)

53. Granville-Barker's description of the Lear of I i: 'more a magnificent portent than a man'. *Prefaces to Shakespeare* (1952) I 285.

54. Richard Buckle, reviewing John Gielgud's 1955 production of *King Lear* in *Observer*, 31 July 1955.

55. *The Times*, 26 Jan 1943, in a review of a performance by Donald Wolfit.

56. James Agate, reviewing John Gielgud's first production, in *Sunday Times*, 19 Apr 1931.

57. *The Times*, in the review above mentioned of Donald Wolfit's performance.

58. Issue of 25 Sept 1946.

59. Gielgud in 1931, 1940, 1950, 1955; Wolfit in 1943, 1944, 1945, and 1953.

60. *The Times*, 16 Apr 1940.

61. Ivor Brown, in *Observer*, 29 Sept 1946.

62. *The Times*, 15 July 1953.

63. *The Times*, 19 Aug 1959.

64. e.g. W. A. Darlington (*New York Times*, 13 Sept 1959) and Muriel St Clare Byrne ('*King Lear* at Stratford-on-Avon, 1959', in *Shakespeare Quarterly*, XI (1960) 191).

65. Ibid. pp. 190, 205.

66. Op. cit. I 271. Gielgud's notes on Barker's hints, set down at the time in his rehearsal copy, may be consulted in his *Stage Directions* (1963), app. I.

67. Program note (quoted in *The Times*, 27 July 1955).

68. 'A Shakespearean Speaks His Mind', in *Theatre Arts*, XLIII (1959) 69–71.

69. Marowitz, op. cit. p. 21.

70. See his 'A Subtext Based on Nothing', in *Tulane Drama Review*, VIII (1963) 122 ff. The quotations below are reprinted by permission.

71. William Empson, *The Structure of Complex Words* (1951) p. 138.

72. Darlington, loc. cit.

73. Richard Buckle, in the *Observer*, 31 July 1955.

74. 'Scofield is a Stalin . . . a guttural upstart whose behavior is so arbitrary and graceless, so jack-booted and ham-fisted, that audiences

may begin by sharing the shocked embarrassment of his family and in-laws. . . . This Lear wolfs his food, hammers the table while he cackles at dirty jokes, and overturns the table in fury when crossed. He even belches in the middle of his farewell to his daughter. . . . And so another aspect of Lear is erased. As well as the King, we have lost the High Priest.' Alan Brien, 'Openings: London', in *Theatre Arts*, XLVII (1963) 58. It is fair to add that Brien found the losses compensated by 'the man of flesh and blood'. Many others including myself looked in vain for such a man.

75. Op. cit. p. 131.

76. Ibid. pp. 128–9. Blau's somewhat different account of his pro-duction in *Theatre Arts*, XLV (1961) 80, may suggest that certain of the effects described above existed more fully in the producer's retro-spective imagination than in the audience's experience at the time. Several spectators have assured me that they were quite unaware of these intentions.

77. Ibid. pp. 122–9.

78. Ibid. p. 124.

79. Op. cit. p. 21.

80. Ibid. pp. 28–9.

81. Ibid. p. 29.

82. One of the more spectacular current instances of directorial reductiveness was Marowitz's *Hamlet*, performed at the Akademie der Künste in West Berlin on 20 Jan 1965. An hour in length, the play had lost several of its characters, including Horatio; lines given in the original to one speaker had been reassigned to another; the part of the prince was played in white clown-face. My point is not that such experiments are wrong, only that they diminish Shakespeare along with our opportunities of seeing what Shakespeare actually wrote.

A. C. Bradley

KING LEAR (1957)

King Lear seems to me Shakespeare's greatest achievement, but it seems to me *not* his best play. And I find that I tend to consider it from two rather different points of view. When I regard it strictly as a drama, it appears to me, though in certain parts overwhelming, decidedly inferior as a whole to *Hamlet*, *Othello* and *Macbeth*. When I am feeling that it is greater than any of these, and the fullest revelation of Shakespeare's power, I find I am not regarding it simply as a drama, but am grouping it in my mind with works like the *Prometheus Vinctus* and the *Divine Comedy*, and even with the greatest symphonies of Beethoven and the statues in the Medici Chapel . . .

The stage is the test of strictly dramatic quality, and *King Lear* is too huge for the stage. Of course, I am not denying that it is a great stage-play. It has scenes immensely effective in the theatre; three of them – the two between Lear and Goneril and between Lear, Goneril and Regan, and the ineffably beautiful scene in the Fourth Act between Lear and Cordelia – lose in the theatre very little of the spell they have for imagination; and the gradual interweaving of the two plots is almost as masterly as in *Much Ado*. But (not to speak of defects due to mere carelessness) that which makes the *peculiar* greatness of King Lear – the immense scope of the work; the mass and variety of intense experience which it contains; the interpenetration of sublime imagination, piercing pathos, and humour almost as moving as the pathos; the vastness of the convulsion both of nature and of human passion; the vagueness of the scene where the action takes place, and of the movements of the figures which cross this scene; the strange atmosphere, cold and dark, which strikes on us as we enter this scene, enfolding these figures and magnifying their dim outlines like a winter mist;

the half-realised suggestions of vast universal powers working in
the world of individual fates and passions – all this interferes
with dramatic clearness even when the play is read, and in the
theatre not only refuses to reveal itself fully through the senses
but seems to be almost in contradiction with their reports. This
is not so with the other great tragedies. No doubt, as Lamb declared, theatrical representation gives only a part of what we
imagine when we read them; but there is no *conflict* between the
representation and the imagination, because these tragedies are,
in essentials, perfectly dramatic. But *King Lear*, as a whole, is
imperfectly dramatic, and there is something in its very essence
which is at war with the senses, and demands a purely imaginative realisation. It is therefore Shakespeare's greatest work, but it
is not what Hazlitt called it, the best of his plays; and its com-
parative unpopularity is due, not merely to the extreme painfulness of the catastrophe, but in part to its dramatic defects, and in
part to a failure in many readers to catch the peculiar effects to
which I have referred – a failure which is natural because the
appeal is made not so much to dramatic perception as to a rarer
and more strictly poetic kind of imagination. For this reason, too,
even the best attempts at exposition of *King Lear* are dis-
appointing; they remind us of attempts to reduce to prose the
impalpable spirit of the *Tempest*.

I propose to develop some of these ideas by considering, first,
the dramatic defects of the play, and then some of the causes of its
extraordinary imaginative effect.

We may begin, however, by referring to two passages which
have often been criticised with injustice. The first is that where
the blinded Gloster, believing that he is going to leap down
Dover cliff, does in fact fall flat on the ground at his feet, and then
is persuaded that he *has* leaped down Dover cliff but has been
miraculously preserved. Imagine this incident transferred to
Othello, and you realise how completely the two tragedies differ
in dramatic atmosphere. In *Othello* it would be a shocking or a
ludicrous dissonance, but it is in harmony with the spirit of *King
Lear*. And not only is this so, but, contrary to expectation, it is

not, if properly acted, in the least absurd on the stage. The imagination and the feelings have been worked upon with such effect by the description of the cliff, and by the portrayal of the old man's despair and his son's courageous and loving wisdom, that we are unconscious of the grotesqueness of the incident for common sense.

The second passage is more important, for it deals with the origin of the whole conflict. The oft-repeated judgment that the first scene of *King Lear* is absurdly improbable, and that no sane man would think of dividing his kingdom among his daughters in proportion to the strength of their several protestations of love, is much too harsh and is based upon a strange misunderstanding. This scene acts effectively, and to imagination the story is not at all incredible. It is merely strange, like so many of the stories on which our romantic dramas are based. Shakespeare, besides, has done a good deal to soften the improbability of the legend, and he has done much more than the casual reader perceives. The very first words of the drama, as Coleridge pointed out, tell us that the division of the kingdom is already settled in all its details, so that only the public announcement of it remains. Later we find that the lines of division have already been drawn* on the map of Britain (line 38), and again that Cordelia's share, which is her dowry, is perfectly well known to Burgundy, if not to France (lines 197, 245). That then which is censured as absurd, the dependence of the division on the speeches of the daughters, was in Lear's intention a mere form, devised as a childish scheme to gratify his love of absolute power and his hunger for assurances of devotion. And this scheme is perfectly in character. We may even say that the main cause of its failure was not that Goneril and Regan were exceptionally hypocritical,

---

* *Kent.* I thought the king had more affected the Duke of Albany than Cornwall.

  Glos. It did always seem so to us: but now, in the division of the kingdom, it appears not which of the dukes he values most.

For (Gloster goes on to say) their shares are exactly equal in value. And if the shares of the two elder daughters are fixed, obviously that of the third is so too.

but that Cordelia was exceptionally sincere and unbending. And it is essential to observe that its failure, and the consequent necessity of publicly reversing his whole well-known intention, is one source of Lear's extreme anger. He loved Cordelia most and knew that she loved him best, and the supreme moment to which he looked forward was that in which she should outdo her sisters in expressions of affection, and should be rewarded by that 'third' of the kingdom which was the most 'opulent'. And then – so it naturally seemed to him – she put him to open shame.

There is a further point, which seems to have escaped the attention of Coleridge and others. Part of the absurdity of Lear's plan is taken to be his idea of living with his three daughters in turn. But he never meant to do this. He meant to live with Cordelia, and with her alone.* The scheme of his alternate monthly stay with Goneril and Regan is forced on him at the moment by what he thinks the undutifulness of his favourite child. In fact his whole original plan, though foolish and rash, was not a 'hideous rashness'[1] or incredible folly. If carried out it would have had no such consequences as followed its alteration. It would probably have led quickly to war,[2] but not to the agony which culminated in the storm upon the heath. The first scene, therefore, is not absurd, though it must be pronounced dramatically faulty in so far as it discloses the true position of affairs only to an attention more alert than can be expected in a theatrical audience or has been found in many critics of the play.

Let us turn next to two passages of another kind, the two which are mainly responsible for the accusation of excessive painfulness, and so for the distaste of many readers and the long theatrical eclipse of *King Lear*. The first of these is much the less important; it is the scene of the blinding of Gloster. The blinding of Gloster on the stage has been condemned almost universally; and surely with justice, because the mere physical horror of such a spectacle would in the theatre be a sensation so violent as to overpower the purely tragic emotions, and therefore the spectacle would seem revolting or shocking. But it is otherwise in reading.

*I loved her most, and thought to set my rest
　On her kind nursery.

For mere imagination the physical horror, though not lost, is so far deadened that it can do its duty as a stimulus to pity, and to that appalled dismay at the extremity of human cruelty which it is of the essence of the tragedy to excite. Thus the blinding of Gloster belongs rightly to *King Lear* in its proper world of imagination; it is a blot upon *King Lear* as a stage-play.

But what are we to say of the second and far more important passage, the conclusion of the tragedy, the 'unhappy ending', as it is called, though the word 'unhappy' sounds almost ironical in its weakness? Is this too a blot upon *King Lear* as a stage-play? The question is not so easily answered as might appear. Doubtless we are right when we turn with disgust from Tate's sentimental alterations, from his marriage of Edgar and Cordelia, and from that cheap moral which every one of Shakespeare's tragedies contradicts, 'that Truth and Virtue shall at last succeed'. But are we so sure that we are right when we unreservedly condemn the feeling which prompted these alterations, or at all events the feeling which beyond question comes naturally to many readers of *King Lear* who would like Tate as little as we? What they wish, though they have not always the courage to confess it even to themselves, is that the deaths of Edmund, Goneril, Regan and Gloster should be followed by the escape of Lear and Cordelia from death, and that we should be allowed to imagine the poor old King passing quietly in the home of his beloved child to the end which cannot be far off. Now, I do not dream of saying that we ought to wish this, so long as we regard *King Lear* simply as a work of poetic imagination. But if *King Lear* is to be considered strictly as a drama, or simply as we consider *Othello*, it is not so clear that the wish is unjustified. In fact I will take my courage in both hands and say boldly that I share it, and also that I believe Shakespeare would have ended his play thus had he taken the subject in hand a few years later, in the days of *Cymbeline* and the *Winter's Tale*. If I read *King Lear* simply as a drama, I find that my feelings call for this 'happy ending'. I do not mean the human, the philanthropic, feelings, but the dramatic sense. The former wish Hamlet and Othello to escape their doom; the latter does not; but it does wish Lear and Cordelia to be saved. Surely, it says, the tragic emotions have been sufficiently stirred already. Surely the tragic outcome of Lear's error and his daughters' ingratitude has been made clear enough and moving enough. And, still more surely, such a tragic catastrophe as this should seem *inevitable*. But this catastrophe, unlike those of all the other mature tragedies, does not seem at all inevitable. It is not even satisfactorily motived.[3] In fact it seems expressly designed to fall suddenly like a bolt from a sky cleared by the vanished storm. And although from a wider point of view one may fully recognise the value of this effect, and may even reject with horror the wish for a 'happy ending', this wider point of view, I must maintain, is not strictly dramatic or tragic.

Of course this is a heresy and all the best authority is against it. But then the best authority, it seems to me, is either influenced unconsciously by disgust at Tate's sentimentalism or unconsciously takes that wider point of view. When Lamb – there is no higher authority – writes, 'A happy ending! – as if the living martyrdom that Lear had gone through, the flaying of his feelings alive, did not make a fair dismissal from the stage of life the only decorous thing for him', I answer, first, that it is precisely this *fair* dismissal which we desire for him instead of renewed anguish; and, secondly, that what we desire for him during the brief remainder of his days is not 'the childish pleasure of getting his gilt robes and sceptre again', not what Tate gives him, but what Shakespeare himself might have given him – peace and happiness by Cordelia's fireside. And if I am told that he has suffered too much for this, how can I possibly believe it with these words ringing in my ears:

> Come, let's away to prison:
> We two alone will sing like birds i' the cage.
> When thou dost ask me blessing, I'll kneel down,
> And ask of thee forgiveness: so we'll live,
> And pray, and sing, and tell old tales, and laugh
> At gilded butterflies?

And again when Schlegel declares that, if Lear were saved, 'the whole' would 'lose its significance', because it would no longer show us that the belief in Providence 'requires a wider range than the dark pilgrimage on earth to be established in its whole extent', I answer that, if the drama does show us that, it takes us beyond the strictly tragic point of view.

A dramatic mistake in regard to the catastrophe, however, even supposing it to exist, would not seriously affect the whole play. The principal structural weakness of *King Lear* lies elsewhere. It is felt to some extent in the earlier Acts, but still more (as from our study of Shakespeare's technique we have learnt to expect) in the Fourth and the first part of the Fifth. And it arises chiefly from the double action, which is a peculiarity of *King Lear* among the tragedies. By the side of Lear, his daughters, Kent, and the Fool, who are the principal figures in the main plot, stand Gloster and his two sons, the chief persons of the secondary plot. Now by means of this double action Shakespeare secured certain results highly advantageous even from the strictly dramatic point of view, and easy to perceive. But the disadvantages were dramatically greater. The number of essential characters is so large, their actions and movements are so complicated, and events towards the close crowd on one another so thickly, that the reader's attention,[4] rapidly transferred from one centre of interest to another, is overstrained. He becomes, if not intellectually confused, at least emotionally fatigued. The battle, on which everything turns, scarcely affects him. The deaths of Edmund, Goneril, Regan and Gloster seem 'but trifles here'; and anything short of the incomparable pathos of the close would leave him cold. There is something almost ludicrous in the insignificance of this battle, when it is compared with the corresponding battles in *Julius Caesar* and *Macbeth*; and though there may have been further reasons for its insignificance, the main one is simply that there was no room to give it its due effect among such a host of competing interests.[5]

A comparison of the last two Acts of *Othello* with the last two Acts of *King Lear* would show how unfavourable to dramatic clearness is a multiplicity of figures. But that this multiplicity is not in itself a fatal obstacle is evident from the last two Acts of *Hamlet*, and especially from the final scene. This is in all respects one of Shakespeare's triumphs, yet the stage is crowded with characters. Only they are not *leading* characters. The plot is single; Hamlet and the King are the 'mighty opposites'; and Ophelia, the only other person in whom we are obliged to take a vivid interest, has already disappeared. It is therefore natural and right that the deaths of Laertes and the Queen should affect us comparatively little. But in *King Lear*, because the plot is double, we have present in the last scene no less than five persons who are technically of the first importance – Lear, his three daughters and Edmund; not to speak of Kent and Edgar, of whom the latter at any rate is technically quite as important as Laertes. And again, owing to the pressure of persons and events, and owing to the concentration of our anxiety on Lear and Cordelia, the combat of Edgar and Edmund, which occupies so considerable a space, fails to excite a tithe of the interest of the fencing-match in *Hamlet*. The truth is that all through these Acts Shakespeare has too vast a material to use with complete dramatic effectiveness, however essential this very vastness was for effects of another kind.

Added to these defects there are others, which suggest that in *King Lear* Shakespeare was less concerned than usual with dramatic fitness; improbabilities, inconsistencies, sayings and doings which suggest questions only to be answered by conjecture. The improbabilities in *King Lear* surely far surpass those of the other great tragedies in number and in grossness. And they are particularly noticeable in the secondary plot. For example, no sort of reason is given why Edgar, who lives in the same house with Edmund, should write a letter to him instead of speaking; and this is a letter absolutely damning to his character. Gloster was very foolish, but surely not so foolish as to pass unnoticed this improbability; or, if so foolish, what need for Edmund to forge a letter rather than a conversation, especially as Gloster appears to be unacquainted with his son's handwriting?[6] Is it in character that Edgar should be persuaded without the slightest demur to avoid his father instead of confronting him and asking him the cause of his anger? Why in the world should Gloster, when expelled from his castle, wander painfully all the way to Dover simply in order to destroy himself (IV i 80)? And is it not extraordinary that, after Gloster's attempted suicide, Edgar should first talk to him in the language of a gentleman, then to Oswald in his presence in broad peasant dialect, then again to Gloster in gentle language, and yet that Gloster should not manifest the least surprise?

Again, to take three instances of another kind: (*a*) only a fortnight seems to have elapsed between the first scene and the breach with Goneril; yet already there are rumours not only of war between Goneril and Regan but of the coming of a French army; and this, Kent says, is perhaps connected with the harshness of *both* the sisters to their father, although Regan has apparently had no opportunity of showing any harshness till the day before. (*b*) In the quarrel with Goneril Lear speaks of his having to dismiss fifty of his followers at a clap, yet she has neither mentioned any number nor had any opportunity of mentioning it off the stage. (*c*) Lear and Goneril, intending to hurry to Regan, both send off messengers to her, and both tell the messengers to bring back an answer. But it does not appear either how the messengers *could* return or what answer could be required, as their superiors are following them with the greatest speed.

Once more, (*a*) why does Edgar not reveal himself to his blind father, as he truly says he ought to have done? The answer is left to mere conjecture. (*b*) Why does Kent so carefully preserve his incognito till the last scene? He says he does it for an important purpose, but what the purpose is we have to guess. (*c*) Why Burgundy rather than France should have first choice of Cordelia's hand is a question we cannot help asking, but there is no hint of any answer.[7] (*d*) I have referred already to the strange obscurity regarding Edmund's delay in trying to save his victims, and I will not extend this list of examples. No one of such defects is surprising when considered by itself, but their number is surely significant. Taken in conjunction with other symptoms it means that Shakespeare, set upon the dramatic effect of the great scenes and upon certain effects not wholly dramatic, was exceptionally careless of probability, clearness and consistency in smaller matters, introducing what was convenient or striking for a momentary purpose without troubling himself about anything more than the moment. In presence of these signs it seems doubtful whether his failure to give information about the fate of the Fool was due to anything more than carelessness or an impatient desire to reduce his overloaded material.

Before I turn to the other side of the subject I will refer to one more characteristic of this play which is dramatically disadvantageous. In Shakespeare's dramas, owing to the absence of scenery from the Elizabethan stage, the question, so vexatious to editors, of the exact locality of a particular scene is usually unimportant and often unanswerable; but, as a rule, we know, broadly speaking, where the persons live and what their journeys are. The text makes this plain, for example, almost throughout *Hamlet*, *Othello* and *Macbeth*; and the imagination is therefore untroubled. But in *King Lear* the indications are so scanty that the reader's mind is left not seldom both vague and bewildered. Nothing enables us to imagine whereabouts in Britain Lear's palace lies, or where the Duke of Albany lives. In referring to the dividing-lines on the map, Lear tells us of shadowy forests and plenteous rivers, but, unlike Hotspur and his companions, he studiously avoids proper names. The Duke of Cornwall, we presume in the absence of information, is likely to live in Cornwall; but we suddenly find, from the introduction of a place-name which all readers take at first for a surname, that he lives at Gloster (i v i). This seems likely to be also the home of the Earl of Gloster, to whom Cornwall is patron. But no: it is a night's journey from Cornwall's 'house' to Gloster's, and Gloster's is in the middle of an uninhabited heath.[8] Here, for the purpose of the crisis, nearly all the persons assemble, but they do so in a manner which no casual spectator or reader could follow. Afterwards they all drift towards Dover for the purpose of the catastrophe; but again the localities and movements are unusually indefinite. And this indefiniteness is found in smaller matters. One cannot help asking, for example, and yet one feels one had better not ask, where that 'lodging' of Edmund's can be, in which he hides Edgar from his father, and whether Edgar is mad that he should return from his hollow tree (in a district where 'for many miles about there's scarce a bush') to his father's castle in order to soliloquise (II iii) – for the favourite stage-direction, 'a wood' (which is more than 'a bush'), however convenient to imagination, is scarcely compatible with the presence of Kent asleep in the stocks. Something of the confusion which bewilders the reader's mind in *King Lear* recurs in *Antony and Cleopatra*, the most faultily constructed of all the tragedies; but there it is due not so much to the absence or vagueness of the indications as to the necessity of taking frequent and fatiguing journeys over thousands of miles. Shakespeare could not help himself in the Roman play; in *King Lear* he did not choose to help himself, perhaps deliberately chose to be vague.

From these defects, or from some of them, follows one result which must be familiar to many readers of *King Lear*. It is far more difficult to retrace in memory the steps of the action in this tragedy than in *Hamlet*, *Othello*, or *Macbeth*. The outline is of course quite clear; anyone could write an 'argument' of the play. But when an attempt is made to fill in the detail, it issues sooner or later in confusion even with readers whose dramatic memory is unusually strong.

The position of the hero in this tragedy is in one important respect peculiar. The reader of *Hamlet*, *Othello*, or *Macbeth*, is in no danger of forgetting, when the catastrophe is reached, the part played by the hero in bringing it on. His fatal weakness, error, wrong-doing, continues almost to the end. It is otherwise with *King Lear*. When the conclusion arrives, the old King has for a long while been passive. We have long regarded him not only as 'a man more sinned against than sinning', but almost wholly as a sufferer, hardly at all as an agent. His sufferings too have been so cruel, and our indignation against those who inflicted them has been so intense, that recollection of the wrong he did to Cordelia, to Kent, and to his realm, has been well-nigh effaced. Lastly, for nearly four Acts he has inspired in us, together with this pity, much admiration and affection. The force of his passion has made us feel that his nature was great; and his frankness and generosity, his heroic efforts to be patient, the

depth of his shame and repentance, and the ecstasy of his reunion with Cordelia, have melted our very hearts. Naturally,
therefore, at the close we are in some danger of forgetting that
the storm which has overwhelmed him was liberated by his own
deed.

Yet it is essential that Lear's contribution to the action of the
drama should be remembered; not at all in order that we may
feel that he 'deserved' what he suffered, but because otherwise
his fate would appear to us at best pathetic, at worst shocking,
but certainly not tragic. And when we were reading the earlier
scenes of the play we recognised this contribution clearly enough.
At the very beginning, it is true, we are inclined to feel merely
pity and misgivings. The first lines tell us that Lear's mind is
beginning to fail with age.[9] Formerly he had perceived how
different were the characters of Albany and Cornwall, but now
he seems either to have lost this perception or to be unwisely
ignoring it. The rashness of his division of the kingdom troubles
us, and we cannot but see with concern that its motive is mainly
selfish. The absurdity of the pretence of making the division
depend on protestations of love from his daughters, his complete blindness to the hypocrisy which is patent to us at a glance,
his piteous delight in these protestations, the openness of his
expressions of preference for his youngest daughter – all make
us smile, but all pain us. But pity begins to give way to another
feeling when we witness the precipitance, the despotism, the
uncontrolled anger of his injustice to Cordelia and Kent, and the
'hideous rashness' of his persistence in dividing the kingdom
after the rejection of his one dutiful child. We feel now the
presence of force as well as weakness, but we feel also the presence
of the tragic $\H{\upsilon}\beta\rho\iota\varsigma$. Lear, we see, is generous and unsuspicious,
of an open and free nature, like Hamlet and Othello, and indeed
most of Shakespeare's heroes, who in this, according to Ben
Jonson, resemble the poet who made them. Lear, we see, is also
choleric by temperament – the first of Shakespeare's heroes who
is so. And a long life of absolute power, in which he has been
flattered to the top of his bent, has produced in him that blindness to human limitations, and that presumptuous self-will,

which in Greek tragedy we have so often seen stumbling against
the altar of Nemesis. Our consciousness that the decay of old age
contributes to this condition deepens our pity and our sense of
human infirmity, but certainly does not lead us to regard the old
King as irresponsible, and so to sever the tragic *nexus* which
binds together his error and his calamities.

The magnitude of this first error is generally fully recognised
by the reader owing to his sympathy with Cordelia, though, as
we have seen, he often loses the memory of it as the play advances. But this is not so, I think, with the repetition of this
error, in the quarrel with Goneril. Here the daughter excites so
much detestation, and the father so much sympathy, that we
often fail to receive the due impression of his violence. There is
not here, of course, the *injustice* of his rejection of Cordelia, but
there is precisely the same ὕβρις. This had been shown most
strikingly in the first scene when, *immediately* upon the apparently cold words of Cordelia, 'So young, my lord, and true',
there comes this dreadful answer:

> Let it be so; thy truth then be thy dower.
> For, by the sacred radiance of the sun,
> The mysteries of Hecate and the night;
> By all the operation of the orbs
> From whom we do exist and cease to be;
> Here I disclaim all my paternal care,
> Propinquity and property of blood,
> And as a stranger to my heart and me
> Hold thee from this for ever. The barbarous Scythian,
> Or he that makes his generation messes
> To gorge his appetite, shall to my bosom
> Be as well neighbour'd, pitied and relieved,
> As thou my sometime daughter.

Now the dramatic effect of this passage is exactly, and doubtless
intentionally, repeated in the curse pronounced against Goneril.
This does not come after the daughters have openly and wholly
turned against their father. Up to the moment of its utterance
Goneril has done no more than to require him 'a little to dis-
quantity' and reform his train of knights. Certainly her manner

and spirit in making this demand are hateful, and probably her
accusations against the knights are false; and we should expect
from any father in Lear's position passionate distress and
indignation. But surely the famous words which form Lear's
immediate reply were meant to be nothing short of frightful:

> Hear, nature, hear; dear goddess, hear!
> Suspend thy purpose, if thou didst intend
> To make this creature fruitful!
> Into her womb convey sterility!
> Dry up in her the organs of increase;
> And from her derogate body never spring
> A babe to honour her! If she must teem,
> Create her child of spleen; that it may live,
> And be a thwart disnatured torment to her!
> Let it stamp wrinkles in her brow of youth;
> With cadent tears fret channels in her cheeks;
> Turn all her mother's pains and benefits
> To laughter and contempt; that she may feel
> How sharper than a serpent's tooth it is
> To have a thankless child!

The question is not whether Goneril deserves these appalling
imprecations, but what they tell us about Lear. They show that,
although he has already recognised his injustice towards Cordelia, is secretly blaming himself, and is endeavouring to do
better, the disposition from which his first error sprang is still
unchanged. And it is precisely the disposition to give rise, in evil
surroundings, to calamities dreadful but at the same time tragic,
because due in some measure to the person who endures them.

The perception of this connection, if it is not lost as the play
advances, does not at all diminish our pity for Lear, but it makes
it impossible for us permanently to regard the world displayed in
this tragedy as subject to a mere arbitrary or malicious power. It
makes us feel that this world is so far at least a rational and a
moral order, that there holds in it the law, not of proportionate
requital, but of strict connection between act and consequence.
It is, so far, the world of all Shakespeare's tragedies.

But there is another aspect of Lear's story, the influence of which modifies, in a way quite different and more peculiar to this tragedy, the impressions called pessimistic and even this impression of law. There is nothing more noble and beautiful in literature than Shakespeare's exposition of the effect of suffering in reviving the greatness and eliciting the sweetness of Lear's nature. The occasional recurrence, during his madness, of autocratic impatience, or of desire for revenge serves only to heighten this effect, and the moments when his insanity becomes merely infinitely piteous do not weaken it. The old King who in pleading with his daughters feels so intensely his own humiliation and their horrible ingratitude, and who yet, at fourscore and upward, constrains himself to practise a self-control and patience so many years disused; who out of old affection for his Fool, and in repentance for his injustice to the Fool's beloved mistress, tolerates incessant and cutting reminders of his own folly and wrong; in whom the rage of the storm awakes a power and a poetic grandeur surpassing even that of Othello's anguish; who comes in his affliction to think of others first, and to seek, in tender solicitude for his poor boy, the shelter he scorns for his own bare head; who learns to feel and to pray for the miserable and houseless poor, to discern the falseness of flattery and the brutality of authority, and to pierce below the differences of rank and raiment to the common humanity beneath; whose sight is so purged by scalding tears that it sees at last how power and place and all things in the world are vanity except love; who tastes in his last hours the extremes both of love's rapture and of its agony, but could never, if he lived on or lived again, care a jot for aught beside – there is no figure, surely, in the world of poetry at once so grand, so pathetic, and so beautiful as his. Well, but Lear owes the whole of this to those sufferings which made us doubt whether life were not simply evil, and men like the flies which wanton boys torture for their sport. Should we not be at least as near the truth if we called this poem *The Redemption of King Lear*, and declared that the business of 'the gods' with him was neither to torment him, nor to teach him a 'noble anger', but to lead him to attain through apparently hopeless failure the very end and aim of life? One can believe that Shakespeare had been tempted at times to feel misanthropy and despair, but it is quite impossible that he can have been mastered by such feelings at the time when he produced this conception.

To dwell on the stages of this process of purification (the word is Professor Dowden's) is impossible here; and there are scenes, such as that of the meeting of Lear and Cordelia, which it seems almost a profanity to touch.[10] But I will refer to two scenes which may remind us more in detail of some of the points just mentioned. The third and fourth scenes of Act III present one of those contrasts which speak as eloquently even as Shakespeare's words, and which were made possible in his theatre by the absence of scenery and the consequent absence of intervals between the scenes. First, in a scene of twenty-three lines, mostly in prose, Gloster is shown, telling his son Edmund how Goneril and Regan have forbidden him on pain of death to succour the houseless King; how a secret letter has reached him, announcing the arrival of a French force; and how, whatever the consequences may be, he is determined to relieve his old master. Edmund, left alone, soliloquises in words which seem to freeze one's blood:

> This courtesy, forbid thee, shall the duke
> Instantly know; and of that letter too:
> This seems a fair deserving, and must draw me
> That which my father loses; no less than all:
> The younger rises when the old doth fall.

He goes out; and the next moment, as the fourth scene opens, we find ourselves in the icy storm with Lear, Kent and the Fool, and yet in the inmost shrine of love. I am not speaking of the devotion of the others to Lear, but of Lear himself. He had consented, merely for the Fool's sake, to seek shelter in the hovel:

> Come, your hovel.
> Poor fool and knave, I have one part in my heart
> That's sorry Lyet for thee.

But on the way he has broken down and has been weeping

(III iv 17), and now he resists Kent's efforts to persuade him to enter. He does not feel the storm:

>   when the mind's free
> The body's delicate: the tempest in my mind
> Doth from my senses take all feeling else
> Save what beats there:

and the thoughts that will drive him mad are burning in his brain:

>   Filial ingratitude!
> Is it not as this mouth should tear this hand
> For lifting food to't? But I will punish home.
> No, I will weep no more. In such a night
> To shut me out! Pour on; I will endure.
> In such a night as this! O Regan, Goneril!
> Your old kind father, whose frank heart gave all, –
> O, that way madness lies; let me shun that;
> No more of that.

And then suddenly, as he controls himself, the blessed spirit of kindness breathes on him 'like a meadow gale of spring', and he turns gently to Kent:

> Prithee, go in thyself; seek thine own ease:
> This tempest will not give me leave to ponder
> On things would hurt me more. But I'll go in.
> In, boy; go first. You houseless poverty –
> Nay, get thee in. I'll pray, and then I'll sleep.

But his prayer is not for himself.

>   Poor naked wretches, whereso'er you are,

it begins, and I need not quote more. This is one of those passages which make one worship Shakespeare.[11]

Much has been written on the representation of insanity in *King Lear*, and I will confine myself to one or two points which may have escaped notice. The most obvious symptom of Lear's insanity, especially in its first stages, is of course the domination of a fixed idea. Whatever presents itself to his senses, is seized on by this idea and compelled to express it; as for example in those words, already quoted, which first show that his mind has actually given way:

> Hast thou given all
> To thy two daughters? And art thou come to this?[12]

But it is remarkable that what we have here is only, in an exaggerated and perverted form, the very same action of imagination that, just before the breakdown of reason, produced those sublime appeals:

> O heavens,
> If you do love old men, if your sweet sway
> Allow obedience, if yourselves are old,
> Make it your cause;

and:

> Rumble thy bellyful! Spit, fire! spout, rain!
> Nor rain, wind, thunder, fire, are my daughters:
> I tax not you, you elements, with unkindness;
> I never gave you kingdom, call'd you children,
> You owe me no subscription: then let fall
> Your horrible pleasure; here I stand, your slave,
> A poor, infirm, weak, and despised old man:
> But yet I call you servile ministers,
> That have with two pernicious daughters join'd
> Your high engender'd battles 'gainst a head
> So old and white as this. O! O! 'tis foul!

Shakespeare, long before this, in the *Midsummer Night's Dream*, had noticed the resemblance between the lunatic, the lover, and the poet; and the partial truth that genius is allied to insanity was quite familiar to him. But he presents here the supplementary half-truth that insanity is allied to genius.

He does not, however, put into the mouth of the insane Lear any such sublime passages as those just quoted. Lear's insanity, which destroys the coherence, also reduces the poetry of his imagination. What it stimulates is that power of moral perception and reflection which had already been quickened by his sufferings. This, however partial and however disconnectedly used, first appears, quite soon after the insanity has declared itself, in the idea that the naked beggar represents truth and reality, in contrast with those conventions, flatteries, and corruptions of the great world, by which Lear has so long been deceived and will never be deceived again:

> Is man no more than this? Consider him well. Thou owest the worm no silk, the beast no hide, the sheep no wool, the cat no perfume. Ha! here's three on's are sophisticated: thou art the thing itself.

Lear regards the beggar therefore with reverence and delight, as a person who is in the secret of things, and he longs to question him about their causes. It is this same strain of thought which much later (IV vi), gaining far greater force, though the insanity has otherwise advanced, issues in those famous Timon-like speeches which make us realise the original strength of the old King's mind. And when this strain, on his recovery, unites with the streams of repentance and love, it produces that serene renunciation of the world, with its power and glory and resentments and revenges, which is expressed in the speech (v iii):

> No, no, no, no! Come, let's away to prison:
> We two alone will sing like birds i' the cage:
> When thou dost ask me blessing, I'll kneel down,
> And ask of thee forgiveness: so we'll live,
> And pray, and sing, and tell old tales, and laugh
> At gilded butterflies, and hear poor rogues
> Talk of court news; and we'll talk with them too.
> Who loses, and who wins; who's in, who's out;
> And take upon's the mystery of things,
> As if we were God's spies: and we'll wear out,
> In a wall'd prison, packs and sets of great ones,
> That ebb and flow by the moon.

This is that renunciation which is at the same time a sacrifice offered to the gods, and on which the gods themselves throw incense; and, it may be, it would never have been offered but for the knowledge that came to Lear in his madness.

I spoke of Lear's 'recovery', but the word is too strong. The Lear of the Fifth Act is not indeed insane, but his mind is greatly enfeebled. The speech just quoted is followed by a sudden flash of the old passionate nature, reminding us most pathetically of Lear's efforts, just before his madness, to restrain his tears:

> Wipe thine eyes:
> The good-years shall devour them, flesh and fell,
> Ere they shall make us weep: we'll see 'em starve first.

And this weakness is still more pathetically shown in the blindness of the old King to his position now that he and Cordelia are made prisoners. It is evident that Cordelia knows well what mercy her father is likely to receive from her sisters; that is the reason of her weeping. But he does not understand her tears; it never crosses his mind that they have anything more than imprisonment to fear. And what is that to them? They have made that sacrifice, and all is well:

> Have I caught thee?
> He that parts us shall bring a brand from heaven,
> And fire us hence like foxes.

This blindness is most affecting to us, who know in what manner they will be parted; but it is also comforting. And we find the same mingling of effects in the overwhelming conclusion of the story. If to the reader, as to the bystanders, that scene brings one unbroken pain, it is not so with Lear himself. His shattered mind passes from the first transports of hope and despair, as he bends over Cordelia's body and holds the feather to her lips, into an absolute forgetfulness of the cause of these transports. This continues so long as he can converse with Kent; becomes an almost complete vacancy; and is disturbed only to yield, as his eyes suddenly fall again on his child's corpse, to an agony which at once breaks his heart. And, finally, though he is killed by an agony of pain, the agony in which he actually dies

is one not of pain but of ecstasy. Suddenly, with a cry represented in the oldest text by a four-times repeated 'O', he exclaims:

> Do you see this? Look on her, look, her lips,
> Look there, look there!

These are the last words of Lear. He is sure, at last, that she
lives: and what had he said when he was still in doubt?

> She lives! if it be so,
> It is a chance which does redeem all sorrows
> That ever I have felt!

To us, perhaps, the knowledge that he is deceived may bring a
culmination of pain: but, if it brings *only* that, I believe we are
false to Shakespeare, and it seems almost beyond question that
any actor is false to the text who does not attempt to express, in
Lear's last accents and gestures and look, an unbearable *joy*.[13]

To dwell on the pathos of Lear's last speech would be an
impertinence, but I may add a remark on the speech from the
literary point of view. In the simplicity of its language, which
consists almost wholly of monosyllables of native origin, composed in very brief sentences of the plainest structure, it presents
an extraordinary contrast to the dying speech of Hamlet and the
last words of Othello to the bystanders. The fact that Lear
speaks in passion is one cause of the difference, but not the sole
cause. The language is more than simple, it is familiar. And this
familiarity is characteristic of Lear (except at certain moments,
already referred to) from the time of his madness onwards, and
is the source of the peculiarly poignant effect of some of his
sentences (such as 'The little dogs and all . . .'). We feel in them
the loss of power to sustain his royal dignity; we feel also that
everything external has become nothingness to him, and that
what remains is 'the thing itself', the soul in its bare greatness.
Hence also it is that two lines in this last speech show, better
perhaps than any other passage of poetry, one of the qualities we
have in mind when we distinguish poetry as 'romantic'. Nothing

like Hamlet's mysterious sigh, 'The rest is silence', nothing like Othello's memories of his life of marvel and achievement, was possible to Lear. Those last thoughts are romantic in their strangeness: Lear's five-times repeated 'Never', in which the simplest and most unanswerable cry of anguish rises note by note till the heart breaks, is romantic in its naturalism; and to make a verse out of this one word required the boldness as well as the inspiration which came infallibly to Shakespeare at the greatest moments. But the familiarity, boldness and inspiration are surpassed (if that can be) by the next line, which shows the bodily oppression asking for bodily relief. The imagination that produced Lear's curse or his defiance of the storm may be paralleled in its kind, but where else are we to seek the imagination that could venture to follow that cry of 'Never' with such a phrase as 'undo this button', and yet could leave us on the topmost peaks of poetry?[14]

The character of Cordelia is not a masterpiece of invention or subtlety like that of Cleopatra; yet in its own way it is a creation as wonderful. Cordelia appears in only four of the twenty-six scenes of *King Lear*; she speaks – it is hard to believe it – scarcely more than a hundred lines; and yet no character in Shakespeare is more absolutely individual or more ineffaceably stamped on the memory of his readers. There is a harmony, strange but perhaps the result of intention, between the character itself and this reserved or parsimonious method of depicting it. An expressiveness almost inexhaustible gained through paucity of expression; the suggestion of infinite wealth and beauty conveyed by the very refusal to reveal this beauty in expansive speech – this is at once the nature of Cordelia herself and the chief characteristic of Shakespeare's art in representing it. Perhaps it is not fanciful to find a parallel in his drawing of a person very different, Hamlet. It was natural to Hamlet to examine himself minutely, to discuss himself at large, and yet to remain a mystery to himself; and Shakespeare's method of drawing the character answers to it; it is extremely detailed and searching, and yet its effect is to enhance the sense of mystery. The results in the two cases differ correspondingly. No one hesitates to enlarge upon Hamlet, who speaks of himself so much; but to use many words about Cordelia seems to be a kind of impiety.

I am obliged to speak of her chiefly because the devotion she inspires almost inevitably obscures her part in the tragedy. This devotion is composed, so to speak, of two contrary elements, reverence and pity. The first, because Cordelia's is a higher nature than that of most even of Shakespeare's heroines. With the tenderness of Viola or Desdemona she unites something of the resolution, power, and dignity of Hermione, and reminds us sometimes of Helena, sometimes of Isabella, though she has none of the traits which prevent Isabella from winning our hearts. Her assertion of truth and right, her allegiance to them, even the touch of severity that accompanies it, instead of compelling mere respect or admiration, become adorable in a nature so loving as Cordelia's. She is a thing enskyed and sainted, and yet we feel no incongruity in the love of the King of France for her as we do in the love of the Duke for Isabella.

But with this reverence or worship is combined in the reader's mind a passion of championship, of pity, even of protecting pity. She is so deeply wronged, and she appears, for all her strength, so defenceless. We think of her as unable to speak for herself. We think of her as quite young, and as slight and small.[15] 'Her voice was ever soft, gentle, and low'; ever so, whether the tone was that of resolution, or rebuke, or love.[16] Of all Shakespeare's heroines she knew least of joy. She grew up with Goneril and Regan for sisters. Even her love for her father must have been mingled with pain and anxiety. She must early have learned to school and repress emotion. She never knew the bliss of young love: there is no trace of such love for the King of France. She had knowingly to wound most deeply the being dearest to her. He cast her off; and, after suffering an agony for him, and before she could see him safe in death, she was brutally murdered. We have to thank the poet for passing lightly over the circumstances of her death. We do not think of them. Her image comes before us calm and bright and still.

The memory of Cordelia thus becomes detached in a manner

from the action of the drama. The reader refuses to admit into it any idea of imperfection, and is outraged when any share in her father's sufferings is attributed to the part she plays in the opening scene. Because she was deeply wronged he is ready to insist that she was wholly right. He refuses, that is, to take the tragic point of view, and, when it is taken, he imagines that Cordelia is being attacked, or is being declared to have 'deserved' all that befell her. But Shakespeare's was the tragic point of view. He exhibits in the opening scene a situation tragic for Cordelia as well as for Lear. At a moment where terrible issues join, Fate makes on her the one demand which she is unable to meet. . . . it was a demand which other heroines of Shakespeare could have met. Without loss of self-respect, and refusing even to appear to compete for a reward, they could have made the unreasonable old King feel that he was fondly loved. Cordelia cannot, because she is Cordelia. And so she is not merely rejected and banished, but her father is left to the mercies of her sisters. And the cause of her failure – a failure a thousand-fold redeemed – is a compound in which imperfection appears so intimately mingled with the noblest qualities that – if we are true to Shakespeare – we do not think either of justifying her or of blaming her: we feel simply the tragic emotions of fear and pity.

In this failure a large part is played by that obvious characteristic to which I have already referred. Cordelia is not, indeed, always tongue-tied, as several passages in the drama, and even in this scene, clearly show. But tender emotion, and especially a tender love for the person to whom she has to speak, makes her dumb. Her love, as she says, is more ponderous than her tongue.[17]

> Unhappy that I am, I cannot heave
> My heart into my mouth.

This expressive word 'heave' is repeated in the passage which describes her reception of Kent's letter:

> Faith, once or twice she heaved the name of 'Father'
> Pantingly forth, as if it press'd her heart:

two or three broken ejaculations escape her lips, and she 'starts' away 'to deal with grief alone'. The same trait reappears with an ineffable beauty in the stifled repetitions with which she attempts to answer her father in the moment of his restoration:

> *Lear.*   Do not laugh at me;
>   For, as I am a man, I think this lady
>   To be my child Cordelia.
> *Cor.*   And so I am, I am.
> *Lear.* Be your tears wet? yes, faith. I pray, weep not;
>   If you have poison for me, I will drink it.
>   I know you do not love me; for your sisters
>   Have, as I so remember, done me wrong:
>   You have some cause, they have not.
> *Cor.*   No cause, no cause.

We see this trait, for the last time marked by Shakespeare with a decision clearly intentional, in her inability to answer one syllable to the last words we hear her father speak to her:

> No, no, no, no! Come, let's away to prison:
> We two alone will sing like birds i' the cage:
> When thou dost ask me blessing, I'll kneel down,
> And ask of thee forgiveness: so we'll live,
> And pray, and sing, and tell old tales, and laugh
> At gilded butterflies. . . .

She stands and weeps, and goes out with him silent. And we see her alive no more.

But (I am forced to dwell on the point, because I am sure to slur it over is to be false to Shakespeare) this dumbness of love was not the sole source of misunderstanding. If this had been all, even Lear could have seen the love in Cordelia's eyes when, to his question 'What can you say to draw a third more opulent than your sisters?' she answered 'Nothing'. But it did not shine there. She is not merely silent, nor does she merely answer 'Nothing'. She tells him that she loves him 'according to her bond, nor more nor less'; and his answer,

How now, Cordelia! mend your speech a little,
Lest it may mar your fortunes,

so intensifies her horror at the hypocrisy of her sisters that she
replies,

Good my lord,
You have begot me, bred me, loved me: I
Return those duties back as are right fit,
Obey you, love you, and most honour you.
Why have my sisters husbands, if they say
They love you all? Haply, when I shall wed,
That lord whose hand must take my plight shall carry
Half my love with him, half my care and duty:
Sure, I shall never marry like my sisters,
To love my father all.

What words for the ear of an old father, unreasonable, despotic,
but fondly loving, indecent in his own expressions of preference,
and blind to the indecency of his appeal for protestations of fondness! Blank astonishment, anger, wounded love, contend within
him; but for the moment he restrains himself and asks,

But goes thy heart with this?

Imagine Imogen's reply! But Cordelia answers,

Ay, good my lord.
Lear. So young, and so untender?
Cor. So young, my lord, and true.

Yes, 'heavenly true'. But truth is not the only good in the world,
nor is the obligation to tell truth the only obligation. The matter
here was to keep it inviolate, but also to preserve a father. And
even if truth *were* the one and only obligation, to tell much less
than truth is not to tell it. And Cordelia's speech not only tells
much less than truth about her love, it actually perverts the truth
when it implies that to give love to a husband is to take it from
a father. There surely never was a more unhappy speech.

When Isabella goes to plead with Angelo for her brother's

life, her horror of her brother's sin is so intense, and her perception of the justice of Angelo's reasons for refusing her is so clear and keen, that she is ready to abandon her appeal before it is well begun; she would actually do so but that the warm-hearted profligate Lucio reproaches her for her coldness and urges her on. Cordelia's hatred of hypocrisy and of the faintest appearance of mercenary professions reminds us of Isabella's hatred of impurity; but Cordelia's position is infinitely more difficult, and on the other hand there is mingled with her hatred a touch of personal antagonism and of pride. Lear's words,

> Let pride, which she calls plainness, marry her![18]

are monstrously unjust, but they contain one grain of truth; and indeed it was scarcely possible that a nature so strong as Cordelia's, and with so keen a sense of dignity, should feel here nothing whatever of pride and resentment. This side of her character is emphatically shown in her language to her sisters in the first scene – language perfectly just, but little adapted to soften their hearts towards their father – and again in the very last words we hear her speak. She and her father are brought in, prisoners, to the enemy's camp; but she sees only Edmund, not those 'greater' ones on whose pleasure hangs her father's fate and her own. For her own she is little concerned; she knows how to meet adversity:

> For thee, oppressed king, am I cast down;
> Myself could else out-frown false fortune's frown.

Yes, that is how she would meet fortune, frowning it down, even as Goneril would have met it; nor, if her father had been already dead, would there have been any great improbability in the false story that was to be told of her death, that, like Goneril, she 'fordid herself'. Then, after those austere words about fortune, she suddenly asks,

> Shall we not see these daughters and these sisters?

Strange last words for us to hear from a being so worshipped and beloved; but how characteristic! Their tone is unmistakable.

I doubt if she could have brought herself to plead with her sisters for her father's life; and if she had attempted the task, she would have performed it but ill. Nor is our feeling towards her altered one whit by that. But what is true of Kent and the fool (who, like Kent, hastens on the quarrel with Goneril) is, in its measure, true of her. Any one of them would gladly have died a hundred deaths to help King Lear; and they do help his soul; but they harm his cause. They are all involved in tragedy.

Why does Cordelia die? I suppose no reader ever failed to ask that question, and to ask it with something more than pain – to ask it, if only for a moment, in bewilderment or dismay, and even perhaps in tones of protest. These feelings are probably evoked more strongly here than at the death of any other notable character in Shakespeare; and it may sound a wilful paradox to assert that the slightest element of reconciliation is mingled with them or succeeds them. Yet it seems to me indubitable that such an element is present, though difficult to make out with certainty what it is or whence it proceeds. And I will try to make this out, and to state it methodically.

(a) It is not due in any perceptible degree to the fact, which we have just been examining, that Cordelia through her tragic imperfection contributes something to the conflict and catastrophe; and I drew attention to that imperfection without any view to our present problem. The critics who emphasise it at this point in the drama are surely untrue to Shakespeare's mind; and still more completely astray are those who lay stress on the idea that Cordelia in bringing a foreign army to help her father was guilty of treason to her country. When she dies we regard her, practically speaking, simply as we regard Ophelia or Desdemona, as an innocent victim swept away in the convulsion caused by the error or guilt of others.

(b) Now this destruction of the good through the evil of others is one of the tragic facts of life, and no one can object to the use of it, within certain limits, in tragic art. And, further, those who because of it declaim against the nature of things, declaim without thinking. It is obviously the other side of the fact that the effects of good spread far and wide beyond the doer of good; and we should ask ourselves whether we really could wish (supposing it conceivable) to see this double-sided fact abolished. Nevertheless the touch of reconciliation that we feel in contemplating the death of Cordelia is not due, or is due only in some slight degree, to a perception that the event is true to life, admissible in tragedy, and a case of a law which we cannot seriously desire to see abrogated.

(c) What then is this feeling, and whence does it come? I believe that we shall find that it is a feeling not confined to *King Lear*, but present at the close of other tragedies; and that the reason why it has an exceptional tone or force at the close of *King Lear*, lies in that very peculiarity of the close which also – at least for the moment – excites bewilderment, dismay, or protest. The feeling I mean is the impression that the heroic being, though in one sense and outwardly he has failed, is yet in another sense superior to the world in which he appears; is, in some way which we do not seek to define, untouched by the doom that overtakes him; and is rather set free from life than deprived of it. Some such feeling as this – some feeling which, from this description of it, may be recognised as their own even by those who would dissent from the description – we surely have in various degrees at the deaths of Hamlet and Othello and Lear, and of Antony and Cleopatra and Coriolanus. It accompanies the more prominent tragic impressions, and, regarded alone, could hardly be called tragic. For it seems to imply (though we are probably quite unconscious of the implication) an idea which, if developed, would transform the tragic view of things. It implies that the tragic world, if taken as it is presented, with all its error, guilt, failure, woe and waste, is no final reality, but only a part of reality taken for the whole, and, when so taken, illusive; and that if we could see the whole, and the tragic facts in their true place in it, we should find them, not abolished, of course, but so transmuted that they had ceased to be strictly tragic – find, perhaps, the suffering and death counting for little or nothing, the greatness of the soul for much or all, and the heroic spirit, in spite of failure, nearer to the heart of things than the smaller, more circumspect, and perhaps even 'better' beings who survived the catastrophe. The feeling which I have tried to describe, as accompanying the more obvious tragic emotions at the deaths of heroes, corresponds with some such idea as this.[19]

Now this feeling is evoked with a quite exceptional strength by the death of Cordelia.[20] It is not due to the perception that she, like Lear, has attained through suffering; we know that she had suffered and attained in his days of prosperity. It is simply the feeling that what happens to such a being does not matter; all that matters is what she is. How this can be when, for anything the tragedy tells us, she has ceased to exist, we do not ask; but the tragedy itself makes us feel that somehow it is so. And the force with which this impression is conveyed depends largely on the very fact which excites our bewilderment and protest, that her death, following on the deaths of all the evil characters, and brought about by an unexplained delay in Edmund's effort to save her, comes on us, not as an inevitable conclusion to the sequence of events, but as the sudden stroke of mere fate or chance. The force of the impression, that is to say, depends on the very violence of the contrast between the outward and the inward, Cordelia's death and Cordelia's soul. The more unmotived, unmerited, senseless, monstrous, her fate, the more do we feel that it does not concern her. The extremity of the disproportion between prosperity and goodness first shocks us, and then flashes on us the conviction that our whole attitude in asking or expecting that goodness should be prosperous is wrong; that, if only we could see things as they are, we should see that the outward is nothing and the inward is all.

And some such thought as this (which, to bring it clearly out, I have stated, and still state, in a form both exaggerated and much too explicit) is really present through the whole play. Whether Shakespeare knew it or not, it is present. I might almost say that the 'moral' of *King Lear* is presented in the irony of this collocation:

Albany. The gods defend her!
        (*Enter* LEAR *with Cordelia dead in his arms.*)

The 'gods', it seems, do *not* show their approval by 'defending' their own from adversity or death, or by giving them power and prosperity. These, on the contrary, are worthless, or worse; it is not on them, but on the renunciation of them, that the gods throw incense. They breed lust, pride, hardness of heart, the insolence of office, cruelty, scorn, hypocrisy, contention, war, murder, self-destruction. The whole story beats this indictment of prosperity into the brain. Lear's great speeches in his madness proclaim it like the curses of Timon on life and man. But here, as in *Timon*, the poor and humble are, almost without exception, sound and sweet at heart, faithful and pitiful. And here adversity, to the blessed in spirit, is blessed. It wins fragrance from the crushed flower. It melts in aged hearts sympathies which prosperity had frozen. It purges the soul's sight by blinding that of the eyes. Throughout that stupendous Third Act the good are seen growing better through suffering, and the bad worse through success. The warm castle is a room in hell, the storm-swept heath a sanctuary. The judgment of this world is a lie; its goods, which we covet, corrupt us; its ills, which break our bodies, set our souls free:

> Our means secure us, and our mere defects
> Prove our commodities.

Let us renounce the world, hate it, and lose it gladly. The only real thing in it is the soul, with its courage, patience, devotion. And nothing outward can touch that.

SOURCE: *Shakespearean Tragedy* (1957).

NOTES

1. It is to Lear's altered plan that Kent applies these words.
2. There is talk of a war between Goneril and Regan within a fortnight of the division of the kingdom (II i 11–12).
3. I mean that no sufficiently clear reason is supplied for Edmund's delay in attempting to save Cordelia and Lear. The matter stands thus.

Edmund, after the defeat of the opposing army, sends Lear and Cordelia to prison. Then, in accordance with a plan agreed on between himself and Goneril, he despatches a captain with secret orders to put them both to death *instantly* (v iii 26–37, 244, 252). He then has to fight with the disguised Edgar. He is mortally wounded, and, as he lies dying, he says to Edgar (at line 162, *more than a hundred lines* after he gave that commission to the captain):

> What you have charged me with, that have I done;
> And more, much more; the time will bring it out;
> 'Tis past, and so am I.

In 'more, much more' he seems to be thinking of the order for the deaths of Lear and Cordelia (what else remained undisclosed?); yet he says nothing about it. A few lines later he recognises the justice of his fate, yet still says nothing. Then he hears the story of his father's death, says it has moved him and 'shall perchance do good' (what good except saving his victims?); yet he still says nothing. Even when he hears that Goneril is dead and Regan poisoned, he *still* says nothing. It is only when directly questioned about Lear and Cordelia that he tries to save the victims who were to be killed 'instantly' (242). How can we explain his delay? Perhaps, thinking the deaths of Lear and Cordelia would be of use to Goneril and Regan, he will not speak till he is sure that both the sisters are dead. Or perhaps, though he can recognise the justice of his fate and can be touched by the account of his father's death, he is still too self-absorbed to rise to the active effort to 'do some good, despite of his own nature'. But, while either of these conjectures is possible, it is surely far from satisfactory that we should be left to mere conjecture as to the cause of the delay which permits the catastrophe to take place. The *real* cause lies outside the dramatic *nexus*. It is Shakespeare's wish to deliver a sudden and crushing blow to the hopes which he has excited.

4. I say 'the reader's', because on the stage, whenever I have seen *King Lear*, the 'cuts' necessitated by modern scenery would have made this part of the play absolutely unintelligible to me if I had not been familiar with it. It is significant that Lamb in his *Tale of King Lear* almost omits the sub-plot.

5. Even if Cordelia had won the battle, Shakespeare would probably have hesitated to concentrate interest on it, for her victory would have been a British defeat.

6. It is vain to suggest that Edmund has only just come home, and that the letter is supposed to have been sent to him when he was 'out'. See 1 ii 38–40, 65–6.

7. The idea in scene i, perhaps, is that Cordelia's marriage, like the division of the kingdom, has really been pre-arranged, and that the

ceremony of choosing between France and Burgundy (1 i 46–7) is a mere fiction. Burgundy is to be her husband, and that is why, when Lear has cast her off, he offers her to Burgundy first (line 192 ff). It might seem from 211 ff that Lear's reason for doing so is that he prefers France, or thinks him the greater man, and therefore will not offer him first what is worthless: but the language of France (240 ff) seems to show that he recognises a prior right in Burgundy.

8. The word 'heath' in the stage-directions of the storm-scenes is, I may remark, Rowe's, not Shakespeare's, who never used the word till he wrote *Macbeth*.

9. Of course I do not mean that he is beginning to be insane, and still less that he *is* insane (as some medical critics suggest).

10. I must however point out that the modern stage-directions are most unfortunate in concealing the fact that here Cordelia sees her father again *for the first time*.

11. What immediately follows is as striking an illustration of quite another quality, and of the effects which make us think of Lear as pursued by a relentless fate. If he could go in and sleep after his prayer, as he intends, his mind, one feels, might be saved: so far there has been only the menace of madness. But from within the hovel Edgar – the last man who would willingly have injured Lear – cries, 'Fathom and half, fathom and half! Poor Tom!'; the Fool runs out terrified; Edgar, summoned by Kent, follows him; and, at sight of Edgar, in a moment something gives way in Lear's brain, and he exclaims:

> Hast thou given all
> To thy two daughters? And art thou come to this?

Henceforth he is mad. And they remain out in the storm.

I have not seen it noticed that this stroke of fate is repeated – surely intentionally – in the sixth scene. Gloster has succeeded in persuading Lear to come into the 'house'; he then leaves, and Kent after much difficulty induces Lear to lie down and rest upon the cushions. Sleep begins to come to him again, and he murmurs,

> 'Make no noise, make no noise; draw the curtains; so, so, so. We'll go to supper i' the morning. So, so, so.'

At that moment Gloster enters with the news that he has discovered a plot to kill the King; the rest that 'might yet have balm'd his broken senses' is again interrupted; and he is hurried away on a litter towards Dover. (His recovery, it will be remembered, is due to a long sleep artificially induced.)

12. III iv 49. This is [1904] printed as prose in the Globe edition, but is surely verse. Lear has not yet spoken prose in this scene, and his next three speeches are in verse. The next is in prose, and, ending in his tearing off his clothes, shows the advance of insanity.

13. [Lear's death is thus, I am reminded, like *père* Goriot's.] This interpretation may be condemned as fantastic, but the text, it appears to me, will bear no other. This is the whole speech (in the Globe text):

> And my poor fool is hang'd! No, no, no life!
> Why should a dog, a horse, a rat, have life,
> And thou no breath at all? Thou'lt come no more,
> Never, never, never, never, never!
> Pray you, undo this button: thank you, sir.
> Do you see this? Look on her, look, her lips,
> Look there, look there!

The transition at 'Do you see this?' from despair to something more than hope is exactly the same as in the preceding passage at the word 'Ha!':

> A plague upon you, murderers, traitors all!
> I might have saved her; now she's gone for ever!
> Cordelia, Cordelia, stay a little.
> Ha!
> What is't thou say'st? Her voice was ever soft,
> Gentle, and low, an excellent thing in woman.

As to any other remarks, I will ask the reader to notice that the passage from Lear's entrance with the body of Cordelia to the stage-direction *He dies* (which probably comes a few lines too soon) is 54 lines in length, and that 30 of them represent the interval during which he has absolutely forgotten Cordelia. (It begins when he looks up at the Captain's words, line 275.) To make Lear during this interval turn continually in anguish to the corpse, is to act the passage in a manner irreconcilable with the text, and insufferable in its effect. I speak from experience. I have seen the passage acted thus, and my sympathies were so exhausted long before Lear's death that his last speech, the most pathetic speech ever written, left me disappointed and weary.

14. The Quartos give the 'Never' only thrice (surely wrongly), and all the actors I have heard have preferred this easier task. I ought perhaps to add that the Quartos give the words 'Break, heart; I prithee, break!' to Lear, not Kent.

15. 'Our last and least' (according to the Folio reading). Lear speaks again of 'this little seeming substance'. He can carry her dead body in his arms.

16. Perhaps then the 'low sound' is not merely metaphorical in Kent's speech in 1 i 153 ff:

> answer my life my judgment,
> Thy youngest daughter does not love thee least;
> Nor are those empty-hearted whose low sound
> Reverbs no hollowness.

17. I i 80. 'More ponderous' is the reading of the Folios, 'more richer' that of the Quartos. The latter is usually preferred, and Mr Aldis Wright says 'more ponderous' has the appearance of being a player's correction to avoid a piece of imaginary bad grammar. Does it not sound more like the author's improvement of a phrase that he thought a little flat? And, apart from that, is it not significant that it expresses the same idea of weight that appears in the phrase 'I cannot heave my heart into my mouth'?

18. Cf Cornwall's satirical remarks on Kent's 'plainness' in II ii 101 ff – a plainness which did no service to Kent's master. (As a matter of fact, Cordelia had said nothing about 'plainness'.)

19. It follows from the above that, if this idea were made explicit and accompanied our reading of a tragedy throughout, it would confuse or even destroy the tragic impression. So would the constant presence of Christian beliefs. The reader most attached to these beliefs holds them in temporary suspension while he is immersed in a Shakespearean tragedy. Such tragedy assumes that the world, as it is presented, is the truth, though it also provokes feelings which imply that this world is not the whole truth, and therefore not the truth.

20. Though Cordelia, of course, does not occupy the position of the hero.

G. Wilson Knight

KING LEAR AND THE COMEDY
OF THE GROTESQUE (1930)

It may appear strange to search for any sort of comedy as a primary theme in a play whose abiding gloom is so heavy, whose reading of human destiny and human actions so starkly tragic. Yet it is an error of aesthetic judgement to regard humour as essentially trivial. Though its impact usually appears vastly different from that of tragedy, yet there is a humour that treads the brink of tears, and tragedy which needs but an infinitesimal shift of perspective to disclose the varied riches of comedy. Humour is an evanescent thing, even more difficult of analysis and intellectual location than tragedy. To the coarse mind lacking sympathy an incident may seem comic which to the richer understanding is pitiful and tragic. So, too, one series of facts can be treated by the artist as either comic or tragic, lending itself equivalently to both. Sometimes a great artist may achieve significant effects by a criss-cross of tears and laughter. Tchehov does this, especially in his plays. A shifting flash of comedy across the pain of the purely tragic both increases the tension and suggests, vaguely, a resolution and a purification. The comic and the tragic rest both on the idea of incompatibilities, and are also, themselves, mutually exclusive: therefore to mingle them is to add to the meaning of each; for the result is then but a new sublime incongruity.

King Lear is roughly analogous to Tchehov where *Macbeth* is analogous to Dostoievsky. The wonder of Shakespearian tragedy is ever a mystery – a vague, yet powerful, tangible, presence; an interlocking of the mind with a profound meaning, a disclosure to the inward eye of vistas undreamed, and but fitfully understood. *King Lear* is great in the abundance and richness of human delineation, in the level focus of creation that builds a massive oneness, in fact, a universe, of single quality from a multiplicity of differentiated units; and in a positive and purposeful working out of a purgatorial philosophy. But it is still greater in the perfect fusion of psychological realism with the daring flights of a fantastic imagination. The heart of a Shakespearian tragedy is centred in the imaginative, in the unknown; and in *King Lear*, where we touch the unknown, we touch the fantastic. The peculiar dualism at the root of this play which wrenches and splits the mind by a sight of incongruities displays in turn realities absurd, hideous, pitiful. This incongruity is Lear's madness; it is also the demonic laughter that echoes in the *Lear* universe. In pure tragedy the dualism of experience is continually being dissolved in the masterful beauty of passion, merged in the sunset of emotion. But in comedy it is not so softly resolved – incompatibilities stand out till the sudden relief of laughter or its equivalent of humour: therefore incongruity is the especial mark of comedy. Now in *King Lear* there is a dualism continually crying in vain to be resolved either by tragedy or comedy. Thence arises its peculiar tension of pain: and the course of the action often comes as near to the resolution of comedy as to that of tragedy. So I shall notice here the imaginative core of the play, and, excluding much of the logic of the plot from immediate attention, analyse the fantastic comedy of *King Lear*.

From the start, the situation has a comic aspect. It has been observed that Lear has, so to speak, staged an interlude, with himself as chief actor, in which he grasps expressions of love to his heart, and resigns his sceptre to a chorus of acclamations. It is childish, foolish – but very human. So, too, is the result. Sincerity forbids play-acting, and Cordelia cannot subdue her instinct to any judgement advising tact rather than truth. The incident is profoundly comic and profoundly pathetic. It is, indeed, curious that so storm-furious a play as *King Lear* should have so trivial a domestic basis: it is the first of our many incongruities to be noticed. The absurdity of the old King's anger is clearly indicated by Kent:

> Kill thy physician, and the fee bestow
> Upon the foul disease.   (I i 166)

The result is absurd. Lear's loving daughter Cordelia is struck from his heart's register, and he is shortly, old and grey-haired and a king, cutting a cruelly ridiculous figure before the cold sanity of his unloving elder daughters. Lear is selfish, self-centred. The images he creates of his three daughters' love are quite false, sentimentalized: he understands the nature of none of his children, and demanding an unreal and impossible love from all three, is disillusioned by each in turn. But, though sentimental, this love is not weak. It is powerful and firm-planted in his mind as a mountain rock embedded in earth. The tearing out of it is hideous, cataclysmic. A tremendous soul is, as it were, incongruously geared to a puerile intellect. Lear's senses prove his idealized love-figments false, his intellect snaps, and, as the loosened drive flings limp, the disconnected engine of madness spins free, and the ungeared revolutions of it are terrible, fantastic. This, then, is the basis of the play: greatness linked to puerility. Lear's instincts are themselves grand, heroic – noble even. His judgement is nothing. He understands neither himself nor his daughters:

> *Regan.* 'Tis the infirmity of his age: yet he hath ever but slenderly known himself.
> *Goneril.* The best and soundest of his time hath been but rash . . .   (I i 296)

Lear starts his own tragedy by a foolish misjudgement. Lear's fault is a fault of the mind, a mind unwarrantably, because selfishly, foolish. And he knows it:

> O Lear, Lear, Lear!
> Beat at this gate that let thy folly in,
> And thy dear judgement out!   (I iv 294)

His purgatory is to be a purgatory of the mind, of madness. Lear has trained himself to think he cannot be wrong: he finds he is wrong. He has fed his heart on sentimental knowledge of his children's love: he finds their love is not sentimental. There is now a gaping dualism in his mind, thus drawn asunder by incongruities, and he endures madness. Thus the theme of the play is

bodied continually into a fantastic incongruity, which is implicit
in the beginning – in the very act of Lear's renunciation, retaining the 'title and addition' of King, yet giving over a king's
authority to his children. As he becomes torturingly aware of
the truth, incongruity masters his mind, and fantastic madness
ensues; and this peculiar fact of the Lear-theme is reflected in the
Lear universe:

> *Gloucester.* These late eclipses in the sun and moon portend no
> good to us: though the wisdom of nature can reason it
> thus and thus, yet nature finds itself scourged by the
> sequent effects: love cools, friendship falls off, brothers
> divide: in cities, mutinies; in countries, discord; in
> palaces, treason; and the bond cracked 'twixt son and
> father. This villain of mine comes under the predic-
> tion; there's son against father: the King falls from bias
> of nature; there's father against child. We have seen
> the best of our time: machinations, hollowness,
> treachery, and all ruinous disorders, follow us dis-
> quietly to our graves.   (I ii 115)

Gloucester's words hint a universal incongruity here: the fantastic incongruity of parent and child opposed. And it will be
most helpful later to notice the Gloucester-theme in relation to
that of Lear.

From the first signs of Goneril's cruelty, the Fool is used as a
chorus, pointing us to the absurdity of the situation. He is
indeed an admirable chorus, increasing our pain by his emphasis
on a humour which yet will not serve to merge the incompatible
in a unity of laughter. He is not all wrong when he treats the
situation as matter for a joke. Much here that is always regarded
as essentially pathetic is not far from comedy. For instance, consider Lear's words:

> I will have such revenges on you both
> That all the world shall – I will do such things –
> What they are, yet I know not; but they shall be
> The terrors of the earth.   (II iv 282)

What could be more painfully incongruous, spoken, as it is, by

an old man, a king, to his daughter? It is not far from the ridiculous. The very thought seems a sacrilegious cruelty, I know: but
ridicule is generally cruel. The speeches of Lear often come near
comedy. Again, notice the abrupt contrast in his words:

> But yet thou art my flesh, my blood, my daughter;
> Or rather a disease that 's in my flesh,
> Which I must needs call mine: thou art a boil,
> A plague-sore, an embossed carbuncle,
> In my corrupted blood. But I'll not chide thee ...
>
> (II iv 224)

This is not comedy, nor humour. But it is exactly the stuff of
which humour is made. Lear is mentally a child; in passion a titan.
The absurdity of his every act at the beginning of his tragedy is
contrasted with the dynamic fury which intermittently bursts
out, flickers – then flames and finally gives us those grand
apostrophes lifted from man's stage of earth to heaven's rain and
fire and thunder:

> Blow, winds, and crack your cheeks! rage! blow!
> You cataracts and hurricanoes, spout
> Till you have drench'd our steeples, drown'd the cocks!
>
> (III ii 1)

Two speeches of this passionate and unrestrained volume of
Promethean curses are followed by:

> No, I will be the pattern of all patience;
> I will say nothing.   (III ii 37)

Again we are in touch with potential comedy: a slight shift of
perspective, and the incident is rich with humour. A sense of
self-directed humour would, indeed, have saved Lear. It is a
quality he absolutely lacks.

Herein lies the profound insight of the Fool: he sees the
potentialities of comedy in Lear's behaviour. This old man,
recently a king, and, if his speeches are fair samples, more than
a little of a tyrant, now goes from daughter to daughter, furious

because Goneril dares criticize his pet knights, kneeling down before Regan, performing, as she says, 'unsightly tricks' (II iv 159) – the situation is excruciatingly painful, and its painfulness is exactly of that quality which embarrasses in some forms of comedy. In the theatre, one is terrified lest some one laugh: yet, if Lear could laugh – if the Lears of the world could laugh at themselves – there would be no such tragedy. In the early scenes old age and dignity suffer, and seem to deserve, the punishments of childhood:

> Now, by my life,
> Old fools are babes again; and must be used
> With checks as flatteries.   (I iii 19)

The situation is summed up by the Fool:

> *Lear.* When were you wont to be so full of songs, sirrah?
> *Fool.* I have used it, nuncle, ever since thou madest thy daugh-
>   ters thy mother: for when thou gavest them the rod,
>   and put'st down thine own breeches . . .   (I iv 186)

The height of indecency in suggestion, the height of incongruity. Lear is spiritually put to the ludicrous shame endured bodily by Kent in the stocks; and the absurd rant of Kent, and the unreasonable childish temper of Lear, both merit in some measure what they receive. Painful as it may sound, that is, provisionally, a truth we should realize. The Fool realizes it. He is, too, necessary. Here, where the plot turns on the diverging tugs of two assurances in the mind, it is natural that the action be accompanied by some symbol of humour, that mode which is built of unresolved incompatibilities. Lear's torment is a torment of this dualistic kind, since he scarcely believes his senses when his daughters resist him. He repeats the history of Troilus, who cannot understand the faithlessness of Cressid. In *Othello* and *Timon of Athens* the transition is swift from extreme love to revenge or hate. The movement of Lear's mind is less direct: like Troilus, he is suspended between two separate assurances. Therefore Pandarus, in the latter acts of *Troilus and Cressida*,

plays a part similar to the Fool in *King Lear*: both attempt to
heal the gaping wound of the mind's incongruous knowledge by
the unifying, healing release of laughter. They make no attempt
to divert, but rather to direct the hero's mind to the present
incongruity. The Fool sees, or tries to see, the humorous
potentialities in the most heart-wrenching of incidents:

> *Lear.* O me, my heart, my rising heart! but, down!
> *Fool.* Cry to it, nuncle, as the cockney did to the eels when she
>   put 'em i' the paste alive; she knapped 'em o' the cox-
>   combs with a stick, and cried 'Down, wantons, down!'
>   'Twas her brother that, in pure kindness to his horse,
>   buttered his hay.   (II iv 122)

Except for the last delightful touch – the antithesis of the other –
that is a cruel, ugly sense of humour. It is the sinister humour at
the heart of this play: we are continually aware of the humour of
cruelty and the cruelty of humour. But the Fool's use of it is not
aimless. If Lear could laugh he might yet save his reason.

But there is no relief. Outside, in the wild country, the storm
grows more terrible:

> *Kent.*   . . . Since I was man
>   Such sheets of fire, such bursts of horrid thunder,
>   Such groans of roaring wind and rain, I never
>   Remember to have heard . . .   (III ii 45)

Lear's mind keeps returning to the unreality, the impossibility
of what has happened:

> Your old kind father, whose frank heart gave all –
> O, that way madness lies; let me shun that;
> No more of that.   (III iv 20)

He is still self-centred; cannot understand that he has been
anything but a perfect father; cannot understand his daughters'
behaviour. It is

> as this mouth should tear this hand
> For lifting food to't . . .   (III iv 15)

It is incongruous, impossible. There is no longer any 'rule in
unity itself'.¹ Just as Lear's mind begins to fail, the Fool finds
Edgar disguised as 'poor Tom'. Edgar now succeeds the Fool as
the counterpart to the breaking sanity of Lear; and where the
humour of the Fool made no contact with Lear's mind, the fantastic appearance and incoherent words of Edgar are immediately
assimilated, as glasses correctly focused to the sight of oncom-
ing madness. Edgar turns the balance of Lear's wavering men-
tality. His fantastic appearance and lunatic irrelevancies, with the
storm outside, and the Fool still for occasional chorus, create a
scene of wraith-like unreason, a vision of a world gone mad:

... Bless thy five wits! Tom's a-cold – O, do de, do de, do de.
Bless thee from whirlwinds, star-blasting, and taking! Do poor
Tom some charity, whom the foul fiend vexes: there could I
have him now – and there – and there again, and there.

(III iv 57)

To Lear his words are easily explained. His daughters 'have
brought him to this pass'. He cries:

Lear. Is it the fashion that discarded fathers
     Should have thus little mercy on their flesh?
     Judicious punishment! 'twas this flesh begot
     Those pelican daughters.
Edgar. Pillicock sat on Pillicock-hill:
     Halloo, halloo, loo, loo!
Fool. This cold night will turn us all to fools and madmen.

(III iv 71)

What shall we say of this exquisite movement? Is it comedy?
Lear's profound unreason is capped by the blatant irrelevance
of Edgar's couplet suggested by the word 'pelican'; then the two
are swiftly all but unified, for us if not for Lear, in the healing
balm of the Fool's conclusion. It is the process of humour, where
two incompatibles are resolved in laughter. The Fool does this
again. Lear again speaks a profound truth as the wild night and
Edgar's fantastic impersonation grip his mind and dethrone his
conventional sanity:

> *Lear.* Is man no more than this? Consider him well. Thou
> owest the worm no silk, the beast no hide, the sheep
> no wool, the cat no perfume. Ha! Here 's three on 's are
> sophisticated! Thou art the thing itself: unaccommo-
> dated man is no more but such a poor, bare, forked
> animal as thou art. Off, off, you lendings! come un-
> button here. (*Tearing off his clothes.*)
> *Fool.* Prithee, nuncle, be contented; 'tis a naughty night to
> swim in.   (III iv 105)

This is the furthest flight, not of tragedy, but of philosophic
comedy. The autocratic and fiery-fierce old king, symbol of
dignity, is confronted with the meanest of men; a naked lunatic
beggar. In a flash of vision he attempts to become his opposite,
to be naked, 'unsophisticated'. And then the opposing forces
which struck the lightning-flash of vision tail off, resolved into
a perfect unity by the Fool's laughter, reverberating, trickling,
potent to heal in sanity the hideous unreason of this tempest-
shaken night: ''tis a naughty night to swim in'. Again this is the
process of humour: its flash of vision first bridges the positive
and negative poles of the mind, unifying them, and then expresses
itself in laughter.

This scene grows still more grotesque, fantastical, sinister.
Gloucester enters, his torch flickering in the beating wind:

> *Fool.* . . . Look, here comes a walking fire.
>   (*Enter* GLOUCESTER, *with a torch.*)
> *Edgar.* This is the foul fiend Flibbertigibbet: he begins at
> curfew and walks till the first cock . . .   (II iv 116)

Lear welcomes Edgar as his 'philosopher', since he embodies that
philosophy of incongruity and the fantastically-absurd which is
Lear's vision in madness. 'Noble philosopher', he says (III iv
176), and 'I will still keep with my philosopher' (III iv 180). The
unresolved dualism that tormented Troilus and was given
metaphysical expression by him (*Troilus and Cressida*, v ii
134–57) is here more perfectly bodied into the poetic symbol of
poor Tom: and since Lear cannot hear the resolving laugh of
foolery, his mind is focused only to the 'philosopher' mumbling

of the foul fiend. Edgar thus serves to lure Lear on: we forget that he is dissimulating. Lear is the centre of our attention, and as the world shakes with tempest and unreason, we endure something of the shaking and the tempest of his mind. The absurd and fantastic reign supreme. Lear does not compass for more than a few speeches the 'noble anger' (II iv 279) for which he prayed, the anger of Timon. From the start he wavered between affection and disillusionment, love and hate. The heavens in truth 'fool' (II iv 278) him. He is the 'natural fool of fortune' (IV vi 196). Now his anger begins to be a lunatic thing, and when it rises to any sort of magnificent fury or power it is toppled over by the ridiculous capping of Edgar's irrelevancies:

> *Lear.* To have a thousand with red burning spits
>   Come hissing in upon 'em –
> *Edgar.* The foul fiend bites my back.   (III vi 17)

The mock trial is instituted. Lear's curses were for a short space terrible, majestic, less controlled and purposeful than Timon's but passionate and grand in their tempestuous fury. Now, in madness, he flashes on us the ridiculous basis of his tragedy in words which emphasize the indignity and incongruity of it, and make his madness something nearer the ridiculous than the terrible, something which moves our pity, but does not strike awe:

> Arraign her first; 'tis Goneril. I here take my oath before this honourable assembly, she kicked the poor king her father.
>   (III vi 49)

This stroke of the absurd – so vastly different from the awe we experience in face of Timon's hate – is yet fundamental here. The core of the play is an absurdity, an indignity, an incongruity. In no tragedy of Shakespeare do incident and dialogue so recklessly and miraculously walk the tight-rope of our pity over the depths of bathos and absurdity.

This particular region of the terrible bordering on the fantastic

and absurd is exactly the playground of madness. Thus the
setting of Lear's madness includes a sub-plot where these same
elements are presented with stark nakedness, and no veiling
subtleties. The Gloucester-theme is a certain indication of our
vision and helps us to understand, and feel, the enduring agony
of Lear. As usual, the first scene of this play strikes the dominant
note. Gloucester jests at the bastardy of his son Edmund, re-
marking that, though he is ashamed to acknowledge him, 'there
was good sport at his making' (I i 23). That is, we start with
humour in bad taste. The whole tragedy witnesses a sense of
humour in 'the gods' which is in similar bad taste. Now all the
Lear effects are exaggerated in the Gloucester-theme. Edmund's
plot is a more Iago-like, devilish, intentional thing than Goneril's
and Regan's icy callousness. Edgar's supposed letter is crude
and absurd:

... I begin to find an idle and fond bondage in the oppression of
aged tyranny ...   (I ii 53)

But then Edmund, wittiest and most attractive of villains, composed it. One can almost picture his grin as he penned those
lines, commending them mentally to the limited intellect of his
father. Yes – the Gloucester-theme has a beginning even more
fantastic than that of Lear's tragedy. And not only are the Lear
effects here exaggerated in the directions of villainy and humour:
they are even more clearly exaggerated in that of horror. The
gouging out of Gloucester's eyes is a thing unnecessary, crude,
disgusting: it is meant to be. It helps to provide an accompanying
exaggeration of one element – that of cruelty – in the horror that
makes Lear's madness. And not only horror: there is even again
something satanically comic bedded deep in it. The sight of
physical torment, to the uneducated, brings laughter. Shakespeare's England delighted in watching both physical torment
and the comic ravings of actual lunacy. The dance of madmen in
Webster's *Duchess of Malfi* is of the same ghoulish humour as
Regan's plucking Gloucester by the beard: the groundlings will
laugh at both. Moreover, the sacrilege of the human body in
torture must be, to a human mind, incongruous, absurd. This

hideous mockery is consummated in Regan's final witticism after Gloucester's eyes are out:

> Go, thrust him out at gates, and let him smell
> His way to Dover.   (III vii 93)

The macabre humoresque of this is nauseating: but it is there, and integral to the play. These ghoulish horrors, so popular in Elizabethan drama, and the very stuff of the *Lear* of Shakespeare's youth, *Titus Andronicus*, find an exquisitely appropriate place in the tragedy of Shakespeare's maturity which takes as its especial province this territory of the grotesque and the fantastic which is Lear's madness. We are clearly pointed to this grim fun, this hideous sense of humour, at the back of tragedy:

> As flies to wanton boys are we to the gods;
> They kill us for their sport.   (IV i 36)

This illustrates the exact quality I wish to emphasize: the humour a boy – even a kind boy – may see in the wriggles of an impaled insect. So, too, Gloucester is bound, and tortured, physically; and so the mind of Lear is impaled, crucified on the cross-beams of love and disillusion.

There follows the grim pilgrimage of Edgar and Gloucester towards Dover Cliff: an incident typical enough of *King Lear* –

> 'Tis the times' plague when madmen lead the blind.
>   (IV i 46)

They stumble on, madman and blind man, Edgar mumbling:

... five fiends have been in poor Tom at once; of lust, as Obidicut; Hobbididance, prince of dumbness; Mahu, of stealing; Modo, of murder; Flibbertigibbet, of mopping and mowing, who since possesses chambermaids and waiting-women ...   (IV i 59)

They are near Dover. Edgar persuades his father that they are climbing steep ground, though they are on a level field, that the sea can be heard beneath:

> *Gloucester*. Methinks the ground is even.
> *Edgar*.   Horrible steep.
>   Hark, do you hear the sea?
> *Gloucester*.   No, truly.
> *Edgar*. Why, then your other senses grow imperfect
>   By your eyes' anguish.   (IV vi 3)

Gloucester notices the changed sanity of Edgar's speech, and
remarks thereon. Edgar hurries his father to the supposed brink,
and vividly describes the dizzy precipice over which Gloucester
thinks they stand:

>   How fearful
> And dizzy 'tis to cast one's eyes so low!
> The crows and choughs that wing the midway air
> Show scarce so gross as beetles: half way down
> Hangs one that gathers samphire, dreadful trade! ...
>   (VI vi 12)

Gloucester thanks him, and rewards him; bids him move off;
then kneels, and speaks a prayer of noble resignation, breathing
that stoicism which permeates the suffering philosophy of this
play:

>   O you mighty gods!
>   This world I do renounce, and, in your sights,
>   Shake patiently my great affliction off:
>   If I could bear it longer, and not fall
>   To quarrel with your great opposeless wills,
>   My snuff and loathed part of nature should
>   Burn itself out.   (IV vi 35)

Gloucester has planned a spectacular end for himself. We are
given these noble descriptive and philosophical speeches to tune
our minds to a noble, tragic sacrifice. And what happens? The
old man falls from his kneeling posture a few inches, flat, face
foremost. Instead of the dizzy circling to crash and spill his life
on the rocks below – just this. The grotesque merged into the
ridiculous reaches a consummation in this bathos of tragedy: it
is the furthest, most exaggerated, reach of the poet's towering

fantastically. We have a sublimely daring stroke of technique, unjustifiable, like Edgar's emphasized and vigorous madness throughout, on the plane of plot-logic, and even to a superficial view somewhat out of place imaginatively in so dire and stark a limning of human destiny as is *King Lear*; yet this scene is in reality a consummate stroke of art. The Gloucester-theme throughout reflects and emphasizes and exaggerates all the per-current qualities of the Lear-theme. Here the incongruous and fantastic element of the Lear-theme is boldly reflected into the tragically-absurd. The stroke is audacious, unashamed, and magical of effect. Edgar keeps up the deceit; persuades his father that he has really fallen; points to the empty sky, as to a cliff:

> . . . the shrill-gorged lark
> Cannot be heard so far . . .   (IV vi 59)

and finally paints a fantastic picture of a ridiculously grotesque devil that stood with Gloucester on the edge:

> As I stood here below, methought his eyes
> Were two full moons; he had a thousand noses,
> Horns whelk'd and waved like the enridged sea;
> It was some fiend . . .   (IV vi 70)

Some fiend, indeed.

There is masterful artistry in all this. The Gloucester-theme has throughout run separate from that of Lear, yet parallel, and continually giving us direct villainy where the other shows cold callousness; horrors of physical torment where the other has a subtle mental torment; culminating in this towering stroke of the grotesque and absurd to balance the fantastic incidents and speeches that immediately follow. At this point we suddenly have our first sight of Lear in the full ecstasy of his later madness. Now, when our imaginations are most powerfully quickened to the grotesque and incongruous, the whole surge of the Glouces-ter-theme, which has just reached its climax, floods as a tributary the main stream of our sympathy with Lear. Our vision has thus been uniquely focused to understand that vision of the grotesque,

the incongruous, the fantastically-horrible, which is the agony
of Lear's mind:

> *Enter* LEAR, *fantastically dressed with wild flowers.*
> (IV vi 81)

So runs Capell's direction. Lear, late 'every inch a king', the
supreme pathetic figure of literature, now utters the wild and
whirling language of furthest madness. Sometimes his words
hold profound meaning. Often they are tuned to the orthodox
Shakespearian hate and loathing, especially sex-loathing, of the
hate-theme. Or again, they are purely ludicrous, or would be,
were it not a Lear who speaks them:

> ... Look, look, a mouse! Peace, peace; this piece of toasted
> cheese will do't ...   (IV vi 90)

It is, indeed, well that we are, as it were, prepared by now for
the grotesque. Laughter is forbidden us. Consummate art has
so forged plot and incident that we may watch with tears rather
than laughter the cruelly comic actions of Lear:

> *Lear.* I will die bravely, like a bridegroom.[2] What!
>   I will be jovial: come, come; I am a king,
>   My masters, know you that?
> *Gentleman.* You are a royal one, and we obey you.
> *Lear.* Then there's life in't. Nay, if you get it, you shall get it
>   with running. Sa, sa, sa, sa.   (IV vi 203)

Lear is a child again in his madness. We are in touch with the
exquisitely pathetic, safeguarded only by Shakespeare's masterful technique from the bathos of comedy.

But indeed this recurrent stress on the incongruous and the
fantastic is not a subsidiary element in *King Lear*: it is the very
heart of the play. We watch humanity grotesquely tormented,
cruelly and with mockery impaled: nearly all the persons suffer
some form of crude indignity in the course of the play. I have
noticed the major themes of Lear and Gloucester: there are
others. Kent is banished, undergoes the disguise of a servant, is

put to shame in the stocks; Cornwall is killed by his own servant resisting the dastardly mutilation of Gloucester; Oswald, the prim courtier, is done to death by Edgar in the role of an illiterate country yokel –

... keep out, che vor ye, or ise try whether your costard or my ballow be the harder ...   (IV vi 247)

Edgar himself endures the utmost degradation of his disguise as 'poor Tom', begrimed and naked, and condemned to speak nothing but idiocy. Edmund alone steers something of an unswerving tragic course, brought to a fitting, deserved, but spectacular end, slain by his wronged brother, nobly repentant at the last:

> *Edmund.* What you have charged me with, that have I done;
>   And more, much more; the time will bring it out:
>   'Tis past, and so am I. But what art thou
>   That hast this fortune on me? If thou'rt noble,
>   I do forgive thee.
> *Edgar.*   Let's exchange charity.
>   I am no less in blood than thou art, Edmund;
>   If more, the more thou hast wrong'd me.
>   My name is Edgar ...   (v iii 164)

The note of forgiving chivalry reminds us of the deaths of Hamlet and Laertes. Edmund's fate is nobly tragic: 'the wheel has come full circle; I am here' (v iii 176). And Edmund is the most villainous of all. Again, we have incongruity; and again, the Gloucester-theme reflects the Lear-theme. Edmund is given a noble, an essentially tragic end, and Goneril and Regan, too, meet their ends with something of tragic fineness in pursuit of their evil desires. Regan dies by her sister's poison; Goneril with a knife. They die, at least, in the cause of love – love of Edmund. Compared with these deaths, the end of Cordelia is horrible, cruel, unnecessarily cruel – the final grotesque horror in the play. Her villainous sisters are already dead. Edmund is nearly dead, repentant. It is a matter of seconds – and rescue comes too late.

She is hanged by a common soldier. The death which Dostoievsky's Stavrogin singled out as of all the least heroic and
picturesque, or rather, shall we say, the most hideous and
degrading: this is the fate that grips the white innocence and re-
splendent love-strength of Cordelia. To be hanged, after the
death of her enemies, in the midst of friends. It is the last hideous
joke of destiny: this — and the fact that Lear is still alive, has
recovered his sanity for this. The death of Cordelia is the last
and most horrible of all the horrible incongruities I have noticed:

> Why should a dog, a horse, a rat have life,
> And thou no breath at all?   (v iii 308)

We remember: 'Upon such sacrifices, my Cordelia, the gods
themselves throw incense' (v iii 20). Or do they laugh, and is the
Lear universe one ghastly piece of fun?

We do not feel that. The tragedy is most poignant in that it is
purposeless, unreasonable. It is the most fearless artistic facing of
the ultimate cruelty of things in our literature. That cruelty
would be less were there not this element of comedy which I
have emphasized, the insistent incongruities, which create and
accompany the madness of Lear, which leap to vivid shape in the
mockery of Gloucester's suicide, which are intrinsic in the texture of the whole play. Mankind is, as it were, deliberately and
comically tormented by 'the gods'. He is not even allowed to
die tragically. Lear is 'bound upon a wheel of fire' and only death
will end the victim's agony:

> Vex not his ghost: O, let him pass! he hates him
> That would upon the rack of this tough world
> Stretch him out longer.   (v iii 315)

King Lear is supreme in that, in this main theme, it faces the very
absence of tragic purpose: wherein it is profoundly different from
Timon of Athens. Yet, as we close the sheets of this play, there is
no horror, nor resentment. The tragic purification of the essentially untragic is yet complete.

Now in this essay it will, perhaps, appear that I have unduly emphasized one single element of the play, magnifying it, and leaving the whole distorted. It has been my purpose to emphasize. I have not exaggerated. The pathos has not been minimized: it is redoubled. Nor does the use of the words 'comic' and 'humour' here imply disrespect to the poet's purpose: rather I have used these words, crudely no doubt, to cut out for analysis the very heart of the play – the thing that man dares scarcely face: the demonic grin of the incongruous and absurd in the most pitiful of human struggles with an iron fate. It is this that wrenches, splits, gashes the mind till it utters the whirling vapourings of lunacy. And, though love and music – twin sisters of salvation – temporarily may heal the racked consciousness of Lear, yet, so deeply planted in the facts of our life is this unknowing ridicule of destiny, that the uttermost tragedy of the incongruous ensues, and there is no hope save in the broken heart and limp body of death. This is of all the most agonizing of tragedies to endure: and if we are to feel more than a fraction of this agony, we must have sense of this quality of grimmest humour. We must beware of sentimentalizing the cosmic mockery of the play.

And is there, perhaps, even a deeper, and less heart-searing, significance in its humour? Smiles and tears are indeed most curiously interwoven here. Gloucester was saved from his violent and tragic suicide that he might recover his wronged son's love, and that his heart might

> 'Twixt two extremes of passion, joy and grief,
> Burst smilingly.   (v iii 200)

Lear dies with the words

> Do you see this? Look on her, look, her lips,
> Look there, look there!   (v iii 312)

What smiling destiny is this he sees at the last instant of racked mortality? Why have we that strangely beautiful account of Cordelia's first hearing of her father's pain:

> . . . patience and sorrow strove
> Who should express her goodliest. You have seen

> Sunshine and rain at once: her smiles and tears
> Were like a better way: those happy smilets,
> That play'd on her ripe lip, seem'd not to know
> What guests were in her eyes; which parted thence,
> As pearls from diamonds dropp'd. In brief,
> Sorrow would be a rarity most beloved,
> If all could so become it.   (IV iii 18)

What do we touch in these passages? Sometimes we know that all human pain holds beauty, that no tear falls but it dews some flower we cannot see. Perhaps humour, too, is inwoven in the universal pain, and the enigmatic silence holds not only an unutterable sympathy, but also the ripples of an impossible laughter whose flight is not for the wing of human understanding; and perhaps it is this that casts its darting shadow of the grotesque across the furrowed pages of *King Lear*.

SOURCE: *The Wheel of Fire* (1930).

NOTES

1. *Troilus and Cressida*, v ii 138.
2. This is to be related to *Antony and Cleopatra*, IV xii 100, and *Measure for Measure*, III i 82; also *Hamlet*, IV iv 62.

Enid Welsford

THE FOOL IN *KING LEAR* (1935)

LIKE others of his profession he is very ready to proffer his cox-comb to his betters, but in doing so he does not merely raise a laugh or score a point, he sets a problem. 'What am I? What is madness?' he seems to ask, 'the world being what it is, do I necessarily insult a man by investing him with motley?'

With this apparently comic question the Fool strikes the key-note of the tragedy of Lear. It is a critical, a crucial question which effects a startling division among the dramatis personae – it being for instance obvious that Goneril, Regan and Edmund are not candidates for the cap and bells. It is also a central ques-tion which at once resolves itself into a question about the nature of the universe. For the full understanding of its import it is necessary to leave for awhile our meditation on the meaning of the words of the Fool, and to consider instead their reverberation in the play as a whole: examining firstly the disposition of the characters, and secondly the movement of events.

It is a critical commonplace that in *King Lear* Shakespeare deals with the tragic aspect of human life in its most universal form. The conflict of good with evil, of wisdom with folly, the hopeless cry to the deaf Heavens for justice, are presented with something of the simplicity of a morality play. For just as in that type of drama the central figure was the soul of man competed for by the conflicting forces of good and ill; so in *King Lear* the two heroes are erring men, warm-hearted, but self-willed whose ruin or salvation depends on the issue of a conflict between two sharply opposed groups of people painted far more uncom-promisingly in black and white than is customary in Shake-spearian tragedy. But if *Lear* has something of the structural simplicity of the morality play it has none of its moral triteness.

Where the medieval playwright furnishes answers, Shakespeare provokes questions and reveals ambiguities. Whether he ever suggests a solution is disputable; but there can be little doubt as to the urgency with which he sets the problem of the nature and destiny of goodness.

In *King Lear* all the 'good' characters have one striking quality in common, they have the capacity for 'fellow-feeling' highly developed. At first, it is true, the imperfect heroes demand rather than give sympathy, but the disinterestedness of their adherents is unlimited. The banished Kent

> Followed his enemy King, and did him service
> Improper for a slave.

Perfect and imperfect alike take it for granted that the capacity for sympathetic love is a very valuable but quite normal attribute of human nature. This attribute makes the good characters peculiarly vulnerable and sometimes almost stupidly helpless. In the first place they instinctively trust their fellows, and this trustfulness does not sharpen their powers of discrimination. The imperfect who crave for affection are particularly liable to make silly mistakes, and their suffering and anger when they think themselves deceived make them still more unable to distinguish friend from foe. The perfectly sympathetic are foolish in a different way. They are blind to their own interests. They save others but themselves they cannot save.

The 'bad' characters are the exact opposite of the good in that they are abnormally devoid of 'fellow-feeling'. They may be hardly more egoistic than some of their opponents, but they differ from them in that they are no more anxious to receive sympathy than they are to give it. They seek only to gratify their physical lust and their will-to-power. A slight personal inconvenience seems to them more important than the agony of their closest kinsman, simply because the sense of sympathy and of human relatedness lies wholly outside their experience. For Goneril, Regan and Edmund the world is the world of Hobbes, a world where every man's hand is against every man's, and the only human ties are contracts which reason and self-interest prompt people to make as the only alternative to mutual annihilation, and which no moral scruple need hinder them from breaking when by doing so they defend their own interests. Up to a point the evil are invulnerable. Their activities are never hampered by a distaste for other people's sufferings, trustfulness never dims their powers of observation, and above all they never put themselves into anyone else's power by a desire for his affection.

The distinction between the good and the bad is clear, there is little ambiguity about the word *knave*. It is the meaning of the word *fool* which is obscure, and its obscurity increases with increasing knowledge of the attitude of the good and evil to one another.

On the whole, and this is true of other plays besides *King Lear*, Shakespeare tends to give more intellectual ability to his sinners than to his saints. Edmund, for instance, is so shrewd and witty that he almost wins our sympathy for his unabashed cruelty. To such an one goodness is simply stupidity:

> A credulous father! and a brother noble,
> Whose nature is so far from doing harms,
> That he suspects none: on whose foolish honesty
> My practices ride easy!

But this is trite; Shakespeare penetrates more profoundly than this into the nature of evil. Sympathy and trustfulness make men easily gullible, and consistently egoistic utilitarians ought to value gulls. But strangely enough they find them most distasteful. 'Well you may fear too far', says Albany, when Goneril suggests that it would be prudent to dismiss her father's train. 'Safer than trust too far', is his wife's characteristic reply. This difference of outlook soon ripens into a real antipathy:

> *Goneril.* My most dear Gloster!   [*Exit* EDMUND
>   O, the difference of man and man! To thee
>   A woman's services are due: *my fool*
>   Usurps my body.
> *Oswald.*   Madam, here comes my lord.   [*Exit*

Enter ALBANY

Goneril. I have been worth the whistle.
Albany.   O Goneril!
   You are not worth the dust which the rude wind
   Blows in your face ...
   She that herself will sliver and disbranch
   From her material sap, perforce must wither,
   And come to deadly use.
Goneril. No more; the text is *foolish*.
Albany. Wisdom and goodness to the vile seem vile:
   Filths savour but themselves. What have you done? ...
Goneril.   Milk-liver'd man!
   That bear'st a cheek for blows, a head for wrongs ...
   With plumed helm thy slayer begins threats;
   Whiles thou, *a moral fool*, sitt'st still, and criest
   'Alack, why does he so?'
Albany.   See thyself, devil!
   Proper deformity seems not in the fiend
   So horrid as in woman.
Goneril.   O vain *fool*!
Albany. Thou changed and self-cover'd thing, for shame,
   Be-monster not thy feature.

Goneril's attitude reminds us of the wise advice which the Fool ironically offered to Kent. To Goneril it is the only conceivable kind of wisdom, to Albany it is just plain knavery, to the Fool it is either wisdom or folly according to your point of view. For the puzzle about evil is not that men do not live up to their principles; it is that men can reverse values and say: 'Evil, be thou my good', and that by reason alone it is not possible to prove them wrong. The bad characters in *Lear* have no fellow-feeling, and therefore act consistently from motives of self-interest. The analytic intellect cannot prove that 'fellow-feeling' is a possibility, still less that it is a duty. Respectable philosophers have founded their systems (though not their practice) on the notion that altruism can always be resolved into egoism. Are not Edmund and Goneril, then, justified in seeing the world as they do see it and acting in accordance with their insight? What have the good to say on this subject? Well, they have no intellectual arguments to offer, but two intuitions or convictions, on which they are prepared to act even at the cost of their own lives. Firstly, if love is lunacy so much the worse for sanity: the good will merely in their turn reverse values and say, 'Folly, be thou my wisdom.' Secondly, love or 'fellow-feeling' is a normal attribute of humanity, and as such it does not need proof, for it is its absence, not its presence, that requires explanation. 'Let them anatomize Regan, see what breeds about her heart. Is there any cause in nature that makes these hard hearts?' Recurrent throughout the play is the sense that the breaking of human ties, especially ties of close blood or plighted loyalty, is so abnormal and unnatural that it must be a symptom of some dread convulsion in the frame of things that must bring about the end of the world unless some Divine Power intervenes to redress the balance before it is too late. And more than that, it is so fundamentally abnormal and inhuman that the mere contemplation of it upsets the mental balance of a normal man. As Lear looks into Goneril's heart his wits begin to turn. To Edmund, on the other hand, it is the most natural thing in the world that he should pursue his own interests, whatever the expense to other people.

Which of these parties sees the truth, or rather, to speak more accurately, which point of view does Shakespeare mean us to adopt as we experience his tragedy? Or is this an instance of his notorious impartiality? Is he giving us a tragic illustration of moral relativity? Do Goneril and Cordelia separate good from evil, wisdom from folly, with very different results, only because they have different but equally valid frames of reference for their measurements? If we join the good characters in the play in asking Heaven to decide, that would seem to be the inescapable conclusion, for both Cordelia and Goneril die prematurely. And if it is a fact that some of the good survive, whereas the evil are shown to be by their nature mutually destructive; yet we may set against this the fact that the good suffer more than the evil, that love and suffering, in this play, are almost interchangeable terms and the driving force of the action is derived from the power of the evil to inflict mental agony upon the good. This is particularly important, because the physical death of the hero is

not really the tragic climax of this play. Lear, after all, is an old
man, and the poignant question about him is not: 'Will he survive?' but rather 'What will happen to his mind?' The real
horror lies not in the fact that Goneril and Regan can cause the
death of their father, but that they can apparently destroy his
human integrity. I say 'apparently', because the whirling ambiguities of the Fool are reflected in the sequence of events as
well as in the opinions of the dramatis personae, and it is only
after a study of the arrangement of the action that we can rightly
decide whether the Heavens are shown as just or wanton, deaf
and dumb or most ironically vocal. For, as Aristotle taught us
long ago, plot is the soul of tragedy.

It has often been pointed out that Lear has a more passive rôle
than most of Shakespeare's tragic characters. Nevertheless he is
involved in an event, and his relationship with the Fool is no
mere static pictorial contrast, but part of the tragic movement
of the play; the movement downwards towards that ultimate
exposure and defeat when the King is degraded to the status of
the meanest of his servants. We watch the royal sufferer being
progressively stripped, first of extraordinary worldly power,
then of ordinary human dignity, then of the very necessities of
life, deprived of which he is more helpless and abject than any
animal. But there is a more dreadful consummation than this
reduction to physical nakedness. Lear hardly feels the storm
because he is struggling to retain his mental integrity, his
'knowledge and reason', which are not only, as he himself calls
them, 'marks of sovereignty', but the essential marks of humanity
itself:

> O, let me not be mad, not mad, sweet heaven!
> Keep me in temper, I would not be mad!
>
> O fool, I shall go mad!

Lear's dread is justified, 'sweet heaven' rejects his prayer, and
the central scenes on the heath are peopled by a blind, half-crazy
nobleman, guided by a naked beggar supposed to be mad, and
by an actually mad King served by a half-witted court-jester –

an amazingly daring version of the culminating moment of the sottie: the great reversal when the highest dignitaries appear as fools, and the World or even Holy Church herself is revealed in cap and bells.

Do we then find at the heart of this greatest of tragedies the satire of the sottie transmuted into despair? That depends on what happens when we test the quality of Lear's unreason, and on how we answer the question already suggested by his brother in folly: 'Do I insult a man by investing him with motley?'

From the time when Lear's agony begins and he feels his sanity threatened he becomes gradually aware of the sufferings of other people:

> My wits begin to turn. . . .
> Poor fool and knave, I've one part in my heart
> That's sorry yet for thee.

And not only are Lear's sympathies aroused, they are broadened. Goneril and Regan break the closest, most fundamental of human ties, they cannot feel even that kind of parental-filial relationship that the animals feel; whereas in his agony, Lear, who had himself been unnatural to Cordelia, suddenly realizes that all men are one in pain:

> . . . Take physic, pomp:
> Expose thyself to feel what wretches feel,
> That thou may'st shake the superflux to them,
> And show the heavens more just.

As Lear's brain reels, his agony increases and his sympathies expand. The same thing happens to Gloucester, whose blindness parallels Lear's madness:

> . . . heavens, deal so still!
> Let the superfluous and lust-dieted man
> That slaves your ordinance, that will not see
> Because he doth not feel, feel your power quickly;

> So distribution should undo excess,
> And each man have enough.

In several passages *seeing* and *feeling* are compared and contrasted with one another. It is feeling that gives the true sight.
'I stumbled when I saw.' Again we are confronted with the
paradoxical reversal of wisdom and folly. At the beginning of
the play both Lear and Gloucester are blind fools:

> O, Lear, Lear, Lear!
> Beat at the gate that let thy folly in
> And thy dear judgment out.

Both the good and the evil would agree that Lear had reason for
self-reproach, but they would disagree as to the nature of the
folly he deplores. To the bad his folly was the folly of trustfulness and affection, to the good it was the folly of distrustfulness
and unkindness. But now that the worst has happened, now that
Lear has lost his sanity, he has enlarged his vision. As his wits
begin to leave him, he begins to see the truth about himself;
when they are wholly gone he begins to have spasmodic flashes
of insight in which, during momentary lulls in the storm of
vengeful personal resentment, he sees the inner truth about the
world. 'Thou wouldst make a good fool', said the Fool to his
master at the beginning of his misfortunes, and he spoke as a
prophet. In his amazing encounter with the *blind* Gloucester, the
mad Lear has something of the wit, the penetration, the quick
repartee of the court-jester. From the realistic point of view it
is no doubt a dramatic flaw that Shakespeare does not account
more clearly for the fate of the real man in motley; but his dis-
appearance was a poetic necessity, for the King having lost
everything, including his wits, has now himself become the
Fool. He has touched bottom, he is an outcast from society, he
has no longer any private axe to grind, so he now sees and
speaks the truth.

And what is the truth? What does the mad Lear see in his
flashes of lucidity? Does he see that Goneril was more sensible
than Cordelia? Is Mr Wyndham Lewis right in suggesting that

it is only the swelling blank verse that differentiates his voice from the disgusted snarling of Thersites? Certainly his vision is a grim one. He sees not one particular event but the whole of human life as a vast sottie:

> *Lear.* What, art mad? A man may see how this world goes,
> with no eyes. Look with thine ears: see how yond
> justice rails upon yond simple thief. Hark, in thine ear:
> change places; and, handy-dandy, which is the justice,
> which is the thief? Thou hast seen a farmer's dog bark
> at a beggar?
> *Gloucester.* Ay sir.
> *Lear.* And the creature run from the cur? There thou mightest
> behold the great image of authority: a dog's obeyed
> in office. . . .
>   . . . Plate sin with gold,
> And the strong lance of justice hurtless-breaks;
> Arm it in rags, a pigmy's straw does pierce it.
> None does offend, none – I say, none; I'll able 'em:
> Take that of me, my friend, who have the power
> To seal th' accuser's lips. Get thee glass eyes;
> And, like a scurvy politician, seem
> To see the things thou dost not.

Already we have watched king and noblemen turned into fools and beggars, now the great reversal of the Saturnalia is transferred from the action of the tragedy into the mind of the tragic hero, who discovers in his dotage, what the evil have known from their cradles, that *in this world there is no poetic justice*:

> When we are born, we cry that we are come
> To this great stage of fools.

This is the favourite common-place of the Enfants-sans-souci transposed into the minor key and made matter not for laughter but for tears.

But it is the falling of these tears (which of course can only be heard through the blank verse or prose rhythm) which differentiates Lear the fool from Thersites the cynic. Thersites gloats over the universality of evil; he never, like Lear, recoils from his

vision of sin with a passionate horror which breaks out into
broken cries reeling between verse and prose, he never begs for
'civet to sweeten his imagination', still less does he include all
under sin that he may have mercy upon all:

> None does offend, none – I say, none; I'll able 'em:
> Take that of me, my friend, who have the power
> To seal th' accuser's lips.

The statement that Shakespeare tends to give more intellectual ability to the evil than to the good needs modification. In
this play, at least, the loving characters when they are perfectly
disinterested or when they have lost everything see equally
clearly and more profoundly than do the cold-hearted. But the
good and evil react very differently to the same facts seen with
equal clearness, and it must not be forgotten that the blind
Gloucester and mad Lear have come to know that to see truly
'how the world goes' is to 'see it feelingly'. And when the world
is seen feelingly, what then? Why then we must be patient.
That is all.

'Patience', like 'wisdom', 'folly', 'knavery', 'nature', is one
of the key words of this tragedy. As soon as Lear begins to
realize the nature of his misfortune, he begins to make pathetic
attempts to acquire it, and when his mental overthrow is complete he recommends it as the appropriate response to the
misery of life:

> If thou wilt weep my fortunes, take my eyes.
> I know thee well enough; thy name is Gloucester:
> Thou must be patient; we came crying hither:
> Thou know'st, the first time that we smell the air,
> We wawl and cry.

Edgar takes the same point of view:

> What! In ill-thoughts again? Men must endure
> Their going hence, even as their coming hither:
> Ripeness is all.

What is meant? Something different from tame submissiveness

or cold stoicism, but completely opposed to that restless activity in pursuit of our own ends which Edmund thinks so preferable to passive obedience to fortune or custom. Patience, here, seems to imply an unflinching, clear-sighted recognition of the fact of pain, and the complete abandonment of any claim to justice or gratitude either from Gods or men; it is the power to choose love when love is synonymous with suffering, and to abide by the choice knowing there will be no Divine Salvation from its consequences.

And here, I think, is the solution of the problem set by the Fool; the problem of apparent moral relativity, 'Wisdom and goodness to the vile seem vile, filths savour but themselves', so that Albany and Goneril have not even sufficient common ground to make a real argument possible. Nevertheless, Shakespeare does not allow us to remain neutral spectators of their debate, he insists that although Goneril's case is as complete and consistent as that of Albany it is *not* equally valid, *not* equally true. In the first place Shakespeare's poetry persuades and compels us to accept the values of the friends rather than of the enemies of Lear. Secondly, Shakespeare makes the fullest possible use of the accepted convention that it is the Fool who speaks the truth, which he knows not by ratiocination but by inspired intuition. The mere appearance of the familiar figure in cap and bells would at once indicate to the audience where the 'punctum indifferens', the impartial critic, the mouthpiece of real sanity, was to be found.

Now the Fool sees that when the match between the good and the evil is played by the intellect alone it must end in a stalemate, but when the heart joins in the game then the decision is immediate and final. 'I will tarry, the Fool will stay – And let the wise man fly.' That is the unambiguous wisdom of the madman who sees the truth. That is decisive. It is decisive because, so far from being an abnormal freakish judgment, it is the instinctive judgment of normal humanity raised to heroic stature; and therefore no amount of intellectual argument can prevent normal human beings from receiving and accepting it, just as, when all the psychologists and philosophers have said their say, normal human beings continue to receive and accept the external world as given to them through sense perception. 'They that seek a reason for all things do destroy reason', notes the judicious Hooker; our data, our premises, we must simply receive, and receive not only through our heads but also through our senses and our hearts. To see truly is to 'see feelingly'.

It would seem, then, that there is nothing contemptible in a motley coat. The Fool is justified, but we have not yet a complete answer to his original query: 'What is folly?' Which is the wise man, which is the fool? To be foolish is to mistake the nature of things, or to mistake the proper method of attaining to our desires, or to do both at once. Even Edmund and Edgar, even Goneril and Albany, could agree to that proposition. But have the perfectly disinterested made either of these mistakes and have not the self-interested made them both? The evil desire pleasure and power, and they lose both, for the evil are mutually destructive. The good desire to sympathize and to save, and their desires are partially fulfilled, although as a result they have to die. Nor have the good mistaken the nature or 'mystery of things' which, after all, unlike Edmund, they have never professed either to dismiss or to understand. It is, indeed, as we have seen, the good who are normal. Lear, in his folly, is not reduced, as he fears, to the level of the beasts, but to essential naked humanity, 'unaccommodated man', 'the thing itself'. It is the evil who 'be-monster' themselves, it is the sight of Goneril which makes Albany fear that

> It will come,
> Humanity must perforce prey on itself,
> Like monsters of the deep.

In this connection it is not without interest that the Elizabethan playwrights made conventional use of the inherited belief in thunder as the voice of the Divine Judge, and that the Divine inspiration of madmen has always been a widespread and deeply rooted popular superstition.

Not that I would suggest that this great tragedy should be regarded as a morality play full of naïve spiritual consolation.

That Shakespeare's ethics were the ethics of the New Testament, that in this play his mightiest poetry is dedicated to the reiteration of the wilder paradoxes of the Gospels and of St Paul, that seems to me quite certain. But it is no less certain that the metaphysical comfort of the Scriptures is deliberately omitted, though not therefore necessarily denied. The perfectly disinterested choose lovingkindness because they know it to be intrinsically desirable and worth the cost, not because they hope that the full price will not be exacted. It is Kent's readiness to be unendingly patient which makes him other than a shrewder and more far-calculating Edmund. If the thunder had ceased at Lear's bidding, then Lear would not have become a sage-fool. What the thunder says remains enigmatic, but it is this Divine ambiguity which gives such force to the testimony of the human heart. Had the speech of the gods been clearer, the apparently simple utterances of the Fool would have been less profound:

> *Fool.* He that has a little tiny wit,
>   With hey, ho, the wind and the rain,
>   Must make content with his fortune's fit,
>   For the rain it raineth every day.
> *Lear.* True, my good boy.

And so we reach the final reversal of values. 'Ay every inch a king', says Lear in his madness, and we do not wholly disagree with him. The medieval clergy inaugurated the Saturnalia by parodying the Magnificat: Shakespeare reverses the process. Lear's tragedy is the investing of the King with motley: it is also the crowning and apotheosis of the Fool.

SOURCE: *The Fool* (1935). Reprinted in Kermode, *Four Centuries of Shakespearian Criticism* (1965).

George Orwell

LEAR, TOLSTOY AND
THE FOOL (1950)

TOLSTOY'S pamphlets are the least-known part of his work, and his attack on Shakespeare[1] is not even an easy document to get hold of, at any rate in an English translation. Perhaps, therefore, it will be useful if I give a summary of the pamphlet before trying to discuss it.

Tolstoy begins by saying that throughout life Shakespeare has aroused in him 'an irresistible repulsion and tedium'. Conscious that the opinion of the civilized world is against him, he has made one attempt after another on Shakespeare's works, reading and re-reading them in Russian, English and German; but 'I invariably underwent the same feelings; repulsion, weariness and bewilderment'. Now, at the age of seventy-five, he has once again re-read the entire works of Shakespeare, including the historical plays, and

I have felt with an even greater force, the same feelings – this time, however, not of bewilderment, but of firm, indubitable conviction that the unquestionable glory of a great genius which Shakespeare enjoys, and which compels writers of our time to imitate him and readers and spectators to discover in him non-existent merits – thereby distorting their aesthetic and ethical understanding – is a great evil, as is every untruth.

Shakespeare, Tolstoy adds, is not merely no genius, but is not even 'an average author', and in order to demonstrate this fact he will examine *King Lear*, which, as he is able to show by quotations from Hazlitt, Brandes and others, has been extravagantly praised and can be taken as an example of Shakespeare's best work.

Tolstoy then makes a sort of exposition of the plot of *King Lear*, finding it at every step to be stupid, verbose, unnatural, unintelligible, bombastic, vulgar, tedious and full of incredible events, 'wild ravings', 'mirthless jokes', anachronisms, irrelevancies, obscenities, worn-out stage conventions, and other faults both moral and aesthetic. *Lear* is, in any case, a plagiarism of an earlier and much better play, *King Leir*, by an unknown author, which Shakespeare stole and then ruined. It is worth quoting a specimen paragraph to illustrate the manner in which Tolstoy goes to work. Act III, scene ii (in which Lear, Kent and the Fool are together in the storm) is summarized thus:

Lear walks about the heath and says words which are meant to express his despair: he desires that the winds should blow so hard that they (the winds) should crack their cheeks and that the rain should flood everything, that lightning should singe his white head, and the thunder flatten the world and destroy all germs 'that make ungrateful man'! The fool keeps uttering still more senseless words. Enter Kent: Lear says that for some reason during this storm all criminals shall be found out and convicted. Kent, still unrecognized by Lear, endeavours to persuade him to take refuge in a hovel. At this point the fool utters a prophecy in no wise related to the situation and they all depart.

Tolstoy's final verdict on *Lear* is that no unhypnotized observer, if such an observer existed, could read it to the end with any feeling except 'aversion and weariness'. And exactly the same is true of 'all the other extolled dramas of Shakespeare, not to mention the senseless dramatized tales, *Pericles, Twelfth Night, The Tempest, Cymbeline, Troilus and Cressida*'.

Having dealt with *Lear* Tolstoy draws up a more general indictment against Shakespeare. He finds that Shakespeare has a certain technical skill which is partly traceable to his having been an actor, but otherwise no merits whatever. He has no power of delineating character or of making words and actions spring naturally out of situations, his language is uniformly exaggerated and ridiculous, he constantly thrusts his own random thoughts into the mouth of any character who happens to be handy, he displays a 'complete absence of aesthetic feeling', and his words 'have nothing whatever in common with art and poetry'.

'Shakespeare might have been whatever you like,' Tolstoy concludes, 'but he was not an artist.' Moreover, his opinions are not original or interesting, and his tendency is 'of the lowest and most immoral'. Curiously enough, Tolstoy does not base this last judgement on Shakespeare's own utterances, but on the statements of two critics, Gervinus and Brandes. According to Gervinus (or at any rate Tolstoy's reading of Gervinus) 'Shakespeare taught . . . that one *may be too good*', while according to Brandes: 'Shakespeare's fundamental principle . . . is that *the end justifies the means*.' Tolstoy adds on his own account that Shakespeare was a jingo patriot of the worst type, but apart from this he considers that Gervinus and Brandes have given a true and adequate description of Shakespeare's view of life.

Tolstoy then recapitulates in a few paragraphs the theory of art which he had expressed at greater length elsewhere. Put still more shortly, it amounts to a demand for dignity of subject matter, sincerity, and good craftsmanship. A great work of art must deal with some subject which is 'important to the life of mankind', it must express something which the author genuinely feels, and it must use such technical methods as will produce the desired effect. As Shakespeare is debased in outlook, slipshod in execution and incapable of being sincere even for a moment, he obviously stands condemned.

But here there arises a difficult question. If Shakespeare is all that Tolstoy has shown him to be, how did he ever come to be so generally admired? Evidently the answer can only lie in a sort of mass hypnosis, or 'epidemic suggestion'. The whole civilized world has somehow been deluded into thinking Shakespeare a good writer, and even the plainest demonstration to the contrary makes no impression, because one is not dealing with a reasoned opinion but with something akin to religious faith. Throughout history, says Tolstoy, there has been an endless series of these 'epidemic suggestions' – for example, the Crusades, the search for the Philosopher's Stone, the craze for tulip growing which once swept over Holland, and so on and so forth. As a contemporary instance, he cites, rather significantly, the Dreyfus case, over which the whole world grew violently excited for no sufficient reason. There are also sudden short-lived crazes for new political and philosophical theories, or for this or that writer, artist or scientist – for example, Darwin who (in 1903) is 'beginning to be forgotten'. And in some cases a quite worthless popular idol may remain in favour for centuries, for 'it also happens that such crazes, having arisen in consequence of special reasons accidentally favouring their establishment correspond in such a degree to the views of life spread in society, and especially in literary circles, that they are maintained for a long time'. Shakespeare's plays have continued to be admired over a long period because 'they corresponded to the irreligious and immoral frame of mind of the upper classes of his time and ours'.

As to the manner in which Shaksepeare's fame *started*, Tolstoy explains it as having been 'got up' by German professors towards the end of the eighteenth century. His reputation 'originated in Germany, and thence was transferred to England'. The Germans chose to elevate Shakespeare because, at a time when there was no German drama worth speaking about and French classical literature was beginning to seem frigid and artificial, they were captivated by Shakespeare's 'clever development of scenes' and also found in him a good expression of their own attitude towards life. Goethe pronounced Shakespeare a great poet, whereupon all the other critics flocked after him like a troop of parrots, and the general infatuation has lasted ever since. The result has been a further debasement of the drama – Tolstoy is careful to include his own plays when condemning the con-temporary stage – and a further corruption of the prevailing moral outlook. It follows that 'the false glorification of Shake-speare' is an important evil which Tolstoy feels it his duty to combat.

This, then, is the substance of Tolstoy's pamphlet. One's first feeling is that in describing Shakespeare as a bad writer he is saying something demonstrably untrue. But this is not the case. In reality there is no kind of evidence or argument by which one can show that Shakespeare, or any other writer, is 'good'. Nor is there any way of definitely proving that – for instance –

Warwick Deeping is 'bad'. Ultimately there is no test of literary merit except survival, which is itself an index to majority opinion. Artistic theories such as Tolstoy's are quite worthless, because they not only start out with arbitrary assumptions, but depend on vague terms ('sincere', 'important' and so forth) which can be interpreted in any way one chooses. Properly speaking one cannot *answer* Tolstoy's attack. The interesting question is: why did he make it? But it should be noticed in passing that he uses many weak or dishonest arguments. Some of these are worth pointing out, not because they invalidate his main charge but because they are, so to speak, evidence of malice.

To begin with, his examination of *King Lear* is not 'impartial', as he twice claims. On the contrary, it is a prolonged exercise in misrepresentation. It is obvious that when you are summarizing *King Lear* for the benefit of someone who has not read it, you are not really being impartial if you introduce an important speech (Lear's speech when Cordelia is dead in his arms) in this manner: 'Again begin Lear's awful ravings, at which one feels ashamed, as at unsuccessful jokes.' And in a long series of instances Tolstoy slightly alters or colours the passages he is criticizing, always in such a way as to make the plot appear a little more complicated and improbable, or the language a little more exaggerated. For example, we are told that Lear 'has no necessity or motive for his abdication', although his reason for abdicating (that he is old and wishes to retire from the cares of state) has been clearly indicated in the first scene. It will be seen that even in the passage which I quoted earlier, Tolstoy has wilfully misunderstood one phrase and slightly changed the meaning of another, making nonsense of a remark which is reasonable enough in its context. None of these misreadings is very gross in itself, but their cumulative effect is to exaggerate the psychological incoherence of the play. Again, Tolstoy is not able to explain why Shakespeare's plays were still in print, and still on the stage, two hundred years after his death (*before* the 'epidemic suggestion' started, that is); and his whole account of Shakespeare's rise to fame is guesswork punctuated by outright misstatements. And again, various of his accusations contradict one another: for example, Shakespeare is a mere entertainer and 'not in earnest', but on the other hand he is constantly putting his own thoughts into the mouths of his characters. On the whole it is difficult to feel that Tolstoy's criticisms are uttered in good faith. In any case it is impossible that he should fully have believed in his main thesis – believed, that is to say, that for a century or more the entire civilized world had been taken in by a huge and palpable lie which he alone was able to see through. Certainly his dislike of Shakespeare is real enough, but the reasons for it may be different, or partly different, from what he avows; and therein lies the interest of his pamphlet.

At this point one is obliged to start guessing. However, there is one possible clue, or at least there is a question which may point the way to a clue. It is: why did Tolstoy, with thirty or more plays to choose from, pick out *King Lear* as his especial target? True, *Lear* is so well known and has been so much praised that it could justly be taken as representative of Shakespeare's best work; still, for the purpose of a hostile analysis Tolstoy would probably choose the play he disliked most. Is it not possible that he bore an especial enmity towards this particular play because he was aware, consciously or unconsciously, of the resemblance between Lear's story and his own? But it is better to approach this clue from the opposite direction – that is, by examining *Lear* itself, and the qualities in it that Tolstoy fails to mention.

One of the first things an English reader would notice in Tolstoy's pamphlet is that it hardly deals with Shakespeare as a poet. Shakespeare is treated as a dramatist, and in so far as his popularity is not spurious, it is held to be due to tricks of stage-craft which give good opportunities to clever actors. Now, so far as the English-speaking countries go, this is not true. Several of the plays which are most valued by lovers of Shakespeare (for instance, *Timon of Athens*) are seldom or never acted, while some of the most actable, such as *A Midsummer Night's Dream*, are the least admired. Those who care most for Shakespeare value him in the first place for his use of language, the 'verbal music' which even Bernard Shaw, another hostile critic, admits to be 'irresistible'. Tolstoy ignores this, and does not seem to realize that a poem may have a special value for those who speak the language in which it was written. However, even if one puts oneself in Tolstoy's place and tries to think of Shakespeare as a foreign poet it is still clear that there is something that Tolstoy has left out. Poetry, it seems, is *not* solely a matter of sound and association, and valueless outside its own language-group: otherwise how is it that some poems, including poems written in dead languages, succeed in crossing frontiers? Clearly a lyric like 'To-morrow is Saint Valentine's Day' could not be satisfactorily translated, but in Shakespeare's major work there is something describable as poetry that can be separated from the words. Tolstoy is right in saying that *Lear* is not a very good play, as a play. It is too drawn-out and has too many characters and sub-plots. One wicked daughter would have been quite enough, and Edgar is a superfluous character: indeed it would probably be a better play if Gloucester and both his sons were eliminated. Nevertheless, something, a kind of pattern, or perhaps only an atmosphere, survives the complications and the *longueurs*. *Lear* can be imagined as a puppet show, a mime, a ballet, a series of pictures. Part of its poetry, perhaps the most essential part, is inherent in the story and is dependent neither on any particular set of words, nor on flesh-and-blood presentation.

Shut your eyes and think of *King Lear*, if possible without calling to mind any of the dialogue. What do you see? Here at any rate is what I see; a majestic old man in a long black robe, with flowing white hair and beard, a figure out of Blake's drawings (but also, curiously enough, rather like Tolstoy), wandering through a storm and cursing the heavens, in company with a Fool and a lunatic. Presently the scene shifts and the old man, still cursing, still understanding nothing, is holding a dead girl in his arms while the Fool dangles on a gallows somewhere in the background. This is the bare skeleton of the play, and even here Tolstoy wants to cut out most of what is essential. He objects to the storm, as being unnecessary, to the Fool, who in his eyes is simply a tedious nuisance and an excuse for making bad jokes, and to the death of Cordelia, which, as he sees it, robs the play of its moral. According to Tolstoy, the earlier play, *King Leir*, which Shakespeare adapted

terminates more naturally and more in accordance with the moral demands of the spectator than does Shakespeare's: namely, by the King of the Gauls conquering the husbands of the elder sisters, and by Cordelia, instead of being killed, restoring Leir to his former position.

In other words the tragedy ought to have been a comedy, or perhaps a melodrama. It is doubtful whether the sense of tragedy is compatible with belief in God: at any rate, it is not compatible with disbelief in human dignity and with the kind of 'moral demand' which feels cheated when virtue fails to triumph. A tragic situation exists precisely when virtue does *not* triumph but when it is still felt that man is nobler than the forces which destroy him. It is perhaps more significant that Tolstoy sees no justification for the presence of the Fool. The Fool is integral to the play. He acts not only as a sort of chorus, making the central situation clearer by commenting on it more intelligently than the other characters, but as a foil to Lear's frenzies. His jokes, riddles and scraps of rhyme, and his endless digs at Lear's high-minded folly, ranging from mere derision to a sort of melancholy poetry ('All thy other titles thou hast given away; that thou wast born with'), are like a trickle of sanity running through the play, a reminder that somewhere or other in spite of the injustices, cruelties, intrigues, deceptions and misunderstandings that are being enacted here, life is going on much as usual. In Tolstoy's impatience with the Fool one gets a glimpse of his deeper quarrel with Shakespeare. He objects, with some justification, to the raggedness of Shakespeare's plays, the irrelevancies, the incredible plots, the exaggerated language: but what at bottom he probably most dislikes is a sort of exuberance, a tendency to take – not so much a pleasure as simply an interest in the actual process of life. It is a mistake to write Tolstoy off as a moralist attacking an artist. He never said that art, as such, is wicked or meaningless, nor did he even say that technical virtuosity is unimportant. But his main aim, in his later years, was to narrow the range of human consciousness. One's interests, one's points of attachment to the physical world and the day-to-day struggle, must be as few and not as many as possible. Literature must consist of parables, stripped of detail and almost independent of language. The parables – this is where Tolstoy differs from the average vulgar puritan – must themselves be works of art, but pleasure and curiosity must be excluded from them. Science, also, must be divorced from curiosity. The business of science, he says, is not to discover what happens but to teach men how they ought to live. So also with history and politics. Many problems (for example, the Dreyfus case) are simply not worth solving, and he is willing to leave them as loose ends. Indeed his whole theory of 'crazes' or 'epidemic suggestions', in which he lumps together such things as the Crusades and the Dutch passion of tulip growing, shows a willingness to regard many human activities as mere ant-like rushings to and fro, inexplicable and uninteresting. Clearly he could have no patience with a chaotic, detailed, discursive writer like Shakespeare. His reaction is that of an irritable old man who is being pestered by a noisy child. 'Why do you keep jumping up and down like that? Why can't you sit still like I do?' In a way the old man is in the right, but the trouble is that the child has a feeling in its limbs which the old man has lost. And if the old man knows of the existence of this feeling, the effect is merely to increase his irritation: he would make children senile, if he could. Tolstoy does not know, perhaps, just *what* he misses in Shakespeare, but he is aware that he misses something, and he is determined that others shall be deprived of it as well. By nature he was imperious as well as egotistical. Well after he was grown up he would still occasion-ally strike his servant in moments of anger, and somewhat later, according to his English biographer, Derrick Leon, he felt 'a frequent desire upon the slenderest provocation to slap the faces of those with whom he disagreed'. One does not necessarily get rid of that kind of temperament by undergoing religious conver-sion, and indeed it is obvious that the illusion of having been reborn may allow one's native vices to flourish more freely than ever, though perhaps in subtler forms. Tolstoy was capable of abjuring physical violence and of seeing what this implies, but he was not capable of tolerance or humility, and even if one knew nothing of his other writings, one could deduce his tendency towards spiritual bullying from this single pamphlet.

However, Tolstoy is not simply trying to rob others of a pleasure he does not share. He is doing that, but his quarrel with Shakespeare goes further. It is the quarrel between the religious and the humanist attitudes towards life. Here one comes back to the central theme of *King Lear*, which Tolstoy does not mention although he sets forth the plot in some detail.

Lear is one of the minority of Shakespeare's plays that are unmistakably *about* something. As Tolstoy justly complains, much rubbish has been written about Shakespeare as a philosopher, as a psychologist, as a 'great moral teacher', and whatnot. Shakespeare was not a systematic thinker, his most serious thoughts are uttered irrelevantly or indirectly, and we do not know to what extent he wrote with a 'purpose' or even how much of the work attributed to him was actually written by him. In the sonnets he never even refers to the plays as part of his achievement, though he does make what seems to be a half-ashamed allusion to his career as an actor. It is perfectly possible that he looked on at least half of his plays as mere pot-boilers and hardly bothered about purpose or probability so long as he could patch up something, usually from stolen material, which would more or less hang together on the stage. However, that is not the whole story. To begin with, as Tolstoy himself points out, Shakespeare has a habit of thrusting uncalled-for general reflections into the mouths of his characters. This is a serious fault in a dramatist, but it does not fit in with Tolstoy's picture of Shakespeare as a vulgar hack who has no opinions of his own and merely wishes to produce the greatest effect with the least trouble. And more than this, about a dozen of his plays, written for the most part later than 1600, do unquestionably have a meaning and even a moral. They revolve round a central subject which in some cases can be reduced to a single word. For example, *Macbeth* is about ambition, *Othello* is about jealousy, and *Timon of Athens* is about money. The subject of *Lear* is renunciation, and it is only by being wilfully blind that one can fail to understand what Shakespeare is saying.

Lear renounces his throne but expects everyone to continue treating him as a king. He does not see that if he surrenders power, other people will take advantage of his weakness: also that those who flatter him the most grossly, i.e. Regan and Goneril, are exactly the ones who will turn against him. The moment he finds that he can no longer make people obey him as he did before, he falls into a rage which Tolstoy describes as 'strange and unnatural', but which in fact is perfectly in character. In his madness and despair, he passes through two moods which again are natural enough in his circumstances, though in one of them it is probable that he is being used partly as a mouthpiece for Shakespeare's own opinions. One is the mood of disgust in which Lear repents, as it were, for having been a king, and grasps for the first time the rottenness of formal justice and vulgar morality. The other is a mood of impotent fury in which he wreaks imaginary revenges upon those who have wronged him. 'To have a thousand with red burning spits come hissing in upon 'em!', and:

> It were a delicate stratagem to shoe
> A troop of horse with felt: I'll put't in proof;
> And when I have stol'n upon these sons-in-law,
> Then kill, kill, kill, kill, kill, kill!

Only at the end does he realize, as a sane man, that power, revenge and victory are not worth while:

> No, no, no, no! Come, let's away to prison ...
> ... and we'll wear out
> In a wall'd prison, packs and sects of great ones
> That ebb and flow by th' moon.

But by the time he makes this discovery it is too late, for his death and Cordelia's are already decided on. That is the story, and, allowing for some clumsiness in the telling, it is a very good story.

But is it not also curiously similar to the history of Tolstoy himself? There is a general resemblance which one can hardly avoid seeing, because the most impressive event in Tolstoy's life, as in Lear's, was a huge and gratuitous act of renunciation. In his old age, he renounced his estate, his title and his copyrights, and made an attempt – a sincere attempt, though it was not successful – to escape from his privileged position and live the life of a peasant. But the deeper resemblance lies in the fact that Tolstoy, like Lear, acted on mistaken motives and failed to get the results he had hoped for. According to Tolstoy, the aim of every human being is happiness, and happiness can only be attained by doing the will of God. But doing the will of God means casting off all earthly pleasures and ambitions, and living only for others. Ultimately, therefore, Tolstoy renounced the world under the expectation that this would make him happier. But if there is one thing certain about his later years, it is that he was *not* happy. On the contrary, he was driven almost to the edge of madness by the behaviour of the people about him, who persecuted him precisely *because* of his renunciation. Like Lear, Tolstoy was not humble and not a good judge of character. He was inclined at moments to revert to the attitudes of an aristocrat, in spite of his peasant's blouse, and he even had two children whom he had believed in and who ultimately turned against him – though, of course, in a less sensational manner than Regan and Goneril. His exaggerated revulsion from sexuality was also distinctly similar to Lear's. Tolstoy's remark that marriage is 'slavery, satiety, repulsion' and means putting up with the proximity of 'ugliness, dirtiness, smell, sores', is matched by Lear's well-known outburst:

> But to the girdle do the gods inherit,
> Beneath is all the fiends';
> There's hell, there's darkness, there's the sulphurous pit,
> Burning, scalding, stench, consumption, etc., etc.

And though Tolstoy could not foresee it when he wrote his essay on Shakespeare, even the ending of his life – the sudden unplanned flight across country, accompanied only by a faithful daughter, the death in a cottage in a strange village – seems to have in it a sort of phantom reminiscence of *Lear*.

Of course, one cannot assume that Tolstoy was aware of this resemblance, or would have admitted it if it had been pointed out to him. But his attitude towards the play must have been influenced by its theme. Renouncing power, giving away your lands, was a subject on which he had reason to feel deeply. Probably, therefore, he would be more angered and disturbed by the moral that Shakespeare draws than he would be in the case of some other play – *Macbeth*, for example – which did not touch so closely on his own life. But what exactly *is* the moral of *Lear*? Evidently there are two morals, one explicit, the other implied in the story.

Shakespeare starts by assuming that to make yourself powerless is to invite an attack. This does not mean that *everyone* will turn against you (Kent and the Fool stand by Lear from first to last), but in all probability *someone* will. If you throw away your weapons, some less scrupulous person will pick them up. If you turn the other cheek, you will get a harder blow on it than you got on the first one. This does not always happen, but it is to be expected, and you ought not to complain if it does happen. The second blow is, so to speak, part of the act of turning the other cheek. First of all, therefore, there is the vulgar commonsense moral drawn by the Fool: 'Don't relinquish power, don't give away your lands.' But there is also another moral. Shakespeare never utters it in so many words, and it does not very much matter whether he was fully aware of it. It is contained in the story, which, after all, he made up, or altered to suit his purposes. It is: 'Give away your lands if you want to, but don't expect to gain happiness by doing so. Probably you won't gain happiness. If you live for others, you must live *for others*, and not as a roundabout way of getting an advantage for yourself.'

Obviously neither of these conclusions could have been pleasing to Tolstoy. The first of them expresses the ordinary, belly-to-earth selfishness from which he was genuinely trying to escape. The other conflicts with his desire to eat his cake and have it – that is, to destroy his own egoism and by so doing to gain eternal life. Of course, *Lear* is not a sermon in favour of altruism. It merely points out the results of practising self-denial for selfish reasons. Shakespeare had a considerable streak of worldliness in him, and if he had been forced to take sides in his own play, his sympathies would probably have lain with the Fool. But at least he could see the whole issue and treat it at the level of tragedy. Vice is punished, but virtue is not rewarded. The morality of Shakespeare's later tragedies is not religious in the ordinary sense, and certainly is not Christian. Only two of them, *Hamlet* and *Othello*, are supposedly occurring inside the Christian era, and even in those, apart from the antics of the ghost in *Hamlet*, there is no indication of a 'next world' where everything is to be put right. All of these tragedies start out with the humanist assumption that life, although full of sorrow, is worth living, and that Man is a noble animal – a belief which Tolstoy in his old age did not share.

Tolstoy was not a saint, but he tried very hard to make himself into a saint, and the standards he applied to literature were other-worldly ones. It is important to realize that the difference between a saint and an ordinary human being is a difference of kind and not of degree. That is, the one is not to be regarded as an imperfect form of the other. The saint, at any rate Tolstoy's kind of saint, is not trying to work an improvement in earthly life: he is trying to bring it to an end and put something different in its place. One obvious expression of this is the claim that celibacy is 'higher' than marriage. If only, Tolstoy says in effect, we would stop breeding, fighting, struggling and enjoying, if we could get rid not only of our sins but of everything else that binds us to the surface of the earth – including love, then the whole painful process would be over and the Kingdom of Heaven would arrive. But a normal human being does not want the Kingdom of Heaven: he wants life on earth to continue. This is not solely because he is 'weak', 'sinful' and anxious for a 'good time'. Most people get a fair amount of fun out of their lives, but on balance life is suffering, and only the very young or the very foolish imagine otherwise. Ultimately it is the Christian attitude which is self-interested and hedonistic, since the aim is always to get away from the painful struggle of earthly life and find eternal peace in some kind of Heaven or Nirvana. The humanist attitude is that the struggle must continue and that death is the price of life. 'Men must endure their going hence, even as their coming hither: Ripeness is all' – which is an un-Christian sentiment. Often there is a seeming truce between the humanist and the religious believer, but in fact their attitudes cannot be reconciled: one must choose between this world and the next. And the enormous majority of human beings, if they understood the issue, would choose this world. They do make that choice when they continue working, breeding and dying instead of crippling their faculties in the hope of obtaining a new lease of existence elsewhere.

We do not know a great deal about Shakespeare's religious beliefs, and from the evidence of his writings it would be difficult to prove that he had any. But at any rate he was not a saint or a would-be saint: he was a human being, and in some ways not a very good one. It is clear, for instance, that he liked to stand well with the rich and powerful, and was capable of flattering them in the most servile way. He is also noticeably cautious, not to say cowardly, in his manner of uttering unpopular opinions. Almost never does he put a subversive or sceptical remark into the mouth of a character likely to be identified with himself. Throughout his plays the acute social critics, the people who are not taken in by accepted fallacies, are buffoons, villains, lunatics or persons who are shamming insanity or are in a state of violent hysteria. *Lear* is a play in which this tendency is particularly well marked. It contains a great deal of veiled social criticism – a point Tolstoy misses – but it is all uttered either by the Fool, by Edgar when he is pretending to be mad, or by Lear during his bouts of madness. In his sane moments Lear hardly ever makes an intelligent remark. And yet the very fact that Shakespeare had to use these subterfuges shows how widely his thoughts ranged. He could not restrain himself from commenting on almost everything, although he put on a series of masks in order to do so. If one has once read

Shakespeare with attention, it is not easy to go a day without quoting him, because there are not many subjects of major importance that he does not discuss or at least mention somewhere or other, in his unsystematic but illuminating way. Even the irrelevancies that litter every one of his plays – the puns and riddles, the lists of names, the scraps of 'reportage' like the conversation of the carriers in *Henry IV*, the bawdy jokes, the rescued fragments of forgotten ballads – are merely the products of excessive vitality. Shakespeare was not a philosopher or a scientist, but he did have curiosity, he loved the surface of the earth and the process of life – which, it should be repeated, is *not* the same thing as wanting to have a good time and stay alive as long as possible. Of course, it is not because of the quality of his thought that Shakespeare has survived, and he might not even be remembered as a dramatist if he had not also been a poet. His main hold on us is through language. How deeply Shakespeare himself was fascinated by the music of words can probably be inferred from the speeches of Pistol. What Pistol says is largely meaningless, but if one considers his lines singly they are magnificent rhetorical verse. Evidently, pieces of resounding nonsense ('Let floods o'erswell, and fiends for food howl on', etc.) were constantly appearing in Shakespeare's mind of their own accord, and a half-lunatic character had to be invented to use them up.

Tolstoy's native tongue was not English, and one cannot blame him for being unmoved by Shakespeare's verse, nor even, perhaps, for refusing to believe that Shakespeare's skill with words was something out of the ordinary. But he would also have rejected the whole notion of valuing poetry for its texture – valuing it, that is to say, as a kind of music. If it could somehow have been proved to him that his whole explanation of Shakespeare's rise to fame is mistaken, that inside the English-speaking world, at any rate, Shakespeare's popularity is genuine, that his mere skill in placing one syllable beside another has given acute pleasure to generation after generation of English-speaking people – all this would not have been counted as a merit to Shakespeare, but rather the contrary. It would simply have been one more proof of the irreligious, earthbound nature of Shakespeare and his admirers. Tolstoy would have said that poetry is to be judged by its meaning, and that seductive sounds merely cause false meanings to go unnoticed. At every level it is the same issue – this world against the next: and certainly the music of words is something that belongs to this world.

A sort of doubt has always hung around the character of Tolstoy, as round the character of Gandhi. He was not a vulgar hypocrite, as some people declared him to be, and he would probably have imposed even greater sacrifices on himself than he did, if he had not been interfered with at every step by the people surrounding him, especially his wife. But on the other hand it is dangerous to take such men as Tolstoy at their disciples' valuation. There is always the possibility – the probability, indeed – that they have done no more than exchange one form of egoism for another. Tolstoy renounced wealth, fame and privilege; he abjured violence in all its forms and was ready to suffer for doing so; but it is not easy to believe that he abjured the principle of coercion, or at least the *desire* to coerce others. There are families in which the father will say to his child, 'You'll get a thick ear if you do that again', while the mother, her eyes brimming over with tears, will take the child in her arms and murmur lovingly, 'Now, darling, *is* it kind to Mummy to do that?' And who would maintain that the second method is less tyrannous than the first? The distinction that really matters is not between violence and non-violence, but between having and not having the appetite for power. There are people who are convinced of the wickedness both of armies and of police forces, but who are nevertheless much more intolerant and inquisitorial in outlook than the normal person who believes that it is necessary to use violence in certain circumstances. They will not say to somebody else, 'Do this, that and the other or you will go to prison', but they will, if they can, get inside his brain and dictate his thoughts for him in the minutest particulars. Creeds like pacifism and anarchism, which seem on the surface to imply a complete renunciation of power, rather encourage this habit of mind. For if you have embraced a creed which appears to be free from the ordinary dirtiness of politics – a creed from which you yourself cannot expect to draw any material advantage – surely that proves that you are in the right? And the more you are in the right, the more natural that everyone else should be bullied into thinking likewise.

If we are to believe what he says in his pamphlet, Tolstoy has never been able to see any merit in Shakespeare, and was always astonished to find that his fellow-writers, Turgenev, Fet and others thought differently. We may be sure that in his un-regenerate days Tolstoy's conclusion would have been: 'You like Shakespeare – I don't. Let's leave it at that.' Later, when his perception that it takes all sorts to make a world had deserted him, he came to think of Shakespeare's writings as something dangerous to himself. The more pleasure people took in Shake-speare, the less they would listen to Tolstoy. Therefore nobody must be *allowed* to enjoy Shakespeare, just as nobody must be allowed to drink alcohol or smoke tobacco. True, Tolstoy would not prevent them by force. He is not demanding that the police shall impound every copy of Shakespeare's works. But he will do dirt on Shakespeare, if he can. He will try to get inside the mind of every lover of Shakespeare and kill his enjoyment by every trick he can think of, including – as I have shown in my summary of his pamphlet – arguments which are self-contra-dictory or even doubtfully honest.

But finally the most striking thing is how little difference it all makes. As I said earlier, one cannot *answer* Tolstoy's pamph-let, at least on its main counts. There is no argument by which one can defend a poem. It defends itself by surviving, or it is indefensible. And if this test is valid, I think the verdict in Shakespeare's case must be 'not guilty'. Like every other writer, Shakespeare will be forgotten sooner or later, but it is unlikely that a heavier indictment will ever be brought against him. Tol-stoy was perhaps the most admired literary man of his age, and he was certainly not its least able pamphleteer. He turned all his powers of denunciation against Shakespeare, like all the guns of a battleship roaring simultaneously. And with what result? Forty years later Shakespeare is still there completely unaffected, and of the attempt to demolish him nothing remains except the yellowing pages of a pamphlet which hardly anyone has read, and which would be forgotten altogether if Tolstoy had not also been the author of *War and Peace* and *Anna Karenina*.

SOURCE: *Shooting an Elephant* (1950).

NOTE

1. *Shakespeare and the Drama.* Written about 1903 as an introduction to another pamphlet, *Shakespeare and the Working Classes*, by Ernest Crosby.

Robert B. Heilman

THE UNITY OF *KING LEAR* (1948)

MARK VAN DOREN prescribes, as one of the duties laid upon the students in a great-books college of which he has written a brief account, the ability to state precisely the unity of *King Lear*. It may be added that when the students are able to pass this test, their understanding of at least one drama ought to satisfy a quite exacting preceptor. For the unity of *King Lear* lies very little on the surface; it can be described only partially in terms of plot relationships; indeed, as in all high art, it is a question of theme; and theme extends itself subtly into the ramifications of dramatic and imagistic constructs. This unity is not much discussed by the professorial gentlemen to whom Mr Van Doren's young men might turn for dramaturgic clues; the various editors of the play, in fact, are intently and innocently questing for sources, and dates, and stage history; and in their busyness they have not much time left, as one of them candidly – and undisturbedly – puts it, for aesthetic criticism. But some of them do desire to show that the master, being the master, has not erred in his duplicity of plot; so Gloucester's family situation and experiences, we are told, heighten the effect produced by Lear's family situation and experiences; and again, the two plots come together in the dealings between Lear and Gloucester, and between Edmund and the two sisters who desire him; and again, in these interrelationships inhere some remarkable ironies which otherwise the play would be without. These points are soundly made, and they are necessary preliminaries. To them we might add, also, that the Gloucester plot is initiated after the Lear plot is firmly under way, and effectually ended while Lear has still much left to do – a kind of chronological discipline of the materials which betokens the author's tact. And in IV vi, in which Lear's madness brings him to a climax of disillusioned insight, so that the gnomic Edgar can distill from this scene the paradox 'Reason in madness', Lear weaves Gloucester into his brilliant synthesis of the world and of the play: '. . . Your eyes are in a heavy case, your purse in a light. You see how the world goes. . . . A man may see how the world goes with no eyes.' Insofar as the subject of the play is Lear's mind, Gloucester has become a part of that subject.

But these considerations are relatively peripheral, and we still need to inquire in what way it is that the two stories of youth-and-age, of father-and-child, are not mere replicas, and what advantage in their coexistence transcends the rhetorical. What, in other words, is the meaning of the Lear plot, and the meaning of the Gloucester plot, and how are the meanings related? To define this fundamental kinship we must first examine the tragic flaws of the protagonists. The flaws may be described, I think, as errors of understanding, and *King Lear* may be read as a play about the ways of perceiving truth: it has a good deal to say about the ways in which the human reason may function, and about the imagination. Our problem then is to discover how this thematic substance receives necessarily different, rather than arbitrarily repetitious, formulations in the Lear plot and in the Gloucester plot.

Lear does not have the pride in reason of, say, Oedipus or Faustus, but he does undertake to reason about certain pheno-mena, and by reasoning faultily he inaugurates a series of tragic consequences. His very first error is typically rationalistic: the introduction of a mensurational standard where it is not appli-cable. He insists upon the untenable proposition that love can be measured, as if it were a material quantum of a certain size or shape. In his intellectual confusion he forgets that deeds rather than words are the symbols of love. The confusion may be described quite literally as a failure of imagination: love must be apprehended by images, and the images are richly available to him – not in verbal shortcuts and formulae, but in the lives of daughters whom he has observed from infancy. Now this kind of evidence, when it is not abstracted by literary art from the full and resistant texture of experience, is vast and inchoate and difficult; Lear shirks a demanding task – the imaginative apprehension of symbols, we all know, is not easy – and seeks an easy rationalistic way out. His failure of understanding here is analogous to his failure to perceive that a king cannot be a king without a crown and cannot maintain his perquisites by a kind of oral recipe or contract, that is, a purely rationalized formulation of a status which involves responsibilities as well as rights. From his endeavor to bound a value by irrelevant standards of measurement, Lear goes on to still another error: his misinterpretation of those verbal measurements of love which his demands have brought forth: he is wholly taken in by the meaningless abstractions and hyperboles of Goneril and Regan and – in another striking failure of imagination – completely misses the import of Cordelia's precise metaphor, 'I love your Majesty / According to my bond; no more nor less.' Lear, then, invites tragedy by three errors of understanding – errors with regard to the nature of kingship, the nature of love, and the nature of language (the value of certain statements about love). Then: these errors are not the negligible slips of a mere observer who has time to check and prove and correct; they are the terrible mistakes of a man of action, of a man whose action is a public action. Lear *imposes* on his world his erroneous conclusions about children and court.

Gloucester accepts rather than imposes: his trouble is inaugurated by Edmund's spontaneously undertaking, without being offered such an opening as Lear gives to Goneril and Regan, to deceive his father. Both fathers, of course, are muddled; even while, ironically, they feel astute, they reason wrongly from the evidence. Like Lear, Gloucester might have consulted his non-rational, experiential awareness of his child's quality. Yet Gloucester is the object of manipulation; his error of understanding is that he too easily falls under the influence exerted upon him. We have other evidence, however, of the nature of his flaw. Edmund's illegitimacy we are never allowed to forget, and near the end Edgar specifically connects Gloucester's suffering with his adultery; he tells Edmund, 'The dark and vicious place where thee he got / Cost him his eyes.' Then there is the even more obvious evidence of Gloucester's attitude to the new Goneril–Regan regime: Gloucester plainly has doubts about the way things are going, but that a principle is involved, a principle which insists that he make a stand, simply does not occur to him. He regrets Cornwall's stocking Lear's follower, Kent; but he himself contributes to the infuriation of Lear by his efforts to 'fix it up' between him and Cornwall. 'You know the fiery quality of the Duke', he tells Lear, and, more maddeningly for Lear, 'I would have all well betwixt you.' Gloucester has hopes that he can 'do business with' Cornwall: despite his genuine discomfort, he is inclined to accept the status quo. Now, what a glance at his whole career tells us is that his conduct is all of a piece: Gloucester is the passive man who is too ready to fall in with whatever influences are brought to bear upon him. He is the man who falls into step with the world, especially when to be out of step would mean a stern quarrel both with the world and with a part of himself. In the liaison of which Edmund is the fruit he fell in with the worldliness that took sexual morality lightly; years later – even in Edmund's hearing, it seems – he refers jauntily to Edmund's origin. Then he falls in with Edmund's suggestions about the evil purposes of Edgar: he becomes the man of the world who knows a plot when he sees one and knows what to do about it, and who is incapable of opposing the immediate pressure by drawing, painstakingly, upon the knowledge which transcends the circumstances of the moment. Finally, as we have seen, he falls in with, does his best to get on with, the Goneril–Regan tyranny. A fine stroke in the management of this part of the play is the ambiguity of the lines in which Gloucester tells Edmund that he intends to aid Lear. His sympathies are unquestionably aroused; that is one part of the picture. But it is also true that he says, 'These injuries the King now bears will be revenged home; there's part of a power already footed; we must incline to the King.' He does pity Lear, but it is equally true that to be pro-Lear may be a good thing; and Gloucester is at least in part maneuvering toward the comfortable stream of things. Not until he suffers for it is his new commitment morally in the clear. His whole tendency toward conformity – toward 'adjustment', as we say in these high times – has already been admirably summarized by his astrological habit of mind, which, we should observe, is shared by no one else in the play. It exactly suits Gloucester. If 'These late eclipses in the sun and moon portend no good to us', what can he do about it? It is Gloucester's flaw never wholly to understand what is implied in the situations in which he finds himself, even though he feels worldlywise enough. Not that he voluntarily seeks what is evil: it is simply that he too easily yields to that in which he should see evil.

Lear, without questioning his own rightness, imposes his will upon others; Gloucester accepts the will of others without effectually questioning their rightness. Thus Lear and Gloucester are, in terms of structure, not duplicates, but complements: this is one key to the unity of *King Lear*. The completeness of the play, its cosmic inclusiveness, which we sense without being able to put our finger upon it, is in part attributable to this double-focused presentation of the tragic error of understanding. We see its basic forms, action and inaction; one tragic character imposes error, the other accepts it. The roles continue consistently throughout the play – Lear as active, Gloucester as passive. Gloucester, it is clear, does at times *act* – enough to become more than an allegorical figure, than a worldlier Griselda. But things keep happening *to* him: whereas Lear combats his daughters furiously and dashes of his own will out into the night, Gloucester is betrayed, is captured, and is tortured. The master touch in the depiction of his career is that his giving in finally becomes giving up: he yields to despair (the Christian anachronisms are familiar to all commentators), suicide is to be his final adjustment. It is wholly right, for the worldly man is one who, by accepting the custom of the time, despairs of the good. But Lear is always a vigorous, aggressive figure; he fights his daughters to the bitter end; even in his madness he imposes his personality upon the others. At the time of his recovery he is contrastingly quiet for a brief while, but again at the end he becomes a commanding, dominating figure beside whom the others seem small. He kills 'the slave that was a hanging thee' (v iii 274) and dies trying to establish that Cordelia is alive.

Lear and Gloucester are tragic heroes: they are essentially good men. We have seen the complementary errors of understanding to which the good man is liable, and thus two kinds of genesis of evil in the world. Now a part of the remarkable fullness of the play is that it shows us not only the release of evil but the subsequent course of evil. In Goneril and Regan, and in Edmund, we see the evil which originates in Lear and Gloucester set free in the world. The old men themselves come to insight through suffering, but they have loosed forces that do terrible damage before they destroy themselves. Yet other children of Lear and Gloucester not only combat the evil forces but also, by their very existence and by positive aid to their unjust parents, contribute to whatever of recovery the old men achieve. The children as a group, that is to say, represent the different elements which are in conflict in the fathers; hence, in a play with an unusually large number of main characters and a great complexity of actions, there is the tightest integration of their component elements. We see good and evil in conflict in the world, but by the structure of the play we are reminded that the conflict is an emanation of that in the individual soul. By the fact of relationship the outer and the inner evil become one, the two struggles are united. The children are not children for nothing; to be the father of Goneril is to create a symbol of the evil brought forth from oneself. The discerning reader of the play will hardly feel that he has done all his duty by hating Goneril.

Edmund's worldliness is an amplification and a positivizing of Gloucester's. Gloucester wants to do as the world does and be comfortable; Edmund wants to have what the world has – 'have lands by wit', as he puts it – and 'grow' and 'prosper' in it. The shallow foxiness which Gloucester exhibits in his imagined detection of Edgar ripens into an effective wiliness in Edmund. Gloucester forgets morality; Edmund flouts it. Edmund is half of Gloucester, liberated from the other half, and matured in its own terms. Gloucester's gullibility – the ironic failure of his self-conscious worldliness – becomes the whole of Edgar as Edgar is seen at the beginning of the play; the emergent moral mastery of Gloucester is paralleled in the development of personal force in Edgar; the kindliness of Gloucester to Lear is the same love and loyalty which come to Gloucester himself from Edgar. Edgar's final defeat of Edmund, Edgar's reunion with his father, and his conquest of his father's despair may all be read as a symbolic version of the gaining of the upper hand, in Gloucester, of the portion of his moral being which had long been in eclipse. But this extension of inner conflicts into conflicting characters who in part objectify the warring subjective elements is most marked in Lear's family. From the start, of course, we discern in Cordelia the sharp insight into people and values of which Lear is capable and to which he is restored by the eventual, tardy revival of his imagination; in her is Lear's submerged tenderness, just as his tempestuousness is echoed in Kent; in the aid which both of them give him we see Lear's better side struggling for the mastery. Yet Cordelia is more complex than some critics have been willing to admit, for there is in her some admixture of what Coleridge called sullenness – of a recusancy, a stubborn antipathy to the disciplining, restricting action which involvement in the world makes inevitable. The unfettered personality may in some contexts be the right moral goal; but it may lead to a narrow protection of self; it is not a moral absolute. Lear will not rule, and he will not understand the terms in which experience speaks; Cordelia will not accept the terms of speech imposed by experience. There is a clash of wills, each combatant bent on self-protection. Lear's withdrawal ironically evokes Cordelia's withdrawal; the daughter springs from the father. In this reading Cordelia becomes a part of the tragic substance rather than a mere innocent and pathetic victim of the forces clashing in the world.

The symbolism of kinship is subtlest and most important in the link between Lear and his elder daughters: here we find the central irony of the play and a fundamental statement of theme. Lear's tragic flaw is the whole being of Goneril and Regan. Lear makes a fatal error of understanding: then his essential method of thought is picked up by his daughters and made their way of life.

In dividing the land, Lear introduces a principle which Goneril and Regan carry on to a logical extreme; they show what happens when an element in him is freed from the restraint imposed by the rest of the personality. In this play, personality is the equilibrium of conflicting forces; evil is ready at all times to break loose from the spiritual whole; autonomy is its end, and any disturbance of tensions may set it on its way. Lear, we have seen, forces the use of the principle of measurement where it is not applicable; he introduces a spirit of calculation; and he is ruthless in punishing what does not contribute to his proposed advantage. Thus Goneril and Regan come to power. And what comes to power with them is the spirit of calculation: in fact, throughout the rest of the play we see Shakespeare tracing the history of three people – Edmund's alliance with the sisters is morally right – in whom the cold calculation of advantage has almost totally excluded adherence to other values. Shelley said of his world that it had substituted calculation for imagination. That is precisely what has happened in the world of the play: Lear's imagination has failed – the value-preserving faculty – and so there have come into control the imagination-less calculators. One by one they dispose of, or plan to dispose of, their enemies. In the final irony they turn on and dispose of each other – a magnificent symbol of the self-destructiveness of their kind of world.

The play, of course, is full of ironic reversals. Of those relevant to the question of unity, the most remarkable is the coming to understanding of Gloucester and Lear. Gloucester gains full insight just as he is blinded; the man who accepts too easily is punished at his one moment of high affirmation – the assertion of the values of the old order against the up-to-date world. Lear's new insight is initially pounded into him in I iv and II iv, the scenes in which he is all but incredulous of the blows poured upon him by Goneril and Regan. These scenes demand our notice because it is they which establish the moral link between Lear and his elder daughters. For in these scenes the main business is the quarrel over the number of retainers Lear is to have: the quarrel takes the form of bargaining, even haggling. But this is not the first haggling in the play: the first dispute over amounts and prices, so to speak, is that brought about in I i by Lear's demanding that his daughters measure their love for him. There, he insisted on an inappropriate calculation; here, he is the victim of an inappropriate calculation by the very daughters who had profited from his own misapplied arithmetic. The daughters' love required a different kind of estimate from that which Lear proposed; likewise his demand for a hundred retainers needs to be estimated by another standard than the rational one of necessity. The daughters apply Lear's own error – the seeking of a rationalistic shortcut through a difficult area of meaning which has to be traversed, in the long run, by extra-rational means. Love must be felt through its proper symbols; the retainers must be imaginatively understood as symbols of position. The utilitarian standard is absolutely irrelevant. So the whole issue is brilliantly summarized in the first line of Lear's last speech before the storm: 'O, reason not the need' (II iv 267). But the reasoning of need in these scenes is a symptom of the new way of life that is to dominate Lear's kingdom. That way of life was prepared for by Lear himself. His daughters might have said to Lear, 'We cannot reason our love.' In effect Cordelia did say it: by using a metaphor rather than the neat logical statement Lear wanted.

King Lear suggests the reasons why it is right for tragedy to use characters 'in high place' and intra-family complications – as it regularly did in Greek and Elizabethan practice. Rulers were public figures; their tragedies became representative; ennoblement through suffering was a general and meaningful, not a shut-off private experience by which many suffered but few were ennobled. Yet in the public plot melodrama is just around the corner: our view of public life always inclines to the melodramatic, for we look for heroes and villains whom we can understand simply. We tend to identify evil with certain figures or groups, and if we can injure or destroy them, we cause the good to triumph. We look for Gonerils and Regans and Edmunds and turn all our wrath upon them; we forget the Goneril and Regan and Edmund that are within us all. The public event may obscure the private reality, the private reality in terms of which the experience is universal. But the ultimate identity of public and private is exactly figured forth in the symbolism of kinship: the family mediates between the soul of man and the community to which he belongs. It is at once a public fact and a projection of the soul; through it the representatively public and the representatively private are seen to be one. By being the father of Goneril and of Cordelia, Lear includes both of them within himself; we cannot then idly hate Goneril as evil but we must recognize the genesis of evil and hence modify our sympathetic identification with Lear so that it includes a sensitiveness to the spiritual trouble within him. Thus we move from melodrama, which represents the externalized conflict as reality, to tragedy, in which the externalized conflict exactly corresponds to the war within the soul – whether the begetting is an affirmation and an imposition of error or a Gloucester-like acquiescence in worldly imperfections. Some such understanding of tragedy, and of the mode of its universality, follows from an examination of the remarkable unity of *King Lear*.

SOURCE: *Sewanee Review* (1948).

Terence Hawkes

'LOVE' IN *KING LEAR* (1959)

THE first scene of *King Lear* has been described as improbable, Lear's question 'How much do you love me?' has been called imponderable and improper, and his equation 'so much love=so much land' is said to be immoral. Such epithets are without doubt justifiable, but their justification may well lie on firmer ground than 'suspension of disbelief', or the traditional facts of the plot. What is certainly present in this first scene is a deliberate probing of the nature of love; a contrasting of love as a spiritual quality with the opposing material elements involved in money, land, and the division of a kingdom. Although this examination is carried out immaculately in terms of character, with the spiritual quality of Cordelia's love poised against the material gains for which Goneril and Regan vie, it is possible to suggest a further, subtler probing of the problem through the words used by these characters, particularly the word *love* itself. The two different, almost opposite meanings which this word could have at the time when Shakespeare was writing hint at, in miniature, the movement of the whole play.

O.E.D. gives as a developed meaning of *Love*, v.[2] (OE. *lofian* 'praise') 'to appraise, estimate or state the price or value of'. This is an entirely different word in origin and phonetic history from *Love*, v.[1] (OE. *lufian*), and was not originally a homophone of it. Its normal development to [bːv] is shown by the sixteenth-century spelling *loave*; but there are fourteenth- and fifteenth-century spellings, *louve* and *lowf*, which indicate a raising of the vowel such as is found before *v* in several words.[1] The apparent development of *Love*, v.[2] into a homophone of *Love*, v.[1] by this process – whether or not followed by shortening – would make possible the punning use quoted by *O.E.D.* from the *Towneley*

Mysteries, in which the meaning of 'to estimate the value of' is made to intrude on the more usual 'to feel affection for'. The pun as used in this particular situation has something of an archetypal nature, for it is Judas who is asked how much he *loves* Jesus Christ; in the punning sense his answer is inevitable:

> *Pilatus.* Now, Iudas, sen he shalbe sold,
>   how *lowfes* thou hym? belyfe let se.
> *Iudas.* ffor thretty pennys truly told
>   or els may not that bargan be.   (xx 238 ff)

As late as 1530 this use of *love* is recognized in John Palsgrave's *Lesclaircissement de la Langue Francoyse*, in the English-to-French section of a 'Table of Verbes':

> I love, as a chapman loveth his ware that he wyll sell. *Je fais.* Come of, howe moche love you it at: *sus, combien le faictiez vous?* I love you it nat so dere as it coste me: . . . I wolde be gladde to bye some ware of you, but you love all thynges to dere. . . .[2]

This sense does not appear in any dictionary after 1530, but seems to have been singled out for close attention here. It seems fair to say, then, that this other verb *to love*, with its clearly defined meaning, was well known at this time, and probably for some time afterwards.

In his book *Words and Sounds in English and French* (Oxford, 1953), Professor John Orr, in the chapter 'On Homonymics', writes of a homonymic 'collision' which took place between the Old French verbs *esmer* and *aimer*. In the evolution of the French language, says Orr, *esmer* 'to reckon, calculate', although later replaced by the modern *priser*, nevertheless tended, in the final stages before *priser* supplanted it, to invade the 'psychological field' of *aimer* 'to love'. To illustrate his point he quotes from the *Roman de Brut* by Wace (one of the sources of the *Lear* story and significantly very like Holinshed's version).[3] Cordelia, disgusted at her sister's flattery, answers, when asked by her father how much she loves him:

> Mes peres iés, jo aim tant tei
> Com jo mun pere amer dei.

> E pur faire tei plus certein,
> Tant as, tant vals e jo tant t'aim.   (1739 ff)

The apparent translation of this last line is 'so much you have, so much you are worth, and so much I love you'. But Orr goes on to show that this line is a recognized proverbial saying, in the manner of a pun, where the equivocation is between *aimer* 'to love' and the similarly pronounced *esmer* 'to estimate the value of'. So the punning translation of this line is now 'So much you have, so much you are worth, *of such a price (or value) you are to me*'.

Thus, the fact that there was a homonymic intrusion of *esmer* into the psychological field of *aimer* is established. It persists in the use of *aimer cher* in the Old and Middle French period, cognate with English 'to love dearly'. Palsgrave and the other evidence of *O.E.D.* shows that a similar intrusion, of the sense of *lofian* into the field of *lufian*, was possible in English at this time.[4]

It is generally accepted that Holinshed's *Chronicles* were among Shakespeare's sources for *King Lear*. Holinshed's version of Cordelia's reply to Lear in the 'division' scene is almost exactly taken from Wace:

... I protest vnto you that I haue loued you euer, and will continuallie (while I liue) loue you as my naturall father. And if you would more vnderstand of the loue that I beare you, assertaine your selfe, that *so much as you haue, so much you are worth, and so much I loue you and no more.*[5]

Whether the pun is intentionally implicit in this version of the line mentioned above is not apparent; but linguistically it is implicit in the two senses of *love* whether Holinshed meant it to be there or not.

Shakespeare's grasping of the pun upon *love*, whether or not from Holinshed, can be detected without doubt in *King Lear*. Not surprisingly, Goneril's *love* presents a fairly precise, tabulated catalogue in the manner of an 'estimate':

Sir, I love you more than words can wield the matter,
Dearer than eye-sight, space, and liberty;
Beyond what can be valued rich or rare;
No less than life, with grace, health, beauty, honour;
As much as child e'er loved or father found;
A love that makes breath poor and speech unable;
Beyond all manner of so much I love you.   (1 i 56 ff)

It is left to Regan to colour this estimate to one in terms of money, which she does with an image of coinage:

Sir, I am made
Of the self-same metal that my sister is,
And prize me at her worth. . . .   (1 i 70 ff)

Cordelia's remark at a very early stage in the proceedings has indicated her direct rejection of the whole immoral nature of *love* as an expressible 'value'. She seizes on the fact that the true sense of *love* implies something which it is impossible to conceive of and 'estimate or state the value of' in any terms. Discarding the punning use of the other verb *to love* which her sisters have offered to Lear she says 'What shall Cordelia do? Love, and be silent' (1 i 63). Her reply to the King comes with all the force of Wace's play:

. . . I love your majesty
According to my bond; nor more nor less   (1 i 93)

SOURCE: *Review of English Studies* (May 1959).

NOTES

1. See E. J. Dobson, *English Pronunciation 1500–1700* (Oxford, 1957) §151 and n 2.
2. Quoted from the Paris edition of 1852, p. 614.
3. See W. Perrett, *The Story of King Lear* (Berlin, 1904).
4. The existence of a punning connexion of the two meanings of *love* for a length of time in literature is not a thing that can be proved,

but it would be ridiculous to suppose that immediately after the publication of *Lesclaircissement* the verb *Love*[2] fell out of use. Often examples of the equivocation crop up unexpectedly, such as in Marvell's *To His Coy Mistress*:

> An hundred years should go to praise
> Thine eyes, and on thy forehead gaze . . .
> For lady you deserve this state,
> *Nor would I love at lower rate.*

The connexion of *love* and *rate* fairly invites the equivocal interpretation of *love* as 'value'.

5. Everyman ed. (1927) p. 226.

Barbara Everett

THE NEW *KING LEAR* (1960)

I T is generally acknowledged that *King Lear* is not only a much better play than its principal source, *King Leir and his three daughters*, but also a quite different one. It is not a pious chronicle-history, but a tragedy in a pagan setting. Yet the orthodox approach to *King Lear* has, in recent years, so much stressed the 'Christian' content and method of the play, that it is sometimes a little difficult to know which of the two plays is in question. It seems, at any rate, a very far cry from the days when Johnson could object that 'Shakespeare has suffered the virtue of Cordelia to perish in a just cause, contrary to the natural ideas of justice, to the hope of the reader, and, what is yet more strange, to the faith of chronicles . . .'[1] Though the pressure of human feeling, and a particular belief in the moral responsibility of the arts, could make Johnson accept with relief the public's decision to allow Cordelia to retire 'with victory and felicity', his own 'sensations' allowed him no doubt as to the real ending of Shakespeare's play: 'I was many years ago so shocked by Cordelia's death, that I know not whether I ever endured to read again the last scenes of the play till I undertook to revise them as an editor.' And it must, surely, be principally of this play that Johnson was thinking when he made the grave charge against Shakespeare that 'he sacrifices virtue to convenience, and is so much more careful to please than instruct, that he seems to write without any moral purpose . . . he makes no just distribution of good and evil . . .'

Johnson is making here a firm judgement on Shakespeare as an artist: that, despite all his great gifts, he failed to satisfy the moral sense in any but the most elementary way ('he that thinks reasonably must think morally'). If one compares this with, for instance, the Introduction to the New Arden *King Lear*, then it is clear that an equally firm judgement is being made, which is precisely opposite to Johnson in its conclusions: 'the symbolic significance of the trial of the two daughters by a mad beggar, a dying Fool, and a serving-man is perfectly clear. *He hath put down the mighty from their seats, and hath exalted the humble and meek* . . . The old Lear died in the storm. The new Lear is born in the scene in which he is reunited with Cordelia. His madness marked the end of the wilful, egotistical monarch. He is resurrected as a fully human being. We can tell from his protest –

> You do me wrong to take me out of the grave

that the awakening into life is a painful process. After the reconciliation, Lear makes only two more appearances. In the scene in which he is being led off to prison he has apparently overcome his desire for vengeance; he has left behind him all those attributes of kingship which had prevented him from attaining his full stature as a man; he has even passed beyond his own pride. At the beginning of the play he is incapable of disinterested love, for he uses the love of others to minister to his own egotism. His prolonged agony and his utter loss of everything free his heart from the bondage of the selfhood. He unlearns hatred, and learns love and humility. He loses the world and gains his own soul. . . . The play is not, as some of our grandfathers believed, pessimistic and pagan; it is rather an attempt to provide an answer to the undermining of traditional ideas by the new philosophy that called all in doubt.' Even so long a quotation as this cannot do justice to Professor Muir's fullness and variety of approach in the Introduction; but it can suggest his ideas on what he calls Shakespeare's 'religious attitude' and on the nature of the work of art he is discussing. Shakespeare, for him, is obviously *not* merely content with 'the real state of sublunary nature', but has imposed upon it something approaching a transcendental design, didactic in intention; and this is (so, I think, the stress of such criticism suggests) the greatest of his great gifts. That a work of art can carry such widely divergent interpretations is a sign of its vitality. But when two such interpretations can seem to be mutually exclusive, it is

perhaps worth while to wonder on what bases the propositions
rest; so that, if they cannot be reconciled, they may, at least, be
clarified.

To suggest that Johnson was not taking the play 'seriously', or
was not 'responding' to it fully, would of course be quite misleading. He feels 'a perpetual tumult of indignation, pity, and hope
. . . So powerful is the current of the poet's imagination, that the
mind, which once ventures within it, is hurried irresistibly along.'
He is, rather, disturbed by that very intensity with which he feels
a piece in which 'the virtuous miscarry'. The quality in the play
which seems to dominate his mind and impress him so deeply is
its logic of action and character, whereby 'villainy is never at a
stop . . . crimes lead to crimes, and at last terminate in ruin'. In his
discussion of the play, the words which recur are 'events . . .
story . . . action'; his reactions are caused by the 'plot', which
presents a spectacle of motivated actions culminating in almost
intolerable suffering.

Those critics who find in the play either a partial, or a total
Christian allegory, are alike in one thing, however different their
respective approaches may be: this is an interest in such parts of
the play as seem to make a statement which is differentiated from
the 'plot' (that is, the story as it would stand as a prose tale). They
are interested in the kind of 'poetic' statements which the play
seems to make, in contradistinction from what actually happens.
Thus Professor Muir quotes the famous lines beginning 'We two
alone will sing like birds i' th' cage . . .' and quotes approvingly
from another critic: 'A life of sins forgiven, of reciprocal charity,
of clear vision, and of joyous song – what is this but the traditional heaven transferred to earth?' And Professor Knight,
stressing the 'purgatorial' aspect of *King Lear*, finds much of the
play's meaning in the lines uttered by Lear on his awakening –
'Thou art a soul in bliss . . .': 'The naturalism of King Lear pales
before this blinding shaft of transcendent light. This is the justification of the agony, the sufferance, the gloom'.[2] Curiously, in the
word 'justification', we come close not only to the world of dis-
tinctively Christian experience, but to the world of 'poetic justice', which Johnson looked for in the play, and could not find.

Such a stress on the 'poetry' of the play is of course a Romantic one, in the sense that one finds the beginnings of such criticism – the 'plot' being poetry, rather than what happens to characters-in-action – in the great Romantic critics. The sense that Shakespeare is creating a great spiritual adventure, to which the outer world – whether of 'what actually happens', or of stage representation – merely offers expendable symbols, is first found in Lamb's famous attack on stage performances of *King Lear*: 'The greatness of Lear is not in corporal dimension, but in intellectual . . . On the stage we see nothing but corporal infirmities and weakness, the impotence of rage; while we read it, we see not Lear, but we are Lear; we are in his mind . . .'.[3] Hazlitt quotes this passage in writing on *King Lear*, and supports Lamb's contention that the poet's work is to 'personate passion, and the turns of passion' with his own: 'the greatest strength of genius is shown in describing the strongest passions . . . our sympathy with actual suffering is lost in the strong impulse given to our natural affections, and carried away with the swelling tide of passion, that gushes from and relieves the heart'.[4] Coleridge, a greater and subtler critic than either Lamb or Hazlitt, stresses, like them, the 'independence of the interest on the story as the ground work of the plot'.[5] It is Lear's 'character, passions, and suffering' which are 'the main subject-matter of the play'. '*Lear* is the most tremendous effort of Shakespeare as a *poet*.' *King Lear* has become King Lear: the play moves us by sympathy for Lear: and that sympathy is created by poetry. We enter, as it were, the poetic element which is Lear's world, and whatever happens is dominated by what is felt (which is principally what Lear feels) and what is felt is found in the poetry. Since 'poetry' used in the Romantic sense is, I think, plot-less – Being, so to speak, rather than Becoming – the stress on the 'unhappy ending' of *Lear*, that Johnson could scarcely 'endure', grows less and less: what is valuable in the play has no 'ending'.

Though these critics stress 'feeling' in *King Lear*, their treatment of the play could scarcely be called transcendental. The first critic of whom the word might be used is, of course, Bradley; though he himself acknowledges his debt to Dowden, who

stresses the sovereignty of the 'moral world' in the play. Bradley's
profound study of the play is remarkable, both for the way in
which he feels a Romantic sympathy for, or participation in, the
central character, to an extreme degree, and also for the way in
which he soberly refuses to take it any further. If he directs the
reader to a more 'transcendental' interpretation of the play, he
does so hesitantly, hedging his observations round with careful
reservations. Thus when he suggests that we should call 'this
poem *The Redemption of King Lear*'[6] (what happens to Lear's
soul outweighing what happens to his body) he does so only in
answer to such criticism as Swinburne's, that stresses the 'pessimism' of the play, and himself affirms the power and partial
verity of such criticism; and the narrowing reference, too, to the
play as 'this poem', is counteracted by the constant analysis of
character and dramatic effect. Again, he closes his essay on the
play with the affirmation that at least a part of its beauty, and at
least a part of its meaning, depend on the feelings aroused by the
death of Cordelia: 'If only we could see things as they are, we
should see that the outward is nothing and the inward is all ...
Let us renounce the world, hate it, and lose it gladly. The only
real thing in it is the soul, with its courage, patience, and devotion. And nothing outward can touch that.' But this very affirmation he balances by saying that 'this strain of thought ... pursued
further and allowed to dominate ... would destroy the tragedy;
for it is necessary to tragedy that we should feel that suffering
and death do matter greatly, and that happiness and life are not
to be renounced as worthless.' Cordelia's death may arouse a sense
of unworldly values, but Cordelia herself is far from perfect, and
fully involved in the tragedy: 'At the moment where terrible
issues join, fate makes on her the one demand which she is unable
to meet.'

Thus, though Bradley is the first to make an impressive appeal
for a more 'mystical' interpretation of *King Lear*, he insists again
and again that it is a 'mystery we cannot fathom', and that no
explicitly religious interpretation will serve: 'Any theological
interpretation of the world on the author's part is excluded from
[the tragedies], and their effect would be disordered or destroyed

equally by the ideas of righteous or unrighteous omnipotence . . . If we ask why the world should generate that which convulses and wastes it, the tragedy gives no answer, and we are trying to go beyond tragedy in seeking one.' His feeling for the intense actuality of Shakespearian characterisation (and the ability to see a dramatic character as a cluster of images is not, perhaps, one that comes without some peculiar habituation) makes him resist any theoretical design overriding such characterisation: 'Perhaps, in view of some interpretation of Shakespeare's plays, it may be as well to add that I do not dream of suggesting that in any of his dramas Shakespeare imagined two abstract principles or passions conflicting, and incorporated them in persons.' For him, the plays stand rather at the point where intensity of experience becomes religious potentiality: but that potentiality finds no fit expression in the world that is the necessary stage for tragedy, and becomes rather aspiration, suffering, moral responsibility. It might perhaps be said that this sense of unfulfilled potentiality is a part of his vision of Shakespearian tragedy.

To turn from Bradley to the criticism of *King Lear* that has appeared over the last twenty or thirty years is to realise to what a startling extent it is indebted to him – startling, in that he has hardly been popular among critics for a very long time. Obviously the 'new' approach to *King Lear* cannot wholly be explained by Bradley's influence. A greater knowledge, both of Elizabethan rhetoric and poetic technique, and of what has been called 'the Elizabethan world picture' in its debt to mediaeval thought, has made readers see the play as a poetic work, whose imagery has as great an effect on the mind as the plot and characters, and also as a work that has a strong strain of the allegorical and even of the didactic. But it is interesting to see so many of Bradley's cautious hints and suggestions purified of their accompanying reservations and now seen as dominating the play. The famous suggestion, for instance, that Lear dies 'in an agony of ecstasy' is now accepted almost universally: what is interesting is its appearance in critics as different as Professor Empson ('He dies of a passion of joy at the false belief that Cordelia has recovered'[7]), Professor Wilson Knight ('what smiling destiny is this he sees at the last instant of racked mortality?'[8]) and Professor Muir ('His actual death-blow is not his bereavement but his joy when he imagines that Cordelia is not dead after all. That joy was based on an illusion. The earlier joy of reconciliation, however shortlived, was not an illusion: it was the goal of Lear's pilgrimage. His actual death was comparatively unimportant'). The mere borrowing of what is certainly a fine, and may be a true, interpretation of Lear's last words is less important than the hypothesis, or suggestion, that accompanies this reading in two of the three: the 'smiling destiny' ('their effect would be disordered or destroyed equally by the ideas of righteous or unrighteous omnipotence') and 'his actual death was comparatively unimportant' ('suffering and death do matter greatly').

What is most remarkable is the predominance of the idea of the feeling of 'reconciliation' at the end of the tragedy, which is Bradley's attempt to answer the question of 'tragic pleasure': since one finds this quite as strong in those who would probably deny keenly any affiliation to Bradley, or even any desire to see the play as a Christian allegory; the sense of a 'happy ending' takes the form of what is called variously the Restoration of Order, or of the Family Bond, or of Reason. In reading such studies, one is impressed by their inner coherence and their cogent force; yet one remembers, perhaps, Bradley's own introduction of such a thesis of 'moral order', and his doubtful conclusion: 'Nor does the idea of a moral order asserting itself against attack or want of conformity answer in full to our feelings regarding the tragic character ... When, to save its life and regain peace from this intestinal struggle, it casts [the tragic heroes] out, it has lost a part of its own substance – a part more dangerous and unquiet, but far more valuable and nearer to its heart, than that which remains ... That this idea, though very different from the idea of a blank fate, is no solution to the riddle of life is obvious; but why should we expect it to be such a solution? Shakespeare was not attempting to justify the ways of God to men, or to show the universe as a Divine Comedy.'

Bradley's *Redemption of King Lear* is tempered by such considerations. The modern King Lear is certainly redeemed: what has disappeared is Bradley's 'honest doubt'. 'Shakespeare makes [*King Lear*] end, not in the final victory of evil, but in the final victory of good ... *King Lear* is, like the *Paradiso*, a vast poem on the victory of true love.'[9] '[*King Lear*] is at least as Christian as the Divine Comedy.'[10] If *King Lear* is to be a Christian allegory, then search must be made for a Christ-figure; Lear, in that he is the *persona patiens*, is given some such characteristics, but he is too completely individualised to serve. Thus stress falls on Cordelia, as both the most beautiful, and the most lightly sketched-in of the characters. 'Divine love, symbolised by Cordelia, enters a kingdom already divided against itself, which is the Christian definition of hell ... If Bradley be right, it is not the chance, but the certainty that she does indeed so live [in resurrection] which causes Lear's hitherto indomitable heart to break, and the great sufferer dies at last, not of sorrow, but in an ecstasy of joy.'[11] Perhaps one ought to remember precisely what Bradley *did* say: 'To us, perhaps, the knowledge that he is deceived may bring a culmination of pain: but if it brings *only* that, I believe we are false to Shakespeare ... All that matters is what she is. How this can be when, for anything the tragedy tells us, she has ceased to exist, we do not ask; but the tragedy itself makes us feel that somehow it is so.' A similar statement of Cordelia's allegorical function can be found elsewhere: 'Cordelia, in that she represents the principle of love, is idealised ...'[12] 'Cordelia cannot stand for individual sanity without at the same time standing for rightness in the relation of man to man — social sanity ... Cordelia for Shakespeare is virtue ... [she] stands for wholeness ... Cordelia is Shakespeare's version of singleness and integration ... She constitutes the apex of the pyramid ... She is the norm itself ...'[13] Again, one returns by contrast to Bradley's patient attempts to trace *all* the strands of characterisation he finds in Cordelia, however much less simple this may make the final effect: 'Yes, "heavenly true". But truth is not the only good in the world, nor is the obligation to tell truth the only obligation. The matter here was to keep it inviolate, but also to preserve a father. And even if truth *were* the one and only obligation, to tell much less than truth is not to tell it.'

Such recent studies have enriched the reading of *King Lear* to
such a degree, by illuminating the strange blend of feelings and
attitudes, of theology and philosophy that the play contains, that
one would be far from wishing to 'prove', in any way, their
inferiority to Bradley, or to Coleridge, or to Johnson. A study
of the genealogy, or growth, of such an interpretation may
simply help to show how a play that must still seem, to the naïf
consciousness, appalling in its content and terrible in its conclusions, can be described as almost a Divine Comedy: 'He unlearns
hatred, and learns love and humility. He loses the world and
gains his own soul.' It is a truism that every age of criticism finds
in Shakespeare precisely what it is looking for: and perhaps what
it looks for is really there, in a potential form. An image, or a
human character, are both potentials, and may be interpreted *ad
infinitum*. And yet, for all the pleasures of eclecticism in criticism,
it is always possible to have reservations about any theory, or
attitude, that is both extreme and exclusive; and criticism that
sees a Shakespearian tragedy as at least tending toward didactic
allegory of a peculiar kind, is surely even more doctrinal in its
assertions than is a 'judging' critic like Johnson, who has a re-
sourceful habit of giving back with one hand, so to speak, what
he has taken away with the other. Johnson's conclusions on *King
Lear* bear out his contention that 'there is always an appeal open
from criticism to nature', and throw open the argument to the
reason of the common reader: 'A play in which the wicked prosper, and the virtuous miscarry, may doubtless be good, because
it is a just representation of the common events of human life:
but since all reasonable beings naturally love justice, I cannot
easily be persuaded, that the observation of justice makes a play
worse . . .' These words are rather hesitant and perplexed, than
bombastic; whereas the reader is, perhaps, a little provoked to
dissent by the very doctrinaire quality evinced in such phrases as
'the *certainty* that she does indeed so live . . .', 'the symbolic
significance of the trial of the two daughters . . . is *perfectly clear*'.

It is obviously impossible to decide, simply, whether or not
King Lear is a 'Christian' play. To set it beside a play that uses
even so great a degree of Christian context, as *Dr Faustus*, is to

realise what one means by the phrase 'a mind naturally Christian'; *King Lear* is not only profoundly concerned with the moral repercussions of desires and actions, nor does it simply present an area of imaginative experience that constantly moves from philosophical into moral and metaphysical speculation, but it also presents these words, 'moral' and 'metaphysical', in a peculiarly Christian way. The splendours of pride, passion, aspiration, are constantly mutating, as it were, into the virtues of humility, gentleness, and endurance. Yet, when all this is said, there remains the fact that there are many kinds of art, and many kinds of statement, that a 'mind naturally Christian' might make. Montaigne also seems, from his writing, to have loved gentleness and courage; yet it would be difficult to make a case for him as a Christian allegorist. The question is not open to solution either way, nor is it, strictly speaking, the critic's business to answer it. All that might be argued is rather the *kind* of statement which Shakespeare is making in *King Lear*; whether or not it is as doctrinal, and as didactic, as it seems in, for instance, Professor Muir's version of the play.

Much of the poetry in the play that is quoted as evidence of Lear's apprehension of 'Heavenly' things – such as, for instance, the two passages mentioned above: 'We two alone will sing like birds i' th' cage . . .' and 'Thou art a soul in bliss . . .' seems to me to be peculiarly conditioned by the way it is used in the play. These passages are of such great beauty that one realises the degree of imaginative potency that they have. And yet Shakespeare often reserves his most 'beautiful' passages, in the tragedies, for a peculiar purpose: to suggest, that is, an imaginative state in ironical opposition to the actual, or to create an atmosphere or a scene that is in some ways irrelevant to the central issues, and heightens them by contrast. One may quote the lyrical phantasies of the mad Ophelia, or the exquisite pastoral of her death, occurring in a play of darkness, corruption, and sophistication; or the elaborate splendour of Othello's 'It is the cause, it is the cause, my soul' – surely the most 'beautiful' speech in the play – which is based on the completely unfounded assumption that Desdemona is unfaithful; or Duncan's and Banquo's praise of the serene calm of the castle that is to hold the blood of one, and the ghost of the other. In both the *King Lear* passages, imagination is 'still, still far wide'. The beautiful and curiously civilised vision of a purgatorial wheel, or the dream of a shared life in a hermit's cell, are both, with their exquisite rhythm and lucid images, in some way apart from what one thinks of as the 'poetic language' of the play, and – to one reader at least – less impressive and moving than this language at its height, as in Lear's and the other characters' speeches in the storm, and Lear's at Cordelia's death. Nor is the poetic vision embodied in such speeches as 'We two alone . . .' of such a power as to outweigh, so to speak, the truth of the action in which they occur. The issue at hand is the battle which, being lost, must result eventually in the death of both Lear and Cordelia. In relation to that issue, Lear's speeches have the nature of decorative art, integral perhaps only in the sense that they contribute to the tragedy of a man in love with 'our lives' sweetness' in a world that refuses to be sweet. The deliberately child-like tone that enters the second of these speeches especially ('And pray, and sing, and tell old tales, and laugh') certainly can be said to have a divine innocence, but it can also be said to reduce the world of the play to something like a child's playground; to be 'God's spies' and to see the flux of human life turn to a game of cards ('wear out packs' may per- haps stand this interpretation) may be a true vision of the 'little world of man', but it is very little indeed, compared to the rest of the play.

The scenes which are most full of explicitly 'Christian' phrasing, or suggestion, or feeling, are confined, on the whole, to one particular part of the play; that is, to the period between the storm-scenes and the last long scene that contains the meeting of Edgar and Edmund and Lear's entry with Cordelia dead in his arms. It is, perhaps, possible that the mood and tone of these scenes may be caused as much by artistic reasons as by moral design. The storm-scenes form the first climax of the play, to which the whole of the first part proceeds with a speed, violence, and – despite the sense of confusion of time and place – an emo- tional logic that brings a feeling of complete inevitability: one action of violence generates another with compulsive force. In the storm-scenes Lear is at his most powerful and, despite moral considerations, at his noblest; the image of a man hopelessly confronting a hostile universe and withstanding it only by his inherent powers of rage, endurance, and perpetual questioning, is perhaps the most purely 'tragic' in Shakespeare. The last scene of all returns to this mood, and forms a second climax, but the tragic mood is altered by the addition of understanding to Lear's character. The presence of purely tragic pain – the desire to 'crack heaven's vault' and deny inevitability by a powerful outcry of feeling – is rarefied, as it were, by a more precise knowledge of the source of that pain: the universal issues are intensified and clarified to the form of a single dead body. It is these parts of the play that provide the dominant tragic effect. The quieter scenes on Dover cliff (with the intellectualised memory or echo of violence in Gloster's 'suicide'), the moment of Lear's awakening and first meeting with Cordelia, and the scene in which they are taken away to prison, form a necessary bridge between the more tragic scenes, designed both to rest and to prepare the mind, and to accumulate a sense of the knowledge or understanding necessary to the second climax of the play – that of Lear's death. Hence they will stress not so much what happens, what is seen and felt, but rather what is intellectually understood; and their tone will become necessarily more contemplative and philosophical. The characters, too, of both Lear and Gloster will suffer a diminishment, absorbed, as it were, into the 'background' –

> As mad as the vex'd sea, singing aloud,
> Crown'd with rank fumiter and furrow weeds . . .

It remains possible that even if one does not lay stress on these particular scenes, and concentrates, rather, on the scenes which show Lear suffering from intense evil, one might make, out of his history, the kind of Christian morality that shows a man 'losing the world and gaining his own soul'; and this remains a permanent possibility, in that any picture of good and evil actions must contain suggestions of Christian experience, especially where the good suffer. One can, perhaps, merely remember the

strength of Bradley's argument – that in the world of Shakespearian tragedy, one single 'nature' generates both good and
evil. *King Lear* surely begins, at least, on an assumption that the
world of 'life' itself – the world, perhaps, of *Twelfth Night* and
Henry IV – is rich, powerful, beautiful, and important. That the
faculties of the mind and body, and the strength and significance
of the individual, should be impaired and lost in the course of a
play, remains in itself *a* tragedy, if not *the* tragedy. A concept
that can include the suggestion that a hero's death is 'comparatively unimportant', is at least a little dangerous – however
'metaphysically' it is taken – in that one of the vital functions of
tragedy is, surely, to ennoble and illuminate the moment of death.
Whatever the structural climax of a Shakespearian tragedy may
be, its emotional climax must remain the moment of its hero's
death. And the lesser forms of death in a tragedy come with only
a slightly smaller impact – loss of profession, loss of love, loss of
friends. The worst performance of *King Lear* – and those seen
by Lamb were presumably far from good – can at any rate present 'an old man tottering about the stage with a walking-stick',
and, with this, at least a part of the tragedy. That Lear should be
forced, by the evil of two of his daughters, to kneel and plead
ironically

> Dear daughter, I confess that I am old:
> Age is unnecessary: on my knees I beg
> That you'll vouchsafe me raiment, bed, and food ...

is terrible, and the moral impact of the moment is great; but that
Lear should choose, because of the goodness of his third daughter, to kneel and confess seriously

> I am a very foolish fond old man
> Fourscore and upward, not an hour more nor less;
> And, to deal plainly,
> I fear I am not in my perfect mind ...

has also something of the terrible in it, and the impact is not,
perhaps, what could be called precisely a 'moral' one. Shake-

spearian tragedy often acts, so to speak, under the level of moral responsibility. Lear's 'compensation' is said to be that at least he learns from his sufferings: he 'loses the world, and gains his soul'. But *what* he learns is that he is 'not ague-proof', that he is 'old and foolish'; and this in itself contains further ranges of common suffering. No moralistic outline that blurs this can be fully satisfying. Such an outline must also, to some degree, blur the character of Lear. A phrase like 'he loses the world' suggests a context of peculiarly Christian experience; that is, it suggests a man (like, for instance, Polyeucte) who makes a conscious and responsible choice, and is aware of at least some of the unhappiness he is willing to suffer. Lear's character is surely scarcely comparable. His greatness lies not in the choice of 'the good', but in the transformation, into something vital and strong, of the suffering that is forced upon him, partly as a result of his own foolishness; and this transformation is a part of that love of the 'pride of life' that is involved in his first mistake, and that never leaves him up to his death. He fights passionately, at his noblest, against the form of death that the Lear of Professor Muir's revised version of the play would accept willingly – the death of self; his last speeches are as much devoted to an infinitely pathetic threnody for his own waning powers, as they are to the dead Cordelia.

That Lear is represented as a character making perpetual discoveries is certainly true, even if it is hard to accept that the moral weight of these discoveries presents some kind of counterpoint to the sufferings he undergoes; since, if he merely 'learns humility', then humility is represented in such a physical way that it contains in itself further active suffering. But perhaps Lear in fact 'learns' something rather different from this, or in a rather different way. That society may be corrupt, that justice may become meaningless in the light of this corruption, that both private and public loyalties may be broken and an old order turned into chaos, that humanity is 'not ague-proof' – none of these is a particularly new or exciting statement. The interest lies, rather, in the light in which these discoveries show themselves to a certain peculiar character. Lear is divested of that degree of civilised intelligence, subtlety and rationality that Hamlet and Macbeth, and perhaps even Othello, possess: that he shows, often, the consciousness of a child, with immense power and will, is a truism of criticism. The one gift that he possesses is a colossal power of life itself: 'We that are young Shall never see so much, nor live so long.' He is represented as feeling – and not only feeling, but living through, enduring, and becoming consciously and responsibly aware of – actions of profound evil; he feels, with a child's intensity, a range of suffering that a child could never meet. All these forms of evil – the weakness of age, the denial of power, the cruelty of his servants and subjects, social corruption and injustice – present themselves to him as a denial of life, at its profoundest and most simply physical; not, as with the other heroes, as a denial of purity, or of honour, or of imagination, or of the spirit. One recalls Berenson's insistence on the quality of what he calls 'life enhancement' by stimulating the sense of 'tactile values' to creativity, in Italian Renaissance painting; similarly Lear commands attention continually by the degree to which the simplest discoveries become, through him, a matter of immediate physical experience, felt both intensely and comprehensively.

This faculty to be found in the play, of an imaginative recreation of a physical awareness both intense and wide-ranging, from 'I feel this pin prick' to 'this great world shall so wear out to nought', is accompanied by something that is in one sense its diametric opposite, and in one sense an extension of itself: which is an apprehension of nothingness. There is a sense in which this apprehension of absolute cessation of being, appearing whenever the word 'nothing' drops into the dialogue, is a worse evil than any of the forms of moral evil that Lear meets. Ironically, the Midas touch of the poet converts even what appals the moral sense into something, if not beautiful, at least intensely interesting, and intensely alive; it is surely not possible to argue that Goneril, who is, in one of Albany's few magnificent phrases

> not worth the dust
> That the rude wind blows in your face –

is less *interesting* than the just and dull Albany himself. The only way, perhaps, in which Renaissance art can convey a sense of evil, or death, is by an antithesis of itself. Thus Lear, whose one heroic quality is a habit of totality of experience, demanding absolutes of love, of power and of truth itself ('who is it who can tell me who I am?'... 'Thou art the thing itself...') is 'rewarded' by an apprehension of the one absolute that the tragic world can offer – the absolute of silence and cessation; and even this apprehension is hedged about by a paradoxical and painful vitality: 'Why should a dog, a rat, a horse have life And thou no life at all?' The silence of the dead Cordelia is a final summary of the presence of what Donne calls 'absence, darkness, death; things which are not', throughout the play, wherever a question is asked and not answered, or a command is not obeyed. That this silence *may* contain, strangely enough, as much potentiality of good as of evil, is suggested by the degree of intense life generated by Cordelia's first 'Nothing'; but one thing, at least, it finishes – the idea of the overriding power of heroic and individual experience. The hero is only a hero insofar as he is able to envisage the limits of the heroic world.

It is perhaps in this way that one could make out a case for a 'metaphysical' *King Lear*; that it shows a world of extreme power and vitality embracing its antithesis. This sense of startling disparities contained within one imaginative world is much more reminiscent of a mind like Pascal's than of the symbolic clarity of a Morality or the simplicity of a mystery play. Intellectual reflection on the play is more likely to need to quote, as it were, phrase after phrase of Pascal's, than to refine from the play itself a pious summary. 'On n'est pas misérable sans sentiment. Une maison ruinée ne l'est pas. Il n'y a que l'homme de misérable. *Ego vir videns* ... La grandeur de l'homme est grande en ce qu'il se connaît misérable. Un arbre ne se connaît pas misérable. C'est donc être misérable que de se connaître misérable; mais c'est être grand que de connaître qu'on est misérable ... Toutes ces misères-là prouvent sa grandeur. Ce sont misères de grand seigneur, misères d'un roi dépossédé.' 'Quand l'univers l'écraserait, l'homme serait encore plus noble que ce qui le tue, parce qu'il sait qu'il meurt; et l'avantage que l'univers a sur lui, l'univers n'en sait rien.'[14] One feels a sense of recognition in such phrases because, though Pascal was a man almost certainly wholly unlike Shakespeare in mind, temperament and way of life, his writing postulates a world in which it is still possible to think both seriously and ironically of 'La grandeur de l'homme', and to see that the conditions on which such grandeur is based are close to those of tragic experience. One of these conditions is a profound doubt – 'une impuissance de prouver' – which perpetually accompanies 'une idée de la vérité'; the only entire certainty is death: 'Le dernier acte est sanglant, quelque belle que soit la comédie en tout le reste.' Pascal's image of man – perhaps one learned from Montaigne – is of a creature bewilderingly made 'un milieu entre rien et tout', perpetually conditioned and limited by his senses, and yet able to comprehend 'all and nothing'.

It is such an image that Lear presents in the closing scene of the play. Whether or not Lear's 'Look there' does, as Bradley interprets it, suggest a belief that Cordelia is still alive, the last half-dozen lines as a whole condense the poetic experience of the play, whereby the physical and the non-physical are shown in their mysterious relationship.

> Thou'll come no more,
> Never, never, never, never, never!
> Pray you, undo this button. Thank you sir.
> Do you see that? Look on her, look, her lips,
> Look there, look there!

It is natural enough that the central character of a poetic tragedy should finish by directing the attention, as it were, finally to the closed mouth of a dead human being, an image which presents most of what can be said about the physical limitations to an aspiring mind. Each of the great tragedies ends similarly with a momentary directing of the attention to the full effect of the tragic action:

> What is it you would see?
> If aught of woe or wonder, cease your search ...
> give order that these bodies

> High on a stage be placed to the view . . .

> Look on the tragic loading of this bed.
> This is thy work.

>   Behold where stands
> Th' usurper's cursed head . . .

That Lear should himself turn chorus – ('Look on her, look . . .)'
and himself endure 'the new acquist Of true experience from this
great event' even while still alive, is consonant with his rôle
throughout the play: his own death is the one thing that cannot be
presented through the heroic consciousness.

Perhaps the chief reason, then, why one feels doubt about an
extremely allegorical interpretation of the play is not that such an
interpretation can be said to be 'wrong', but simply that the play
succeeds so well in another way. Rather than setting up an absolute dichotomy between the 'world' and 'the soul', between
concretes and abstracts, it shows a continual relation between the
two that strengthens and enriches both; so that a sense of extreme evil can be conveyed in a phrase of casual malice – ('What
need one?' 'And all night, too') and a sense of extreme good in
the commonest expression of a woman's kindness:

>   Mine enemy's dog,
> Though he had bit me, should have stood that night
> Against the fire; and wast thou fain, poor father,
> To hovel thee with swine and rogues forlorn
> In short and musty straw? Alack, alack!

It also fulfils that function by which tragedy makes the unendurable endurable by bringing it within an artistic design, while
retaining its essential truth; the forms of suffering in the play are
transformed not so much by being seen '*sub specie aeternatis*', but
rather by being seen as forms of intense life. If the play exhilar-
ates, it is less because 'Cordelia, from the time of Tate, has always
retired with victory and felicity', whether temporal or spiritual,
than because it exhibits a poetic power in the writing of the play
itself, in the consciousness given to its central character, and in

the responsive awareness of audience or reader, that can understand and endure imaginatively actions of great suffering, and by
understanding can master them: '... L'homme serait encore plus
noble que ce qui le tue, parce qu'il sait qu'il meurt.' If 'Hamlet
and Lear are gay', and if tragedy does exist to 'give a great kick
at human misery', then this is perhaps more because of the gaiety
of mastery inherent in the creative act than because of any cheerful propositions made by tragedy itself. The more terrible the
propositions, the greater is the mastery; the greater the degree of
the 'un-tragic', the 'un-sublime', contained – the ugly, the humiliating, the petty, the chaotic, the ridiculous, the mad, the gross,
the casual and the carnal – then the greater is the act that can
turn these into 'the good, the beautiful, and the true', and yet
retain the nature of the things themselves. Whether this is, in
itself, a highly moral act is a question too difficult to answer; but
it is, perhaps, not best answered by turning *King Lear* into a
morality play.

SOURCE: *Critical Quarterly* (Winter, 1960).

NOTES

1. Johnson, *Preface and Notes to Shakespeare* (1765).
2. G. Wilson Knight, *The Wheel of Fire* (1949).
3. Lamb, 'On the Tragedies of Shakespeare', in *The Reflector* (1810–1811).
4. Hazlitt, *Characters of Shakespeare's Plays* (1817–18).
5. Coleridge, *Shakespearian Criticism*, ed. T. M. Raysor (1936).
6. Bradley, *Shakespearean Tragedy* (1957).
7. Empson, *Structure of Complex Words* (1951).
8. G. Wilson Knight, op. cit.
9. R. W. Chambers, *King Lear* (1939).
10. J. F. Danby, *Shakespeare's Doctrine of Nature* (1949).
11. G. Beckersteth, *The Golden World of King Lear*, B.A. Lecture, 1936.
12. G. Wilson Knight, op. cit.
13. J. F. Danby, op. cit.
14. Pascal, *Pensées*.

John Holloway

KING LEAR (1961)

King Lear, a play set (unlike *Macbeth*) in the legendary pre-
history of Britain, depicts a world which is remote and primaeval.
This is not to deny that it has life and meaning for all times: its
permanent relevance is what follows from having the quality of
legend, and the primaeval as subject. Nor is it a merely trite
observation about the play. To apprehend this fact is to be led
to a decisive truth. The action of *King Lear* comprises an event
which today has largely lost its meaning; though one, indeed,
which points back to men's original and deepest fears and convictions, and seems to have been part of their consciousness from
primitive times.

This by now largely archaic idea is present elsewhere in the
tragedies. It is brought before the mind in the guards' words at
the death of Antony:

> *Second Guard.*   The star is fall'n.
> *First Guard. And time is at his period.*   (IV xiv 106)

It is in Macduff's words at Duncan's murder:

> Shake off this downy sleep, Death's counterfeit,
> And look on death itself. Up, up, and see
> *The great doom's image*! Malcolm! Banquo!
> *As from your graves rise up* and walk like sprites
> To countenance this horror!   (II iii 74)

The point here is that the king's end is like the end of the world:
not the Day of Judgement, but the universal cataclysm which
was to precede it. Twice, in *Lear*, the idea is mentioned explicitly.
Kent, when he sees Lear enter with Cordelia dead in his arms,
says:

> Is this the promis'd end?

and Edgar replies:

> Or image of that horror?   (V iii 263)

The mad Lear and the blinded Gloucester meet:

> *Glou.* O, let me kiss that hand!
> *Lear.* Let me wipe it first, it smells of mortality.
> *Glou.* O ruin'd piece of nature! *This great world*
> *Shall so wear out to nought.*   (IV vi 132)

The idea of a universal deflection of Nature towards evil and disaster (as prelude to final salvation) seems to call forth an echo elsewhere in the play. Gloucester's well-known reference to 'these late eclipses of the sun and moon' (I ii 99) re-echoes the words of St Luke on the end of the world:

> And there shalbe signes in the Sunne, and in the Moone, & in the starres; and upon the earth trouble among the nations, with perplexitie, the sea and the water roring: And mens hartes fayling them for feare, and for looking after those thinges which are comming on the worlde: for the powers of heaven shalbe shaken.
> (21: 25–6)

The storm on the heath recalls what the Book of Revelation says of Armageddon:

> And there folowed voyces, thundringes, and lightnynges: and there was a great earthquake, such as was not since men were upon the earth ...   (16: 18)

For the Elizabethans, the End of the World was a living conviction and even something of a current fear. We touch here on one of the oldest of traditions: that notion of the world's turning upside down which Archilochus already employs when, having unexpectedly seen an eclipse of the sun, he says that the fish might as well now come and feed on land, or wolves feed in the sea. Repeated incessantly, by Shakespeare's time this was a long-established commonplace; but when Hooker (though merely adapting Arnobius) finds his imagination kindled by this thought, and turns from detailed analysis to write with the full range of his eloquence, the idea is present in all its power and solemnity:

Now if nature should intermit her course ... if those principal and mother elements of the world ... should lose the qualities which they now have; if the frame of that heavenly arch erected over our heads should loosen and dissolve itself; if celestial spheres should forget their wonted motions ... if the moon should wander from her beaten way, the times and seasons of the year blend themselves by disordered and confused mixture, the winds breathe out their last gasp, the clouds yield no rain, the earth be defeated of heavenly influence, the fruits of the earth pine away as children at the withered breasts of their mother no longer able to yield them relief; what then would become of man himself?

The reader of Shakespeare has thus to recognize that the 'Elizabethan World Picture' pictured an order quite different from anything which would now come to mind as order. Coherent and providential system as it was, it included within itself a standing potentiality for progressive transformation into chaos. Paradoxically, the more that the world is conceived in religious terms, the easier is it for a potentiality of deflection into chaos to stand as no radical infringement, but a genuine ingredient of order. Further than this, for Shakespeare's time collapse into universal chaos was not merely a permanent possibility in a fallen (though divinely created) Nature: it was a foreordained part of created Nature's route to salvation; and to envisage it, to dwell on it, to comprehend what it could be like, was part of what went to make up a comprehension of God's governance of the world.

How *Lear* is in part a rehearsal of this terrible potentiality of Nature becomes plainer, if one bears in mind that what the descent into chaos would be like was delineated by tradition. It already had its familiar contours and features. There is no need here to do more than hint briefly at the length and strength of this tradition. If we go back, for example, to Mark 13, which is the chapter in that gospel corresponding to Luke 21 (the account of the final calamity of the world which was briefly quoted above) we see the major concerns of *Lear* emerge one by one: 'There shal nation rise against nation, & kingdome against kingdome: and there shalbe earthquakes ... the brother shall betray the brother to death, and the father the sonne: and the children shal rise against their fathers and mothers, and shal put them to death.' From this one might turn to Wulfstan's *Sermon to the English People*, composed in response to the chaos overtaking England when the Danish invasion was at its height: '. . . the father did not stand by his child, nor the child by the father, nor one brother by another . . .' and – sign of the traditional combination of ideas from which Lear itself emerged – Wulfstan goes on immediately to speak of how treachery, unlawfulness and infidelity to one's lord have spread everywhere throughout the land.

What must have been a passage familiar to all of Shakespeare's audience, the Homily of 1574 *Against Disobedient and Wilful Rebellion*, also clearly sees dissension between parents and children as the predictable counterpart of dissension in the body politic: 'when the subjects unnaturally do rebel against their prince . . . countrymen to disturb the public peace and quietness of their country, for defence of whose quietness they should spend their lives: the brother to seek, and often to work the death of his brother; the son of the father, the father to seek or procure the death of his sons, being at man's age, and by their faults to disinherit their innocent children. . . .' Donne's well-known reference to how 'new philosophy calls all in doubt' in the First Anniversary belongs to the same train of thought. These words, so often quoted in bleak and misleading isolation, easily misrepresent the main weight of Donne's argument. This by no means expresses a new-found disquiet resulting from new astronomy or anything like it. All that such things do for Donne is provide mere topical confirmation of that fallen condition which is established on other grounds and by the longest of traditions.

> Then, as mankinde, so is the worlds whole frame
> Quite out of joynt, *almost created lame*:
> For, before God had made up all the rest,
> Corruption entred, and deprav'd the best:
> It seis'd the Angels . . .
> The noblest part, man, felt it first; and then
> Both beasts and plants, curst in the curse of man.
> *So did the world from the first houre decay. . . .*

Here is the beginning of Donne's discussion. The reference to 'new philosophy' has a subordinate place in the middle of it. The poet goes straight on to rehearse the traditional counterparts of chaos in Nature (counterparts, needless to say, having nothing to do with 'new philosophy'), and these take us straight back to *Lear*:

> 'Tis all in peeces, all cohaerence gone;
> All just supply, and all Relation:
> *Prince, Subject, Father, Sonne are things forgot,*
> For every man alone thinkes he hath got
> To be a Phoenix, and that then can bee
> None of that kinde, of which he is, but hee . . .

Finally, a passage from Burton's *Anatomy of Melancholy*, resuming the same point, also relates it directly to the twin threads of action which run through the movement of the play: 'Great affinity is there is betwixt a political and an economic body [i.e. a house or family]; they differ only in magnitude; *as they have both likely the same period* . . . six or seven hundred years, so many times they have the same means of their vexation and overthrow; as namely riot, a common ruin of both.'

Disruption in the kingdom, disruption in the family, linked by tradition, were facets of that universal disruption of Nature, that Descent into Chaos, which for millennia had been a standing dread of mankind and at the same time one of mankind's convictions about providential history in the future.

King Lear is an exploration of this potentiality to quite a different degree from, say, *Macbeth*. The nadir of that play, the point at which Macbeth's own evil nature seems to diffuse evil throughout his whole country, falls short of what happens even at the very start of *Lear*. In *Macbeth* the evil emanates from one man (or one couple) quite alone. In *Lear* it seems, from the first, like an infection spreading everywhere, affecting a general change in human nature, even in all nature. Those, like Kent and Cordelia, who stand out against its progress, manifest its influence even in doing so: as if Burton's 'riot' could be countered (which may be true, indeed) only by riot of another kind. The disease is general; antidotes are helpless or non-existent; the course must be run.

In its details, the play sometimes displays an extraordinary realism. Lear's hesitation before he demands to see the supposedly sick Duke of Cornwall and his inability to believe that his messenger has been set in the stocks, Edgar's impersonation of the peasant, the whole dialogue in Act v scene iii between Albany, Edmund, Goneril and Regan, are all instances of unforgettable rightness and richness in catching the complex and individualized movements of minds vehemently working and intently engaged. Yet for a sense of the play as a whole this has less weight than what is almost its opposite: an action deliberately stylized so that its generic quality and its decisive movement should stand out more than its human detail. This is true, notably, of the division of the kingdom with which the play opens. We must see this as stylized not merely in its quality as it takes place on the stage, but in how it points forward. Time and again this kind of event occurs in contemporary drama (*Gorboduc*, *The Misfortunes of Arthur*, *Selimus*, *Woodstock*, *Locrine* are examples). Its status as decisively misguided or evil is not in doubt; and it is the established sign or first step in a movement which threatens chaos or actually brings it. The direction and nature of what is to happen in *Lear* need not be inferred by the spectator through his detailed response to the behaviour and dialogue of the actors. Richly as it may be confirmed and elaborated in these things, its essence stands starkly before him in the stylization of a known kind of opening event. The intricate complication of the story, the detailed characterization, do nothing to obscure what is clear in the almost folk-tale quality of how the play begins. '*We have seen the best of our time.*'

Those words of Gloucester are essentially dynamic words, and this movement and dynamic ought to be seen in an aspect of *King Lear* which has been so much discussed that here it need not be discussed in full: its imagery. That the characters in the play are repeatedly likened to the lower orders of creation, for example, gives no mere general or pervasive tinge to the work, and embodies no merely general idea about humanity at large.

It cannot be found in the opening scene. It arrives as the action begins to move, and becomes dominant as the quality of life which it embodies becomes dominant in the play. Just as it is not enough for Professor Muir to say that the plot of Lear 'expressed the theme of the parent–child relationship' – for it expressed no mere problem or issue, because it depicts a particular movement which begins when that relationship fails in a definite way – so it is not enough for him to refer to 'the prevalence of animal imagery' and to add merely: 'This imagery is partly designed to show man's place in the Chain of Being, and to bring out the subhuman nature of the evil characters, partly to show man's weakness compared with the animals, and partly to compare human life to the life of the jungle.' The hedge-sparrow that fed the cuckoo, the sea-monster that is less hideous than ingratitude in a child, ingratitude itself sharper than a serpent's tooth, the wolfish visage of Goneril, are not scattered through the play as mere figurative embodiments of those discursive or philosophical interests. They burst upon the audience altogether, at the close of Act I. If they throw out some general and discursive sugges-tion about 'human life', that is far less prominent than how they qualify the phase of the action which comes at that point, crowd-ing the audience's imagination, surrounding the human characters with the subhuman creatures whose appearance they are fast and eagerly assuming.

Likewise, when Kent (II ii 67–89) speaks of the rats 'that bite the holy cords atwain', and the men who follow their masters like ignorant dogs or are no different from cackling geese, we are offered no general comment upon human life, but a context in imagery for the conduct of Oswald which preoccupies here and now. The society of the play, in its descent into animality, had reached this point. Edgar, shortly after, underlines the change going on before our eyes:

> I will preserve myself; and am bethought
> To take the basest and most poorest shape
> That ever penury in contempt of man
> *Brought near to beast.*   (II iii 6)

The descent continues; Regan, Cornwall, Gloucester and Edgar
are all drawn in as its ministers or its victims; and now the images
gain a new quality. They do indeed become general, for the
disease they reflect and stress has become general. The play is
indeed coming to depict, in Hooker's phrase, an earth 'defeated
of heavenly influence'; and the Fool's

Horses are tied by the heads, dogs and bears by th' neck, mon-
keys by th' loins, and *men* by the legs ...   (II iv 7)

underlines this. 'Man's life is cheap as beast's', Lear adds a moment
later (II iv 266).

All this is enforced by the progressive transformation, as Act II
advances, of the settled society of men, with their fixed abodes,
into a confusion of people constantly leaving their homes, constantly on horseback and riding recklessly from place to place.
Lear's own words, towards the close of this movement, make the
point of it:

> They have travelled all the night! Mere fetches!
> *The images of revolt and flying off.*   (II iv 87)

Yet Lear himself, quitting Goneril, is the first to break with the
settled order:

> ... Darkness and devils!
> Saddle my horses; call my train together.
>
> ... Prepare my horses.
>
> ... Go, go, my people.
>
> ... Away, away!   (I iv 251–2, 258, 272, 289)

Goneril, in the person of her messengers, is quick to follow his
example:

> Take you some company, and away to horse ...
>   (I iv 337)

Next, it is Cornwall of whom Edmund, at his father's castle, says:

> He's coming hither now, *i' th' night, i' th' haste*,
> And Regan with him.   (II i 24)

And Kent explains that this hurried journey was the immediate
result, like the spreading of an infection, of a letter from Goneril:

> ... Which presently they read; on whose contents
> They summoned up their meiny, straight took horse,
> Commanded me to follow ...   (II iv 33)

Regan has already set the tone of her journey more fully than she
intended:

> *Cornwall.* You know not why we came to visit you.
> *Regan.* Thus *out of season, threading dark-eyed night*.
>   (II ii 118)

The last appearance of this motif of the horse and the homeless
rider comes once again from Lear himself:

> *Glo.* The king is in high rage.
> *Corn.*   Whither is he going?
> *Glo.* He calls to horse; but will I know not whither ...
> Alack, the night comes on, and the high winds
> Do sorely ruffle; for many miles about
> There's scarce a bush.

Nothing could lead on more clearly to the idea that the society
of men is becoming the chaotic world of the outlaw.

This descent from humanity, however, is something which
cannot be envisaged fully through the idea of the brute and its
animal life alone. It is a descent, embodied in the action, enriched
by imagery, and confirmed by what is said as comment, far below
brutality. Lear does not only 'choose ... To be a comrade with
the wolf and owl' (II iv 207). He sinks lower still: recreant against
Nature and outcast among its creatures:

This night, wherein the cub-drawn bear would crouch,
The lion, and the belly-pinched wolf
Keep their fur dry, unbonneted he runs,
And *bids what will* take all.   (III i 12)

Edgar joins him ('What art thou that dost grumble there i' th'
straw?' asks Kent, III iv 43). The spectacle is of man below the
animals, since he combines the vices of all of men in his single self:

Hog in sloth, fox in stealth, wolf in greediness, dog in madness,
lion in prey . . .   (III iv 91)

It is only now, when all left of humanity seems to be a madman,
a beggar and a jester surrounded by the storm, that the extreme
is reached, and the thought of it put forward at last:

> *Lear.* Why, thou wert better in a grave than to answer with thy
> uncover'd body this extremity of the skies. Is man no
> more than this? Consider him well.

[this 'him' means Edgar as much as man in general]

> Thou ow'st the worm no silk, the beast no hide, the
> sheep no wool, the cat no perfume. Here's three on us
> are sophisticated! Thou are the thing itself: unaccom-
> modated man is no more but such a poor, bare, forked
> animal as thou art. Come, off, you lendings! Come,
> unbuttoned here.   (III iv 100)

Regan and Goneril also seem to pass down through, and out
of, the whole order of Nature; though they are its monsters not
its remnants. The word itself, already recurrent in the present
discussion, is explicitly used of each of them (III vii 101; IV ii
62–3); and Albany, in two of the comments which he makes about
his wife, draws attention not only to the kind of movement which
the play has displayed so far, but also – and it is an important new
point – to that further movement with which it will close. He
asserts that what has happened so far is bringing his society (again
the stress is upon the movement, upon its being *brought*) to the

condition of the sea, with its universal war, unlimited in savagery, of all against all:

> If that the heavens do not their visible spirits
> Send quickly down to tame these vile offences,
> *It will come*
> Humanity must perforce prey on itself,
> Like monsters of the deep. (IV ii 46)

Besides this, he indicates what may be expected to ensue:

> That nature which condemns its origin
> Cannot be border'd certain in itself;
> She that herself will sliver and disbranch
> From her material sap, perforce must wither
> And come to deadly use ... (IV ii 32)

The thought is near to that of Cornwall's servants:

> *Second Serv.* I'll never care what wickedness I do
>   If this man come to good.
> *Third Serv.*   If she live long,
>   And in the end meet the old course of death,
>   Women will all turn monsters. (III vii 98)

Lear's part in this change is a special one. He is not only the 'slave' of the elements; he is also the man to whom Kent said '... you have that in your countenance that I would fain call master ... authority' (I iv 27). But his special part is best understood by dwelling upon something which has seldom received much attention: the clear parallel (though it is also a clearly limited one) between the condition of Lear, and that in the Old Testament of Job. This follows on naturally from how the play brings men down to animals, because Gloucester's 'I' th' last night's storm I such a fellow saw / Which made me think a man a worm' (IV i 33), recalls Job's 'I sayde ... to the wormes, You are my mother, and my syster' (17: 14). Again, Albany's 'O Goneril! / You are not worth the dust which the rude wind / Blows in your face' sees Goneril as less than the dust, and thus

echoes a thought constant in Job: 'nowe must I sleepe in the
dust'; 'Thou madest me as the mould of the earth, and shalt bring
me into dust agayne'; 'our rest together is in the dust'; 'one dyeth
in his ful strength ... another dyeth in the bitternesse of his
soule ... they shal sleepe both alike in the earth and the wormes
shal cover them'; 'all fleshe shall come to nought at once, and al
men shal turne agayne unto dust' (7: 21; 10: 9; 21: 23–6; 34: 15).

Yet these two points are merely the beginning of a much wider
resemblance. Job's patience is something that Lear early claims
for himself (II iv 229; cf 'I will be the pattern of all patience'
(III ii 37), and that Gloucester ultimately acquires:

> henceforth I'll bear
> Affliction till it do cry out itself
> 'Enough, enough,' and die.   (IV vi 75)

There are many other links in matters, comparatively speaking,
of detail. 'Thou puttest my fete also in the stockes' (13: 27); 'for
the vehemencie of sorowe is my garment changed, which com-
passeth me about as the coller of my coat' (30: 18; cf 'come,
unbutton here', III iv 106; and 'pray you undo this button', v iii
309); 'Wherefore do wycked men liue, come to theyr olde age,
and encrese in ryches' (21: 7; cf 'Is there any cause in nature that
makes these hard hearts', III vi 76, and the servant's '... if she
live long, / And in the end meet the old course of death ...',
III vii 99).

Besides these sharp if local resemblances, there are passages in
Job that seem to resume whole sections of the play: 'They cause
the poore to turne out of the way ... they cause the naked to
lodge wythout garment and wythout coveryng in the colde.
They are wet wyth the showres of the mountaynes, and embrace
the rocks for want of a covering' (24: 4–8). 'Heare then the
sound of his voice, & the noyse that goeth out of his mouth. He
directeth it under the whole heaven, and his lyght [= lightning]
unto the endes of y^e world. A roryng voyce foloweth ...
thundreth marveylously wyth his voyce ... He commandeth the
snow, and it falleth upon earth: he geueth the rayne a charge, &

the shouers have their strength and fal downe' (37: 2–6). Finally (though it still remains, to discuss exactly what light these parallels throw) in one passage Lear's whole situation is summed up: 'Myne owne kinsfolkes haue forsaken me and my best acquaynted haue forgotten me. The seruantes and maydes of myne owne house tooke me for a stranger, and I am become as an aliant [= alien] in theyr sight. I called my seruant, and he gaue me no answere . . . Al my most familiers abhorred me: and they whome I loued best are turned agaynst me' (19: 14–18).

A resemblance, even a massive resemblance such as exists here, is one thing; light thrown on the exact contour of *King Lear* is another. Yet light is certainly thrown, and abundantly. How this is so may perhaps best be seen through taking note of something both plain and remarkable about the action of the play: what might be called not its *action*, but its *protraction*. In one sense, *Lear* is a much longer play than it need have been – need have been, that is, to have been less ambitiously tragic. By the middle of Act IV (or even the end of Act III) something of an ordinary tragic action has been completed. Lear has fallen from being the minion of Fortune (when the play opens he is presented as in one sense a king of kings) to being its chief victim. Through the ordeal of this fall, his eyes have been opened. From being one who 'hath ever but slenderly known himself' (I i 292), he has come to say 'Here I stand your slave, / A poor infirm, weak and despised old man' (III ii 19). He has learnt, moreover, or re-learnt, the central and traditional lessons that good kings must know:

> Poor naked wretches, wheresoe'er you are,
> That bide the pelting of this pitiless storm,
> How shall your houseless heads and unfed sides,
> Your loop'd and window'd raggedness, defend you
> From seasons such as these? O, I have ta'en
> Too little care of this! Take physic, pomp;
> Expose thyself to feel what wretches feel. . . .
>
> (III iv 28)

The lines express something of what Piers Plowman learns from Hunger, and the facts to which they point are those explicit in the

Wakefield *Second Shepherds' Play*, and implicit indeed in the
Magnificat. The twin passages which begin:

> Tremble, thou wretch
> That hast within thee undivulged crimes
> Unwhipped of justice ...   (III ii 51)

and

> Thou rascal beadle, hold thy bloody hand.
> Why dost thou lash that whore? Strip thy own back;
> Thou hotly lusts to use her in that kind
> For which thou whip'st her ...   (IV vi 160)

are not well seen as philosophical passages about appearance and
reality. Their import is moral. They are conventional and traditional, their power lying in this very embodiment of the familiar
facts of human hypocrisy in all their brutal force and immediacy;
and their point of origin is St Paul: '... Thou therfore which
teachest another, teachest thou not thy selfe? thou that preachest,
A man should not steale, doest thou steale? Thou that sayest, A
man should not commit adulterie, doest thou commit adultery?
thou that abhorrest idoles, committest thou sacriledge? Thou that
gloriest in the Lawe, through breaking the Law dishonourest thou
God ...?' (Romans 2: 21–3). Moreover, Lear had learned to
repent: '... these things sting / His mind so venomously that
burning shame / Detains him from Cordelia' (IV iv 45); and by
the end of Act IV it partly seems that his madness has ceased:
'Be comforted, good madam. The great rage, / You see, is killed
in him' (IV iv 78).

The completeness of this change must not be insisted on
beyond a certain point (though that there is something of the
same kind in Gloucester's situation seems clear enough). A transition from blindness and injustice, through suffering, to self-
knowledge, responsibility and repentance, is not the final import
even of this long central section of the play. Nevertheless, it is
there plainly enough. The materials exist for a more conventional
and less protracted tragedy which could have ended well before
the beginning of Act v. If we ask what extends the play further,
the Book of Job reveals the answer.

What makes the situation of Job unique may be brought out by starting from the position of Job's comforters: Eliphaz's 'Who ever perished being an innocent?' or where were the upright destroyed' (4: 7), and Bildad's 'if thou be pure and upright, then surely he wil awake up unto thee' (8: 6). The comforters are orthodox. The men God punishes are sinners. Those who live piously under affliction, he restores; and so far as they are concerned, the sinister implications in Job's case are plain enough. But Job's protracted afflictions are a challenge to this orderly and consoling doctrine. When, despite his miseries, he 'holdeth fast to his integrity' ('In all this Job sinned not') his miseries are simply redoubled. This is the extraordinary event, the terrifying paradox indeed, which begins and demands the discussion that occupies the rest of the work. If there is any order of Nature at all, good must now replace evil; instead, evil returns twofold and is prolonged far beyond its proper span.

The action of *Lear* is also prolonged by this same conception. Repeatedly, we are made to think that since Nature is an order (though doubtless a stern one) release from suffering is at hand; but instead, the suffering is renewed. Act IV, the Act in which the play takes on its second and more remarkable lease of life, conspicuously begins with this very turn of thought and situation. Edgar, seeing himself at the very bottom of Fortune's wheel, finds cause for hope (living as he thinks in a world of order) in that fact alone:

> To be worst,
> The lowest and most dejected thing of fortune,
> Stands still in esperance, lives not in fear.
> The lamentable change is from the best;
> The worst returns to laughter. Welcome, then,
> Thou unsubstantial air that I embrace! (IV i 2)

At this very moment, he encounters his father and sees that he has been blinded; and his response is to recognize the very potentiality of life which was embodied in the story of Job:

> O gods! Who is't can say 'I am at the worst'?
> I am worse than e'er I was . . .

> And worse I may be yet. The worst is not
> So long as we can say 'This is the worst'.   (IV i 26)

The bitter reversal of events comes again and again. It is less than the full truth to say (as was suggested on p. 215) that Lear recovers from his madness during Act IV. The 'great rage' may be killed in him, but among his first words to Cordelia, when he is awakened out of sleep and we hope momentarily for his recovery, are:

> If you have poison for me, I will drink it.   (IV vii 72)

Cordelia's army, coming to rescue her father, succeeds only in putting her as well as him into the hands of their worst enemies. Later it seems as if Lear and Cordelia are to find a kind of private happiness in prison together. Yet even as this vision forms in our minds, we recall Edmund's threat, and realize that

> The good years shall devour them, flesh and fell,
> Ere they shall make us weep . . .   (v iii 24)

is hopeless fantasy on Lear's part, and only too soon to be proved so. Later still, the threat appears to be removed; for as he is dying Edmund confesses to his plot, and the Captain is sent hurrying to save Cordelia from death. But again, we are worse than e'er we were: the only result, the immediate result, is Lear's entry with Cordelia in his arms.

Perhaps this ironic turn in events, this constant intensifying of disaster at the moment when disaster seems to be over, is represented yet once again in the play: in the very moment of Lear's death. Conceivably, Lear is meant to think for a moment that Cordelia is alive; and dies before he realizes his mistake. Certainly, our hopes for Lear himself are, in a limited sense, raised once more by the words of Albany which immediately precede Lear's last speech. On either or both these counts, it seems as if some kind of remission is at hand; but at this moment Lear suffers the last infliction of all. Nor is it possible to accept, as true in anything but an incomplete and strained sense, R. W. Chambers' opinion that both Lear and Gloucester 'die of joy'. Edgar has already given the audience the exact truth of Gloucester's death:

> But his flaw'd heart –
> Alack, too weak the conflict to support! –
> 'Twixt two extremes of passion, joy and grief,
> Burst smilingly.   (v iii 196)

The last two words confirm a paradoxical combination of joy and grief, they do not convert it to a state of bliss; and it is a somewhat bold interpretation of the moment of Lear's death, one which without the parallel to Gloucester (and perhaps with it) would be over-bold, to assert that there, joy lies even in equal balance with grief. That Lear's heart breaks is clear from the words of Kent ('Break heart, I prithee break'); and that this is the culmination of an ordeal of torment renewed almost beyond belief, is what we are instructed to see by what this reliable authority says next:

> Vex not his ghost. O, let him pass! He hates him
> That would *upon the rack* of this rough world
> Stretch him out longer.   (v iii 312)

This in fact is the note sounded throughout the closing scenes. The world can be to mankind, and has been to Lear, a rack: a scene of suffering reiterated past all probability or reason. It can be a place of which Edgar was able to say, at the beginning of Act IV:

> World, world, O world!
> But that thy strange mutations make us hate thee,
> Life would not yield to age.   (IV i 10)

Later, only a few moments before the play closes, he goes on from the account of his father's death to hint plainly at the coming death of Kent:

> *Edmund.*   ... but speak you on;
>   You look as you had something more to say.

Albany. If there be more, more woeful, hold it in;
   For I am almost ready to dissolve,
   Hearing of this.
Edgar.   This would have seem'd a period
   To such as love not sorrow; but another,
   To amplify too much, would make much more,
   And *top extremity*.
   While I was big in clamour, came there in a man ...
   ... His grief grew puissant, and the strings of life
   Began to crack.

This is to underline once more the idiom of the play's later movement, its reiteration of suffering, to 'top extremity', when it seems
that suffering must surely be over.

At this stage in the discussion, one must try to record the note
upon which *King Lear* is resolved. It is not easy to do so, and it is
less easy than more than one distinguished critic has allowed.
One interpretation, certainly, has attracted many readers. We
may frame it, with Professor Chambers, as 'the victory of Cordelia and of Love'; or with Professor Knights, as the 'complete
endorsement of love as a quality of being', or with Professor
Wilson Knight, as 'the primary persons, good and bad, die into
love'. It is better to see the play thus, than to regard its close as
the embodiment only of cynicism, chaos and despair. But one
should remind oneself at this point of what, surely, is familiar
knowledge: that love (unless that word is taken, as I fear it is
often taken, to mean every good thing) is a value with a great
but finite place in human life; and that if it is a full description of
the affirmation on which the play closes, that affirmation is a
limited one; is indeed, curiously inadequate, curiously out of
scale with the range, power and variety of the issues of life on
which this incomparable work has touched. Those for whom the
word 'love' is a talisman will find this suggestion objectionable.
That may be an argument in its favour.

With these considerations in mind, one may incline to see the
close of *Lear* in another light. The survivors of Cleopatra, say,
and of Brutus and Coriolanus, indeed speak as though these
characters enjoyed a kind of victory or triumph even in death.

When, at the close of *Lear*, Shakespeare characteristically gives those who survive the protagonist lines which suggest what the audience is to see in his end, it is not to any victory or triumph, through love or anything else, that he makes them direct our attention. He causes them to agree that there has never been such a case of a man stretched out on the rack of the world, and released at last. At the close of *Macbeth* there is much emphasis on a movement of regeneration, a restoration of good at the level of the body politic. Lear ends more sombrely. 'Our present business ... is general woe', says Albany, appealing to Kent and Edgar for nothing more optimistic than to help him rule and 'the *gor'd* state *sustain*' – the modest ambition of that last word should not be missed. The last speech of all, that of Edgar, seems peculiarly significant, for all its bald rhyming:

> The weight of this sad time we must obey:
> *Speak what we feel, not what we ought to say,*
> The oldest hath borne most; *we that are young*
> *Shall never see so much nor live so long.*

The ordeal has been unique in its protraction of torment, and the note is surely one of refusal to hide that from oneself, refusal to allow the terrible potentialities of life which the action has revealed to be concealed once more behind the veil of orthodoxy and the order of Nature. If there is such an order, it is an order which can accommodate seemingly limitless chaos and evil. The play is a confrontation of that, a refusal to avert one's gaze from that. Its affirmation is as exalted, humane and life-affirming as affirmation can be, for it lies in a noble and unflinching steadiness, where flinching seems inevitable, in the insight of its creator.

To turn to a more intimate awareness of the personal bonds on which the play closes is to extend and amplify this, and still to see something other than what deserves the name of 'love' *tout court*. Perhaps there is a clue in the fact that it is Edmund ('Yet Edmund was beloved', v iii 239) and only Edmund, who speaks of love by itself. We are meant, of course, to see it as embodied always in what Cordelia does; but in her sole reference to this in the later

scenes of the play, what she at once goes on to speak of is not
her love but, in effect, her duty:

> No blown ambition does both our arms incite,
> But love, dear love, *and our ag'd father's right.*
>   (IV iv 26)

This stress, not on loving alone, but on doing and being what it
falls to one to do and be, is so insistent that its having been left
unregarded is surprising. Cordelia's first speech of any substance
to the re-awakened Lear confirms its relevance for both her and
him:

> O look upon me, sir,
> And hold your hands in benediction o'er me.
> No, sir, you must not kneel.   (IV vii 57)

What she wants is for him to do what it is a father's duty to do:
not what it is *her* duty to do in return. The same kind of thought
is prominent in Lear's first speech after capture:

> When thou dost ask me blessing, I'll kneel down,
> And ask of thee forgiveness.   (V iii 10)

Each of them is to do what (paradoxically, in Lear's case) it is
appropriate for them to do: the idea is of service and duteousness,
not love in any simple or emotional sense. In just this light, too,
are we invited to see Edgar's bond with his father:

> *Albany.* How have you known the miseries of your father?
> *Edgar.* By nursing them, my Lord . . .
>   . . . became his guide,
> Led him, begg'd for him, sav'd him from despair;
> Never – O fault! – reveal'd myself unto him
> Until some half-hour past, when I was arm'd;
> Not sure, though hoping, of this good success,
> I asked his blessing, and from first to last
> Told him my pilgrimage.   (V iii 180–96)

Kent's devotion to Lear is of course one in which feeling means service:

> I am the very man . . .
> That from your first of difference and decay
> Have followed your sad steps. (v iii 285)

> I have a journey, sir, shortly to go.
> My master calls me; I must not say no.
>
> (v iii 321)

The bond which remains, at the play's close, among the other (or perhaps only) survivors, is of the same kind:

> *Albany.* . . . Friends of my soul, you twain
> Rule in this realm, and the gor'd state sustain.
>
> (v vii 319)

With these many pointers in mind, perhaps the final import of the reconciliation of Lear to Cordelia, or Gloucester to Edgar, may also be seen as meaning more than the word 'love' can easily mean, at least in our own time; and as being, in the end, one with the whole of what happens at the close of the drama. That the closing phase is one in which the evil in the play proves self-destructive, is well known. Evil has come, it has taken possession of the world of the play, it has brought men below the level of the beasts, it has destroyed itself, and it has passed. Good (I have argued) is far from enjoying a triumphant restoration: we are left with the spectacle of how suffering can renew itself unremittingly until the very moment of death.

If, at the close, some note less despairing than this may be heard, it comes through our apprehending that in an austere and minimal sense, Edmund's words 'the wheel has come full circle' extend, despite everything, beyond himself. Below the spectacle of suffering everywhere in possession, is another, inconspicuous but genuine: that the forces of life have been persistently terrible and cruel, but have also brought men back to do the things it is their part to do. Union with Cordelia barely proves Lear's salvation: his salvation is what Kent says, release from a life of torment. But that union is the thing to which he rightly belongs.

He deviated from it, and life itself brought him back. So with Gloucester. To follow the master, to sustain the state, to bless one's child, to succour the aged and one's parents – this idea of being brought back to rectitude is what the play ends with. These are the things which it falls to living men to do; and if the play advances a 'positive', I think it is that when men turn away from how they should live, there are forces in life which constrain them to return. In this play, love is not a 'victory'; it is not that which stands at 'the centre of the action', and without which 'life is meaningless'; it does not rule creation. If anything rules creation, it is (though only, as it were, by a hairsbreadth) simply rule itself. What order restores, is order. Men tangle their lives; life, at a price, is self-untangling at last.

In view of these things, how fantastic it would be to call *King Lear* a play of intrigue! Yet this idea, immediate though its rejection must be, does indeed suggest the many things going on, and being intricately fitted together, which mark the closing scenes of the play. This very fact is what leads back from the attitudes of the play to what is more intimate with its substance, and with the experience which it offers to us in its sequence. The war with France, the intrigue between Edmund and the sisters, the emergence of Albany, Edmund's plot with the captain and his duel with Edgar, densen into a medium of something like quotidian life, through which and beyond which Lear's own situation stands out in isolation. It is the very variety in the strands of life which brings out how, at the end, life as it were stands back from Lear; and affords him a remoteness, a separation from his fellows, in which his ordeal is completed.

This is the culmination, moreover, of how he begins. As in the tragedies which have been discussed already, at the outset the protagonist is at the focal point of all men's regard. But Lear's progressive isolation does not steal upon him, or his audience, unawares. Relinquishing the kingdom, repudiating Cordelia, banishing Kent, cursing Goneril (I iv 275–89), departing wrathfully from Regan:

> He calls to horse, and will I know not whither . . .
>
> (II iv 296)

– all these actions set Lear, of his own free will, apart from his fellows; and are the prelude to how he sets himself apart, first from human contact of any kind whatsoever:

> No, rather I abjure all roofs, and choose
> To wage against the enmity o' th' air ...
>
> (II iv 207)

and then from the whole of Nature:

> This night, wherein the cub-drawn bear would crouch,
> The lion, and the belly-pinched wolf
> Keep their fur dry, unbonneted he runs,
> And *bids what will take all.*
>
> (III i 12)

Yet Lear's position is ambiguous. In his first speech on the heath he is not only the almost satanic enemy of Nature, cursing it in its entirety; but also its victim.

> Strike flat the thick rotundity o' th' world
> Crack nature's moulds, all germens spill at once,
> That make ingrateful man. ...
>
> (III ii 7)

is followed almost at once by:

> ... Here I stand, your slave,
> A poor, infirm, weak and despis'd old man.

If the tenor of the first passage is unmistakably like that of Macbeth's giant defiance ('though the treasure / Of nature's germens tumble all together / Even till destruction sicken – answer me / To what I ask you ...)', the second has its counterpart in *Macbeth* as well. Macbeth's 'They have tied me to a stake; I cannot fly' has its closest parallel, indeed, in Gloucester's 'I am tied to the stake, and I must stand the course' (III vii 53); but if Gloucester is like Macbeth in that his fate is more of an execution than anything else, so is Lear. Kent's thought of him on the rack is a variant of his own

> I am bound
> Upon a wheel of fire; that mine own tears
> Do scald like molten lead.   (IV vii 46)

The parallel with Macbeth is a strange and clear one; and the full currency in Shakespeare's own mind of the image through which we see the king in the later part of the play must be brought to attention and life. Today, the direction 'enter Lear, fantastically dressed with weeds' can easily seem mere fantasy without a background, or have merely some kind of enrichment in generalized associations with fertility and its converse. For Shakespeare, Lear's status in this scene must have been much more exact and significant. The figure

> Crown'd with rank fumiter and furrow weeds,
> With hardocks, hemlock, nettles, cuckoo-flow'rs,
> Darnel and all the idle weeds that grow
> In our sustaining corn ...   (IV iv 3)

whose first words are 'I am the King himself', who jests and preaches (IV vi 181), who is filled with a conviction that he is soon to be killed ('I will die bravely, like a smug bridegroom', IV vi 200; 'If you have poison for me, I will drink it', IV vii 72), who can say: 'Nay, an you get it, you shall get it by running', and run away dressed in his flowers and pursued by the attendants – this figure is easily recognizable. He is a Jack-a-Green, at once hero and victim of a popular ceremony. For a moment, he is a hunted man literally, as he is in spirit throughout the play. Nor is such a level of interest in any way out of place for Lear. There is much of the quality of folk thinking or acting, of the folk-tale, about his whole career. This shows in the stylized opening scene, in the formality and symmetry of his break with the three sisters, in his mock court in the outhouse and in this Jack-a-Green spectacle, right through to his final entry – which cannot but call up the legendary 'Come not between the dragon and his wrath' of the opening tableau, and in which Lear and Cordelia must appear not as king and princess, but, beyond normal life, as emblems of the extremes of what is possible in life.

Over the four plays which have been discussed so far there seems by now to emerge, with increasing clarity, a repeated and recognizable pattern. In *Lear* it is surely inescapable. Despite the rich detail and realism of this play, the action and the staging are stylized largely throughout. The protagonist (followed, less fully but in some ways more plainly, by Gloucester) pursues a well-marked rôle. He is the man who begins as centre of his whole world, but who is progressively set, both by the other characters and by himself, apart from it and against it. 'Against' means above, in solitary defiance, and below, in an ordeal of protracted suffering which takes on the quality of a hunt. His response to this may indeed be a growing awareness and comprehension of where he stands; but if this makes the onward movement of the action profounder and more impressive, it in no way retards or redirects it; and its end is a death which, though realistically the outcome of the human situation of the play, has at the same time the quality of stylized and ritual execution. All is foreseen, nothing can be delayed or hastened or mitigated. We are led, in fact, to envisage a new metaphor for the status of the tragic rôle in these plays; to see running through the work, besides its other interests, its detailed representation of life, its flow of ideas, its sense of good and evil, something which might be called the vertebrate structure of its intrinsic design; the developing line, unabridged, of a human sacrifice.

SOURCE: *The Story of the Night: Shakespeare's Major Tragedies* (1961).

C. J. Sisson

JUSTICE IN *KING LEAR* (1962)

NOWHERE, in the whole range of Shakespeare's work, is the desire so acutely felt as in *King Lear* to be able to consult Shakespeare himself upon the words he had written and upon their significance in his mind.

The desperate painfulness of the tragic ending of *King Lear* led the stage, when the brave Elizabethan days were past, to accept for almost two hundred years Tate's sentimentalized version with a happy ending, Lear surviving and Cordelia suitably married to Edgar. It is a rare, indeed an amiable, confession of weakness that led A. C. Bradley to wish that Shakespeare had saved Lear and Cordelia from the general wreck to enjoy peace and happiness together, though he is careful to insist that his wish rests upon principles of dramatic perfection, not upon sentiment. Yet never did Shakespeare take a more deliberate or a more striking decision than to reject version after version of the story, in Spenser, in Holinshed, or in the old play in which this happy ending closes an episode in British history. We may well feel that if there has been revulsion against Shakespeare's desperate conclusions here, no less instinctive and powerful was Shakespeare's revulsion against the epilogue to this happy ending in Holinshed, the renewal of civil war, the defeat of Cordelia Queen of Britain, and her death at her own hands. Shakespeare's story, at any rate, had a conclusion in which everything was concluded, and if Cordelia was hanged, she did not hang herself as in Holinshed.

There is no subject upon which Bradley is more guarded and more inconclusive, than the question of poetical justice. Yet through a maze of words it would seem that his conception of dramatic principles, as applied to *King Lear*, is offended by the gross disproportion between cause and effect in the catastrophe of this tragedy. He agrees that we may not measure the consequences of flaws in character in precise proportion to their results, and the logic of tragedy is not the logic of justice. Yet for him, here in *King Lear*, the vast sway of moral equilibrium in the universe is wanting, and there is consequently aesthetic dissatisfaction. Bradley's dissatisfaction finds itself reflected in the not uncommon estimate of the play as a tragedy of pessimistic outlook upon the world of men, and undue stress is still frequently laid upon Gloucester's words:

> As flies to wanton boys, are we to the gods;
> They kill us for their sport.

Too much stress has certainly been laid on what is described as the fairy-tale basis of the story of *King Lear*, with a consequent tendency to interpret the play in terms of cloudy symbolism for want of problems of human reality. What King in his senses, it is argued, would in real life divide his kingdom among his three daughters, abdicate, and spend his days thereafter in rotation with each in turn? How could a drama of living men and women emerge from such a fanciful theme? The modern world indeed might come closer in reality to Lear's action, in the avoidance of destruction of an estate by death-duties, with the device of deeds of gift to children. But in Elizabethan days funeral expenses were a far greater tax upon an estate than the claims of the Exchequer. Admittedly, the story was history, and was fact, to Shakespeare and the Elizabethans. Holinshed tells it, with a portrait of King Lear himself, bearded and helmeted, and a revolting woodcut of Cordelia, to illustrate it. There are parallels in classical history, and indeed in the early Elizabethan drama, as in *Gorboduc*, but we may perhaps distinguish between history and fairy-tale legend.

What we cannot do, is to deny the evidence of recorded contemporary events that such actions, not by kings certainly, but by men of great estate, were of frequent occurrence in Shakespeare's time. Some bear unexpected resemblances to the story of Lear as Shakespeare tells it. There was, for example, the Yorkshireman Ralph Hansby, who divided his great estates among his three daughters upon their marriage. He had no son, and he abdicated his greatness to continue it only in the advancement of his daughters. Two of them were ungrateful, but the third was his Cordelia, who married Sir John York. The career of Lady Julian York, a steadfast, loyal, obstinate soul, may be followed in state records up to her long imprisonment by King James for recusancy. Cordelia, we may well hold, would have been a recusant, Catholic or Puritan, in Shakespeare's day, averse by her nature to commodious conformity, to her great loss. In the story of the life of Brian Annesley, it has been recorded that the name of the youngest of his three daughters was actually Cordelia.[1]

Closest of all in some respects is the story of Sir William Allen, a very wealthy old Londoner, about which there is the fullest detail in Chancery records, a very lamentable story indeed.[2] Sir William was for long a leading figure in the Company of Merchant Adventurers. He had his day of quasi-royalty, for he was Lord Mayor of London, and was knighted by the Queen in his year of office, in 1571. He lived on to be over eighty years of age, and found his great possessions a heavy burden from which he desired relief. He had moreover found himself growing forgetful in his great old age.

> Methinks I should know you, and know this man,
> Yet I am doubtful. For I am mainly ignorant
> What place this is; and all the skill I have
> Remembers not these garments; nor I know not
> Where I did lodge last night.

Sir William had three daughters, all married, one of them to a Frenchman, Francis Verzelin. So he divided his great properties among the three daughters, and arranged that he should stay with each of them in turn, at one of the houses that had been his own. But once they had entered into possession, they treated him very ill, and grudged him all service and comfort. Being so very old a man, he felt the cold bitterly, and desired warmth. But his daughters, so the Court was told, 'limited his fire', kept him short of wood and coal, and treated his childish querulous protests with scorn and disdain. Coal was very dear, they said, an unnecessary expense. So Goneril and Regan with Lear's knights. 'What need *one?*' said Regan, 'this house is little.'

> Dear daughter, I confess that I am old;
> Age is unnecessary, on my knees I beg
> That you'll vouchsafe me raiment, bed and food.

And he kneels to Regan. What could be said for these pelican daughters?

> *Goneril.* His knights grow riotous, and himself upbraids us
> On every trifle . . .
> You strike my people, and your disordered rabble
> Make servants of their betters.

So Sir William's daughters complained that he was rude to their servants, called them 'fussocks', awkward, unhandy – surely very mild abuse.[3] So at last he died, in great misery, and died with a father's curse upon them. There was no Cordelia among these three.

Sir William probably was in truth an obstinate, self-willed old man, as indeed Lear was with perhaps more justification, by virtue of his kingship. Sir William had a wife, Lady Mary Allen, who possibly resisted in vain his dangerous decision. A mother knows her own daughters, and a woman is more practical-minded, more critical of ideas. Lear, it may be noted, has no Queen in the play to defend her own crown as well as his. Like Hansby and Allen, he also has no son. There was none of power to question his self-will in the solitary absoluteness of his royalty. We must not put from our consideration the part of truth in what Goneril and Regan have to say in their judgment of his character and of his action in the very first scene, even in the first flush of their rich succession.

> *Regan.* 'Tis the infirmity of his age; yet he hath *ever* but
> slenderly known himself.
> *Goneril.* The best and soundest of his time hath been but rash,
> then must we look from his age to receive not alone
> the imperfections of long-ingrafted condition, but

therewithal the unruly waywardness that infirm and choleric years bring with them.

It is something more than a coincidence that the Lear story first emerged on the London stage soon after the great stir which the story of Sir William Allen made in London. The case occupied the Court of Chancery for a long time in 1588 to 1589, and the early play, *The True Chronicle History of King Leir*, upon which in some measure Shakespeare founded his great tragedy, followed perhaps a year later. It may well be that this first play was designed to take advantage of the reflection on the stage of a current *cause célèbre* in actual London life. At all events, it must be conceded that no Elizabethan would accept the dismissal of the preliminary action of the play as a fairy-tale theme, remote from actuality. We may reasonably believe that Shakespeare knew this story of Sir William and his daughters, for he was certainly in London at the time when it was the talk of the town. How, we may well ask, would this knowledge affect his treatment of the story of King Lear when he turned one day to this old play which was in print in 1605, and saw in it material for the supreme exercise of his tragic genius?

It is a far cry from a Christian merchant-knight of Shakespeare's London to a pagan King of Britain in that remote world in which history merges into legend. What could be common to these two, save the mere story? The knowledge of this contemporary affair would surely lend immediacy and poignancy to these figures from the ancient past, and to their problems, in the chronicled story of Holinshed, partially recreated in the old play. And it would help Shakespeare to penetrate to the common elements of human nature involved in such a story as it affected two such various sets of people and sets of facts. It would impel him, finally, to seek out some philosophic significance in which these events could be reconciled with the ultimate order and meaning of the universe of God and man, to arrive indeed at what we call tragic reconciliation.

The story of Sir William Allen is merely desperate, it would seem, and totally devoid of that measure of poetic justice which marks the story that came to Shakespeare from Holinshed. There he found one daughter among the three who was a loving child, and in the end right triumphs. Goneril and Regan are defeated, retribution falls upon them, Lear is restored to his throne, and Cordelia succeeds him as Queen. So the old play tells the story, and so Spenser tells it again in *The Faerie Queene*. But as Shakespeare concludes his play he seems to be deliberately depriving it of all poetic justice and of all apparent moral significance. The loving daughter is involved in the general disaster of the House of Lear, against all authority of history or stage. So also in the parallel sub-plot of Gloucester and his sons, introduced from Sidney's *Arcadia*, the happy ending of Sidney's story is changed to tragedy. In the end, the storm of untoward events, reflected in the thunder and lightning and great wind of the conflicting elements, passes. There remains, said Coleridge, 'the closing in of night, and the single hope of darkness'.

A considerable chorus of comment has chimed in with this grievous verdict upon the greatest of tragedies. Robert Bridges tells us that if Shakespeare's object in *Othello* is to excite his audience, in *Macbeth* to terrify it, and in *Hamlet* to mystify it, in *King Lear* his object is to harrow it. For Miss Lena Ashwell, a great Shakespearean actress of this century, as for Tolstoy also, the play is a dead march of pessimism. 'We find Greek pessimism in *Lear*', she wrote.[4] Ruskin's complaint is that we do not find Greek optimism in *Lear*. The enemy in Shakespeare is blind fate, as Miss Ashwell also complained. The fault of haste or indiscretion beings results terrible beyond all bounds.

At the close of a Shakespeare tragedy, nothing remains but dead march and clothes of burial. At the close of a Greek tragedy there are far-off sounds of a divine triumph, and a glory as of resurrection.[5]

It is perhaps odd that Aristotle did not feel this in Greek tragedy, or at any rate did not express this feeling. But we may well hold that this is precisely what we feel in *King Lear*, if not in Greek tragedy.

The only philosophy that can possibly see in *King Lear* the mere fall of black night upon a shipwreck of human life and love is materialism, which encloses life within final limits of time and space. In such a view a famous couplet of Pope might well express the cosmic significance of the play.

> Thy hand, great Anarch, let the curtain fall
> And universal darkness cover all.

But indeed the truth would be more disastrous. For such a philosophy the world has neither Ruler nor Anarch, neither order nor monarchy, neither God nor Devil in command, but is a ship not only without a compass or a captain, but without a sea.

Much play has been made of the setting of *King Lear* in a pagan world of pre-Christian Britain, and of Shakespeare's possible exclusion of Christian thought from its moral and spiritual atmosphere.[6] This has led to interpretations of the play as resting upon a stoic philosophy, along with a materialistic view of life and of the universe, though these are inconsistent one with another, and are also remote from the truth. Certainly the stoic attitude towards life preserves the invulnerability of the virtuous philosopher, who may justly take refuge in suicide, in contempt for the incalculable, uncontrolled circumstance that destroys him. But of this, whatever we may find in *Julius Caesar*, there is nothing in *King Lear*. Lear himself is certainly the least invulnerable of men, and furthest of all from the Senecal man of Chapman's admiration. Othello does not take refuge in death, he executes justice upon himself, well aware that this act does not close his account. Hamlet considers the stoic solution, only to reject it. Iago comes nearest to stoic self-sufficiency, disdainful of the final disastrous throw of the dice, silent and impassive. Gloucester sets aside the temptation, as Hamlet does:

> You ever gentle gods,
> Let not my worser spirit tempt me again
> To die before you please.

Nor does Edmund fall into this pit, though there was excuse for him. It is worth noting that Shakespeare reduces the guilt of the

Edmund whom he took from the *Arcadia*. There it is Edmund himself who with revolting cruelty tears out his father's old eyes. In Shakespeare he is not even present when Cornwall, before Regan's eyes, does the hideous deed. But he is born to contempt in the society in which he is an unwelcome intruder, even to his father, for whom he is the visible memory of his 'pleasant vices', as Edgar put it. For Albany, he is 'half-blooded fellow'. He stands from his very birth 'in the plague of custom', bastard and base-born. And yet in the end of all, he seeks to make amends. 'Some good I mean to do', and dies true brother to Edgar after all, and no brother to Iago.

There is in fact poetic justice enough in *King Lear*. Goneril, Regan, Cornwall and Edmund, all perish in their sins. Evil is destroyed. Towards the end of the play Albany proclaims the restoration of the old King to his absolute power, and of Edgar and Kent to their just rights:

> All friends shall taste
> The wages of their virtue, and all foes
> The cup of their deservings.

But poetic justice seems to be of little moment. When Edmund's death is reported to Albany, he truly comments, 'that's but a trifle here', as indeed it is. When the news of the desperate deaths of Goneril and Regan comes to Lear, he puts it aside carelessly as an irrelevance, 'Ay, so I think.' And hard upon Albany's proclamation, to which the old king pays no attention, it is cancelled by Lear's death. As for Kent, restored to his rights, and more, he has a journey shortly to go, to join his master. Albany's justice beats the air. Of what avail indeed would it be to set Lear and Cordelia, Gloucester and Kent, afloat again in that 'ebb and flow of great ones' that Lear mocks so gently, but so irrevocably.

The truth is that greater issues are afoot in this play than the verdicts of justice or the nice balance of rights and wrongs in the universe. We have long ago learned to recognise in its action and development a theme which might justify the title *The Redemption of King Lear* in place of *The Tragedy of King Lear*, pointing to a happy ending of deeper truth than Tate's or that desired by

Bradley. It is a theme that recurs elsewhere in Shakespeare, in comedy as in tragedy. It is something of a key to the significance of *The Taming of the Shrew*, in which Katherine finds her true self and with it happiness. In *Troilus and Cressida* again, Troilus, lost in love, perplexed and frustrated by Cressida's weak disloyalty, comes at last to his full manhood as a Prince of Troy at war against her enemies, pursuing duty instead of his own private ends, and goes forth to certain death in battle with the mantle of dead Hector upon him. So with Lear who has hitherto, as Goneril justly says, but slenderly known himself, and comes to fuller knowledge and with it a deeper understanding of the world of men and of their universe, through the desperate evils let loose by his own act. From overweening pride, security, and obstinacy, he moves through rebellious anger, despair, and madness to patience, to humility, and to a new recognition of truth and goodness. In the great storm of events he suffers a sea-change, purged by suffering. Much has been made, as by Bradley and later critics, of the apparent paradox of Lear's passivity throughout the movement of the play, though he is its principal character, as if he were something like a soul in purgatory. But his activity is within the microcosmos of his own conscious being, and it is intense. Deep within the very core of this activity lies the problem of justice, that justice which in the catastrophe of the play appears to be contemned and almost irrelevant.

In Shakespeare's later plays the question of the operation of justice comes constantly into dramatic consideration, which vividly reflects the poet's deep concern with the problem. In *Measure for Measure* the whole action rests upon an image of the delegation of the powers of justice from God to Kings, as trustees for divine justice. So the Duke vests his royal powers in his deputy Angelo, and is content to observe unseen. The tyranny of formal laws, the fallibility of their human instrument, and their corruption and abuse in practice, lead to the Duke's intervention and to his resumption of his supreme function so that right may be done. In the bankruptcy of justice, mercy and charity make amends, extended even to the corrupt justicer. It is difficult to refrain from pursuing the image further, into the robe of religion worn by the Duke, a symbol of his divine function, into the noviceship of Isabella whose plea is throughout for mercy, and into the marriage of justice and mercy in their persons with which the play concludes.

In *The Tempest* we have a rightful Duke in exile upon an island where he is sole master, determining events and controlling destinies, inflicting punishment and showing mercy, with spirits at his call and with the elements in his command as instruments of his will. His power is supernatural, and is wielded by himself in his absolute decision. The law and the justice of Prospero upon his island reflect in its limited sphere something closely akin to a world controlled by a constant and sufficient intervention of divine justice in direct operation upon human destinies and actions, by a law of visitations, in the Elizabethan sense of the word. He is capable of anger at evil, like the wrath of God. He puts men's hearts to test. There is mercy and forgiveness for penitence in the evildoer, in which Caliban also has his share. So the island which Gonzalo would govern in all the simplicity and beauty of the golden age has also a form of justice that is utopian, and yet rules the universe. In the world of men it is indeed utopian. When Prospero returns from his island to that world, to his Dukedom and to Milan, he breaks his staff, buries his book, and abdicates those powers that surpass royal power.

These two plays are comedies, and in them the dramatic treatment of the question of justice is not incompatible with a mind that is merely curious in its analysis of the operation of justice in human life. In the tragedies of *Macbeth*, *Othello*, and *Hamlet*, specific problems of justice are met, and solved. But in *King Lear* it may well seem that that analysis has become destructive, that a logical dilemma has moved into a philosophic quandary, that the function of justice itself has come into question, a devastating thought. It is, of course, a familiar thought in the Christian world. 'Though thou slay me, yet will I trust in thee.' But this trust rests upon the admission of ignorance of the evidence, and upon a faith overcoming individual judgment. It is another doubt altogether that questions the validity of the principle and its significance in human life.

When this tragedy opens, Lear himself, like the Emperor Valentinian in Fletcher's play, *is* justice and wields that power by virtue of his kingship. The very first scene in the play shows that power in direct action, even as Stuart London from time to time saw King James sitting himself, as he was entitled to do, on the Bench of his Court of Star Chamber. Lear is engaged upon one of the two main limbs of justice as it appeared to Aristotle and as it appears also to our modern world, Distributive Justice and Retributive Justice. In the modern world we are accustomed to Distributive Justice, the lean kine, swallowing up the once fat kine of Retributive Justice. And we are becoming gradually less inclined to consent even in works of imagination to the operation of justice as retributive. King Lear, surprisingly, is exercising distributive justice from the throne, though he rests his judgment upon merit, contrary to the enlightened modern view of social justice. Goneril and Regan satisfy the claims of merit, as Lear has formulated it, but against all his expectation Cordelia fails the test, and retributive justice also comes at once into action, upon an ungrateful daughter and a rebellious servant Kent, Lear nothing doubting his right to exercise it nor questioning his own decision. Yet he is not by nature tyrannical or unjust or given to hatred. From these decrees the dread train of events flows inevitably, in which Lear's whole world suddenly gives way under his feet. The idea upon which the play rests is indeed the consequence of a grave error and abuse of justice by the king within whose powers justice lies.

As the action develops, Lear himself is led to consider power more closely, and with it justice, the sword of power. Here Shakespeare makes a significant change in the story of Lear as Holinshed tells it. In Holinshed, Lear retains the half of his royal estate, and retains his throne, content to give great rewards to his daughters and to assure to them the succession to all. But in Shakespeare he gives all at once, and his crown too, and with it he abdicates also from his power to dispense justice, and becomes subject to justice for the first time. No longer a king, no longer hedged about with divinity, a mere 'idle old man', as Goneril puts it scornfully, he is the better able now to examine kingship, the sanctions of royal power, and justice, with eyes no longer veiled by their exercise in his own person. 'I think the King is but a man', says Shakespeare's Henry the Fifth, and philosophises a good deal upon the theme. But it is all very theoretical, such an essay as that absolute monarch Henry the Eighth might have written for his tutor. But heaven help the tutor if the essay were not applauded with an *alpha plus*. King Hal's essay is something like a report of a Royal Commission of one, signed *Henry R*.

> No, thou proud dream,
> I am a king that find thee, and I know.

It is vastly different with Lear.

> I *was* a king that find thee, and I know.

When the rain came to wet me once, and the wind to make me chatter; when the thunder would not peace at my bidding; there I found 'em, there I smelt 'em out. Go to, they are not men o' their words; they told me I was everything. 'Tis a lie, I am not ague-proof.

As the play opens with the King doing justice, so other, briefer, trial-scenes comment further upon power and justice. The mad parody of a trial in Act III, scene vi is prefaced by the Fool's searching question:

Prithe nuncle tell me, whether a madman be a gentleman or a yeoman,

to which Lear replies, 'A king, a king'. The Justices in this trial are madmen too, save one. There are three, Edgar as Poor Tom, the Fool, and Kent added to the Bench as an afterthought. Lear is the accuser, and he too is mad. The honourable assembly of judges sitting upon his cause is a crazy phantasmagoria that shifts and dissolves into nothingness. The scene is followed hot-foot by Cornwall's brief trial of Gloucester. He has scruples not concerning justice, but concerning the forms of justice, which forbid the execution of Gloucester. Yet he diverts justice to the vengeance

of wrath served by mere power beyond men's control, in the
execution of Gloucester's eyes. And in this doing of injustice the
false justicer himself meets his death-wound at the hands of one
of his servants, of one of those whose control he mocks. Such is
the exercise of power, the master of justice.

In the next act we have further scathing analysis of justice in
action:

See how yond justice rails upon yond simple thief. Hark in
thine ear. Change places; and handy-dandy, which is the justice,
which is the thief?

Gloucester, like justice, is blind, yet may well see how the world
goes, with no eyes. A farmer's dog barking at a beggar is 'the
great image of authority – a dog's obeyed in office'. The dis-
pensers and the instruments of justice are corrupt and evil themselves. Plaintiff and defendant alike are but guilty in different
ways. And justice is merely impotent. The kingship itself is not
left unscathed in Lear's sharp irony: 'No, they cannot touch me
for coining; I am the King himself.'

Finally, there is the great storm and wind, the heavens and
earth at war. In the old play the storm stands for divine anger.
The thunder and lightning are the signs of the coming intervention of Jupiter, of divine justice. But in Shakespeare, deliberately
and plainly, this is changed into a reflection of disorder and chaos,
the elements in hideous battle, driven into strife at the will of the
purposeless, violent gods above, as if the universe were distraught.
And this is what breaks Lear's already precarious sanity. It is
the ultimate doubt concerning justice, that even in the heavens
there is no certainty or security. Power and justice are weighed
in the balance – the vaunted image of dispassionate justice – and
are found wanting.

When we think of this appalling analysis of justice, we may
well wonder why so much comment has been concentrated upon
Lear's outburst against luxury and lechery, as if that were the
core and heart of his revolt of the spirit, as if it were an explosion
of Shakespeare's own personal revolt against sex, of his utter dis-

illusionment. But in comparison this is formal, commonplace, trite, and insignificant.

How are we then to think of the complex, profound re-birth of the spirit in Lear out of these depths that he has plumbed, and out of which he emerges into a new light? Is the true subject and conclusion of this tremendous play the purging of Lear through suffering, an *exemplum* of the theological concept of the Problem of Pain? It has even been put that Lear's Purgatory is here and now in this world, not in the world to come, though Purgatory is peopled only by souls already redeemed. It would be gravely disturbing to the spirit if this were indeed the final teaching of the play, the true interpretation of its action as Shakespeare conceived and created it. If the world of Lear was truly purgatorial in this sense, then Lear's concern was for his own salvation. Having been subjected to a deep educative process, he submits to it and accepts it, so that he may pass an all-important examination. The gods do not after all kill us for their sport; they only kill us for our own good, a far more desperate conclusion. But it is indeed not so in *King Lear*.

When the tide turns and the light begins to shine again upon Lear's troubled being, it is not of himself that he is thinking, not even of his immortal soul. 'In boy, go first,' he says to the shivering Fool – out of the bitter storm into the poor shelter of the hovel.

> Nay get thee in. I'll pray, and then I'll sleep.
> Poor naked wretches, wheresoe'er you are
> That bide the pelting of this pitiless storm,
> How shall your houseless heads, and unfed sides,
> Your looped and windowed raggedness, defend you
> From seasons such as this? O I have ta'en
> Too little care of this.

So Gloucester too, to his son Edgar, poor Tom:

> In fellow there, into the hovel; keep thee warm.

The Christian concept of charity is sweeping like a great tide into his soul, as into Gloucester's, the tide in which Cordelia and Kent have ever floated as in their own native element. In such an element forgiveness becomes a superfluity, an irrelevance:

> *Lear.* I know you do not love me, for your sisters
>   Have, as I remember, done me wrong.
>   You have some cause, they have not.
> *Cor.* No cause, no cause.

Love casteth out doubt also. We recall two kneelings of Lear to daughters. He kneels before Regan in Act II, scene iv. There he kneels in outraged satire, in parody of submission, an 'unsightly trick' as Regan calls it at once. In Act v he is about to kneel to Cordelia:

> When thou dost ask my blessing, I'll kneel down,
>   And ask of *thee* forgiveness.

'No cause, no cause.' If there is a truly theological basis for this play, it is that evil is to be known and feared because it is the absence of good, that hatred is dreadful because it arises out of the absence of love. The end of the play is surely the triumph of love, of positive goodness.

Edgar reveals himself to Gloucester, and asks his blessing. And Gloucester, overcome by this revelation of unshakeable love, torn between joy and grief, dies in ecstasy. 'His flawed heart . . . burst smilingly.' Kent asks no reward for the steadfast loyalty of his love for Lear. That love is beyond reason or purpose.

> I have a journey, sir, shortly to go.
>   My master calls me, I must not say no.

Love, as Shakespeare had written before he wrote *King Lear*,

> Love is not love,
> Which alters when it alteration finds . . .
> O no, it is an ever fixed mark
> That looks on tempests and is never shaken.

Cordelia's husband, the King of France, echoes these words early in this play:

> Love's not love
> When it is mingled with regards that stand
> Aloof from the entire point.

Beyond the facile satisfaction of an old fairy tale, beyond the defiance of a Prometheus or the stoic fortitude of Eteocles in Greek tragedy, beyond the stony anaesthesia of Shelley's Beatrice Cenci, 'all fear and pain being subdued', is the reconciliation in *King Lear* that comes despite the evil of the world, the apparent injustice of fate impartial in its destruction of good and evil alike, in the fulfilment of a soul's destiny – that too, not in 'calm of mind, all passion spent', as with Milton's Samson, but shaken still by mortality, as Christ was in the Garden of Gethsemane.

So we are led back to the deep criticism of power and justice upon which this play has so much to say. It has but little to say upon divine justice in direct intervention or indirect, though this was so familiar and accepted a feature of the Elizabethan moral landscape. And what it says is all incidental, and contradictory. The gods are just, and use our vices to plague us, says Edgar, yet Gloucester accuses these gods whom elsewhere he calls 'kind', and 'ever-gentle', of slaying men for their wanton sport. Lear himself invokes the judgment of Heaven and the just cause of the goddess Nature, yet considers whether the gods themselves have not set his daughters upon him to plague him. Both are at one with Eteocles in the *Seven against Thebes* in their dark moments. 'The only favour the gods enjoy from us is our death,' he complains, and he dies submissive to impotence against the evils sent down upon man by the gods. But praise and blame of the gods alternate in *King Lear* and are little more than expletives. Only Albany speaks in terms of conviction of a judgment of the heavens that falls upon Goneril and Regan. It seems to be the true conclusion of *King Lear* that power and justice, human or divine, are none of them ultimately important after all.

There are crucial phrases in the four tragedies that are the more significant here because the word 'cause' is so deeply coloured in Elizabethan use by its judicial associations. 'It is the cause, it is the cause,' says Othello. 'All causes must give way,' says Macbeth. 'Report me and my cause aright,' says Hamlet to Horatio. 'No cause, no cause,' says Cordelia in pure love. And so in the universe, in God's love for man, and man's love for God, and man's love for man, if we did but understand it. The concepts of the less or more, the fine balance of right and wrong, even the most well meant of human attempts to reflect the divine assessment of God's creatures, all are mortal, and fallible. And when we know this, and come to live by this knowledge, then we are at one with the true power and with the ultimate justice that reigns causeless in the universe, with 'the love that moves the sun and all the stars', the shining vision that is the supreme bliss of eternal life.

SOURCE: *Shakespeare's Tragic Justice* (1962).

NOTES

1. G. M. Young, 'Shakespeare and the Termers', in *Proceedings of the British Academy*, XXXIII. The Hansby-York material is unpublished.
2. PRO C24/210/Verzelyn v Allen; C24/211/Allen v Verzelyn.
3. *N.E.D.* cites *fussock* as first occurring in the eighteenth century.
4. *Reflections upon Shakespeare* (1927).
5. *Modern Painters*, IX ii 15.
6. It has not, however, been sufficiently observed that it is a deliberate variation from the old play of *Leir*, in which we have a Christian world, with a Saviour, a Church, and even an accusation of Puritanism levelled at Cordelia.

W. R. Elton

DOUBLE PLOT IN
KING LEAR (1966)*

ACCORDING to Bradley, the double plot chiefly contributes to
Lear's 'structural weakness', 'the secondary plot fills out a story
which would by itself have been somewhat thin', and 'the sub-
plot simply repeats the theme of the main story'.[1] Although the
double action is thus held to be fatally defective and to be filling
which is 'simply' repetitive, some critics have excused it on the
grounds that it universalizes ingratitude and intensifies the tragic
effect. Since Shakespeare succeeded, however, in the neighboring
tragedies of *Othello* and *Macbeth*, in achieving intensity and universality without recourse to such devices, a further attempt to
account for its unique and apparently uneconomic occurrence
may be appropriate.

Among other explanations for the double plot is that which
identifies in Lear and Gloucester traditional aspects of the sensitive soul: the irascible and the concupiscible matching the protagonists' anger and lechery. This traditional dualism could,
because of its medieval and Renaissance conventionality, tend to
dramatic recognition.

Following Plato's conventional division,[2] Erasmus' Folly
believes Jupiter has set up against our diminutive reason 'two . . .
masterless tyrants'. These are 'anger, that possesses the region of
the heart, and consequently the very fountain of life, the heart
itself; and lust, that stretches its empire everywhere'.[3] King
James's teacher, George Buchanan, in *De jure regni apud Scotos*
points out that

---

* Quotations from *King Lear* are from the Arden edition, ed. Kenneth Muir (1952). Quotations from other Shakespearean plays are
from the Globe edition of the *Works*, ed. William George Clark and
William Aldis Wright (1952).

two most loathsome monsters, anger and lust, are clearly apparent in mankind. And what else do laws strive for or accomplish
than that these monsters be made obedient to reason? ... He,
therefore, who releases a king, or anyone else, from these bonds
does not merely release a man, but sets up two exceedingly cruel
monsters in opposition to reason. ....[4]

In addition, the second book of the *Faerie Queene* presents the
familiar opposition of wrath and lust, the irascible in cantos i–vi,
the concupiscible in cantos vii–xii. Guillaume Du Vair's *The
Moral Philosophie of the Stoicks*, translated by Thomas James
(1598), speaks of the senses as disturbing 'that part of the soule
where concupiscence and anger dooth lodge' and raising a 'tumult
... in the mind, that reason during this furie can not bee heard'.[5]
Huarte de San Juan's *The Examination of Mens Wits* (1594)
notes, regarding their ability to repress inferior powers, that 'our
first parents ... lost this qualitie, and the irascible and concupiscible remained ... ' (p. 250). Montaigne's influential disciple,
Pierre Charron, in *De la sagesse* (1601) distinguishes between
'*Concupiscible*, and *Irascible* Faculties'.[6] Lodowick Bryskett's *A
Discourse of Civill Life* (1606) identifies 'the two principall
appetites, the irascible and the concupiscible' (p. 48).[7]

Because in Renaissance drama differences in rank may imply
other personal distinctions, the royal Lear represents the higher
portion of the human creature, his reason being closer to the
divine; while the more lowly Earl of Gloucester represents its
nether portion. Rank also has its afflictions. Tommaso Buoni's
Problemes of Beautie and All Humane Affections, whose translation appeared in 1606, attempts to explain an accepted fact: 'Why
are great Princes commonly afflicted with the griefes of the mind,
and men of baser condition with those of the body' (p. 235).[8]
Since passions, as Du Vair's *The Moral Philosophie of the Stoicks*
remarks, 'darken and obscure the eye of reason' (p. 62), anger and
madness assail the king, who suffers most in the mind, putting out
his reason's light; while the 'dark place' of physical lust and
'nether crimes', as well as the physical darkness of blinding,
attend his fellow *persona patiens*. Mankind's upper half, closer to

the angels, and the nether half, bestial, are symbolized, for example, in Lear's centaur speech (IV vi 126–34).[9]

Before the end of the fourth Act the protagonists, in this last of meeting places, grope together, minds dim and eye sockets empty, like creatures out of Bruegel's 'Parable of the Blind'.[10] Lacking even the compensatory vision of the mad Cassandra or the blind Tiresias, they enact a parable of the limitations of human knowledge. Yet, if Lear and Gloucester cannot, in a sense, 'know' or 'see', they can feel; but the irony is that their hard-earned gift of feeling only makes them suffer more. The limit of their knowledge, like Edgar's, is the suffering it brings. As do Montaigne[11] and Sidney's *Arcadia* (I 227), Webster's *The Duchess of Malfi* (III v 81–4), for example, expresses the Sophoclean position:

> Thou art happy, that thou hast not understanding
> To know thy misery: For all our wit
> And reading, brings us to a truer sence
> Of sorrow. . . .

According to the traditional irascible–concupiscible distinction, Lear's intellectual error of anger receives the conventional punishment of madness (*ira furor brevis*), and Gloucester's physical sin of lechery the conventional retribution of blindness. Yet it is evident that Gloucester, in addition to such irascible passions as fear and despair, also participates in Lear's angry propensities; the earl's rash and premature fury at Edgar parallels Lear's outburst at Cordelia. 'I am almost mad myself' (III iv 170), Gloucester confesses to Kent. On the other hand, Lear, at least figuratively, shares Gloucester's blindness. Blind from the start, dim of sight at the end ('Mine eyes are not o' th' best', v iii 279), he anticipates both Gloucester and the darkening of his own mind's eye: 'Old fond eyes, / Beweep this cause again, I'll pluck ye out' (I iv 310–11).

A further iterated parallel is that between joy and sorrow, both of which were usually ascribed to the concupiscent faculty. Renaissance psychology recognized the perverse and convulsive effects of such extremes. For example, Nashe speaks of 'many whom

extreame joy & extreame griefe hath forced to runne mad' (II
114–15), and Timothy Bright in *A Treatise of Melancholie* (1586),
which Shakespeare probably knew, remarks, 'What marvell . . .
if contraries in passions bring forth like effects; as to weepe &
laugh, both for joy & sorow? For as it is oft seene that a man
weepeth for joy, so is [it] not straunge to see one laugh for griefe'
(pp. 148–9).[12]

In this regard, the similarity between the deaths of Gloucester
and Lear accentuates their difference: Gloucester perishes between
extremes of grief and of joy at the knowledge that his son was
'miraculously' preserved (v iii 196–9); Lear dies between extremes
of a kind of joy in his desperate illusion of her lips' movement and
of grief in his emphatic knowledge that his daughter was need-
lessly butchered. While such emotional extremities were divisive,
immoderateness of joy alone could cause death. 'Sudden Joy',
says the Renaissance proverb (Tilley J86), 'kills sooner than
excessive grief.' 'For it is not possible', declares Mabbe's 1623
translation of Alemán's *Guzman de Alfarache*, 'that any mans
heart should dissemble a sudden joy. Though it sometimes so
hapneth, that excesse of joy, doth suffocate the naturall heat, and
deprive it of it's life.'[13] Especially in an old or enfeebled man, the
extremes themselves could wrenchingly cause violence. Apropos,
the *Celestina* in Mabbe's translation (1631) remarks:

on the one side he is oppressed with sadness and melancholy . . .
on the other side transported with that gladsome delight and
singular great pleasure. . . . And thou knowest that, where two
such strong and contrary passions meet, in whomsoever they
shall house themselves with what forcible violence they will
work upon a weak and feeble subject.[14]

Analogous to the above, as well as to the microcosmic weather
analogy of Lear (cf III i, ii), is Cordelia's own joy and grief as
described by the Gentleman (IV iii 18–20):

> You have seen
> Sunshine and rain at once; her smile and tears
> Were like, a better way. . . .[15]

Proverbially reflected in the *Arcadia* and in other parallels, the contrast is echoed also in S.S.'s *The Honest Lawyer*: 'So I have seene (me thinkes) Sun-shine in raine' (1616, sig. B).[16] Finally, as in Bright, cited earlier, it is anticipated in the perversity of the Fool:

> *Then they for sudden joy did weep,*
> *And I for sorrow sung.* (i iv 182–3)[17]

Progressively skeptical and Epicurean with regard to the gods, Lear is set up against the superstitious and eventually 'Stoic' Gloucester, their differences, like their similarities, being great. In crediting the ominousness of eclipses, Gloucester, although Epicurean on a sensual level, assumes an un-Epicurean position, for followers of Epicurus rejected such prognostication. On the other hand, Gloucester's belief in omens could, like his later tenuous acceptance of 'ripeness', associate him with a Stoic view, which also vigorously defended both intuitive and inductive divination.[18]

Further, in an earlier tragedy Shakespeare had already employed the classical distinction as a measure of a character's shifting viewpoint; the scornful and Epicurean Cassius, at a moment of defeat, partially repudiates his previous rejection of omens:

> You know that I held Epicurus strong
> And his opinion: now I change my mind,
> And partly credit things that do presage.
> (v i 77–9)[19]

As it does with regard to attitudes toward thunder and the stars, *Julius Caesar*'s opposition of the Epicurean Cassius and the Stoic Brutus foreshadows a similar antithesis in *King Lear*. Still earlier, the *Taming of the Shrew* (i i 27–40) had philosophically posed Epicurean delights against Stoic repressions. In Jacobean, Caroline, and Restoration comedy, moreover, the opposition between Stoic and Epicurean continues, and that duality, as a recent study of Etherege reminds us,[20] underlies works of such dramatists as Chapman, Jonson, Thomas Nabbes, and Fletcher.

As superstitious 'over-believer' and skeptical 'under-believer',

Gloucester and Lear tend to two of the best-known pagan philosophical attitudes in the Renaissance. In 1604 Andrew Willet's *Thesaurus ecclesiæ* juxtaposes those points of view:

First, both the Stoickes and Epicures (which were two of the most famous sects of Philosophers amongst the Gentiles, as we may reade Act. 17.18.) are confuted: The first whereof did bring in a fatall necessitie, making all things to depend, not upon the will and providence of God, but upon a certain connexion of causes, to the which the divine power it selfe should be subject: like as vaine Astrologers and star-gazers do attribute all to their constellations and aspects of starres. But the Scripture teacheth us, *that the Lord doth in heaven and earth whatsoever it pleaseth him*, Psal. 135–6: he is not forced by, or tyed to any such fatall conjunction of causes.

Having piously derogated the fatalistic, astrological, and Stoic pattern, Willet turns next to its equally contemned Epicurean counterpart, which removes God's providence from earthly cares:

The Epicures ... [like] many carnall men ... cannot look into Gods providence, as the Preacher speaketh in the person of such, Eccle. 9.10 *Time and chance cometh to all*. Ambrose hereof writeth well. ... *The Epicures thinke, that God taketh no care of us: and Aristotle, that Gods providence descendeth no lower then the Moone: but what workeman doth cast off the care of his worke?*[21]

Of the four ancient schools most esteemed by the humanists – Platonism, Aristotelianism, Stoicism, and Epicureanism – the last is espoused by More's Utopians, who regard the Stoics as their particular adversaries.[22] 'I wil no Stoickes of my Jury', pronounces Sir John Harington in *An Apologie* (1596, sig. Cc 1ᵛ); 'of the twoo extreames, I would rather have Epicures'. Yet in a chapter on 'the opposite opinions of the Stoicks and Epicures' Thomas Jackson's *A Treatise of the Divine Essence and Attributes*, part II (1629), notes that 'The Stoicks did well in contradicting the Epicures, which held *fortune* and *Chance* to rule all things ...' (p. 179).

Moreover, cosmic Epicureanism and Stoicism had personal

corollaries, which are attacked, for instance, in Miles Mosse's *Scotlands Welcome* (1603), assailing contemporary atheists: '*Epicures* they are, for they hunt after pleasure as after their chiefest good. . . . *Stoikes* they are: for though they love to dispute of Action and Practise, yet themselves covet to sit in ease and quietnesse' (p. 76). In addition, William Fulbeck's *A Booke of Christian Ethicks or Moral Philosophie* (1587) describes the alternatives facing his contemporaries, who may seem, according to their actions, 'fooles to the Stoikes, blockes to the Epicures' (sig. E). It is such want of feeling that evokes Marullus's outcry in *Julius Caesar*, 'You blocks, you stones, you worse than senseless things!' (i i 40), as well as Montaigne's repeated attacks upon 'Stoicall impassibility'; compare the commonplace jest in *Taming of the Shrew* on 'stoics' and 'stocks' (i i 31). Speaking of a philosopher, Montaigne says, 'Hee would not make himselfe a stone or a blocke, but a living, discoursing and reasoning man . . .', and the essayist admits himself not 'begotten of a blocke or stone'.[23] Sidney's *Arcadia*, too, following the tale of the 'Paphlagonian' king, observes,

> Griefe is the stone which finest judgement proves:
> For who grieves not hath but a blockish braine.
>
> (i 227)[24]

As Edgar has been shown above to provide indications contrary to Stoicism, so Lear, whom he parallels, repudiates such unfeeling impassiveness. 'Howl, howl, howl! O! you are men of stones . . .' (v iii 257).

Indeed, anger marks both Lear's opening scene, when he rages at Cordelia, and his closing scene, when at her death he storms at the heavens. Although anger was associated with the irascibility of old age, the emotion was not always discredited. On the one hand, 'in age', notes *The Pilgrimage of Man* (1606), 'man is wonderfully changed, he is prompt to wrath . . .' (sig. D2), as the evil daughters agree, 'You see how full of changes his age is . . . the unruly waywardness that infirm and choleric years bring with them' (i i 287, 298–9). Yet, on the other hand, in Kent's reply to Cornwall, 'but anger hath a privilege' (ii ii 71; cf *King*

John, IV iii 32), and in Lear's prayer for 'noble anger' (II iv 278)
may be heard an attitude antithetical to the Stoic injunction. As
King James himself confesses, 'I love not one that will never bee
Angry: For as hee that is without *Sorrow*, is without *Gladnesse*: so
hee that is without *Anger*, is without *Love*',[25] while Bacon points
out, 'To seek to extinguish Anger utterly is but a bravery of the
Stoics.'[26] Similarly, William Sclater's *An Exposition ... upon the
First Epistle to the Thessalonians* (1619) argues against Stoic re-
pression of such emotions and, like Lear, indicts 'men of stones':

> The opinion of Stoickes, not allowing to their Wise man any use
> of Affections, not to sigh or change countenance at any crosse
> accident, sorts neither with Religion nor Reason.... Another
> sort of men wee have, in practice more then Stoicall; whom no
> crosse from God or men can affect to sorrow ... their patience
> is it, or rather their blockish senselesnesse?   (p. 317)

Indeed, a Renaissance point of view, like Lear's, exalted a virtuous
anger. Ficino and the Florentine humanists, for example, helped
effect a change with regard to the traditional sin of *ira*, trans-
forming it partly to a 'noble rage',[27] as in Lear's desired 'noble
anger', which, instead of bursting forth, comes deliberately called.

Similar in their deaths, the protagonists provide a basis for
comparison also in their lives. Although both are, as Lamb said,
on the 'verge of life', for Gloucester the verge is symbolized by a
physical cliff, while for Lear it is the more terrible Dover of the
mind, as in Gerard Manley Hopkins's

> O the mind, mind has mountains; cliffs of fall
> Frightful, sheer, no-man-fathomed.

Yet the common language of their renunciation-resolves, Lear's
'To shake all cares and business from our age' (I i 39) and Gloucester's presuicidal

> This world I do renounce, and in your sights
> Shake patiently my great affliction off (IV vi 35–6)

in light of the consequence of such attempts, may suggest that
human suffering is unshakable; the attempt to escape leads only to

further suffering. Whereas the abject Gloucester falls undignifiedly, Lear stands erect as he challenges the elements to 'Singe my white head!' (III ii 6). The latter's attitude to life as well as to death seems summed up in several lines of *Choice, Chance, and Change* (1606), regarding one who, being 'moulded of a noble mind', has 'steele unto the backe' and 'Cries not with feare, to heare a thunder cracke.' Such a person

> Stoupes not to death untill the heart do crack:
> Lives like himselfe, and at his latest breath,
> Dies like himselfe. . . .   (sig. [K3])

If *Hamlet* shows the mature Shakespeare deliberately exploiting parallel ideas for dramatic effect – for example, the various attitudes toward the ghost of the sentinels, Hamlet, and Horatio in Act 1 – the more complex *Lear* reveals him employing such ideas to provide the very structure of the play itself. Moreover, Renaissance conventions may adequately account for Shakespeare's unprecedented duplication; and I suggest that there may be no real loss of economy, since Lear and Gloucester stand for recognizably antithetical religious positions in this tragedy of man's relation to the heavens.

Conventionally paired, superstition and skepticism (or atheism) assumed a relation of polarity as well as, inevitably, of similarity: extremes to the mean of faith, they were both irreligious. Suggested by Plutarch in 'Of Superstition',[28] the concept of true faith as the *via media* between superstition and skepticism was restated, in terms favorable to itself, by Renaissance Calvinism, which conveniently consigned Catholicism to a superstitious or atheistic limbo. Marking the distinction, Hooker, after castigating atheists, turns his ire on practicers of superstition: 'Wherefore to let go this execrable crew [of atheists and Machiavellians], and to come to extremities on the contrary hand.'[29] James's *Basilicon Doron* (Edinburgh, 1603), advises his son, regarding his conscience, 'especially . . . to keepe it free from two diseases, wherewith it useth oft to be infected; to wit, Leaprosie, & superstition: the former is the mother of Atheisme, the other of Heresies' (p. 15). Elsewhere James utters the aphorism, 'The Devill alwaies avoydes the meane, and waites upon extremities; So hath he sought to devide the world betwixt *Athisme*, and *Superstition*.'[30] That superstition was the counterpart of atheism, that both were irreligious, is, typically, the conviction of Joseph Hall, who, in his *Characters of Vertues and Vices* (1608), observes: 'The Superstitious hath too manie Gods, the Prophane man hath none at all . . .' (p. 93).

Between reason, the soul's left hand, and faith, her right, true religion walked; any deviation to the left led to atheism, any excess to the right led to superstition. Among numerous texts illustrative of the dichotomy, Burton may be cited: 'For methods sake I will reduce them [the fallacious doctrines] to a twofold division, according to those two extreames of *Excesse* and *Defect*, impiety and Superstition, idolatry and Athisme.'[31] A mock prognostication of 1608, *The Penniles Parliament of Threed-bare Poets* (sig. B3), announces, 'Athistes, by the Law, shall be as Odious, as they are Carles: and those that depend on Destiny, and not on God, may chaunce looke through a narrow Lattice at Footemans Inne', meaning prison. As Bacon observes in his essay 'Of Superstition', the one, atheism, 'is unbelief', while 'the other', superstition, 'is contumely: and certainly superstition is the reproach of the Deity'. Just as atheism, he supposes, is related to wariness, so superstition is totally unreasonable and therefore the greater threat to political stability; it 'bringeth in a new *primum mobile*, that ravisheth all the spheres of government'.[32] By virtue of their superstition, especially, pagans were led to atheism, polytheism tending to break down men's faith. Fitzherbert's *Second Part of a Treatise*, cited above, alludes to the pagan inclination to both atheism and superstition. In like fashion, what has been termed the first sixteenth-century English pantheon of the heathens' gods, Stephen Batman's *The Golden Booke of the Leaden Goddes* (1577) in its dedication claims to show 'into what . . . Atheisme . . . Idolatrye, and Heresie, they have . . . affiaunced their beleeves'.

Finally, while the superstitious–concupiscible character might be seen as passively accepting, the skeptical–irascible might be regarded as a dynamically rejecting type. Contemporary ideas of belief and unbelief, of the passive and the active, could also in this manner be assimilated to antithetical structural elements. Ironically, while at the start Lear is caught by belief in his evil daughters and disbelief in his good daughter, he is throughout the middle portion of the play torn between his previous belief and disbelief in his daughters as well as in his gods. For Lear, belief is sanity, and its loss becomes insanity. Having 'caught' Cordelia (v iii 21) and having again lost her, Lear in his last words composes a tension of nihilistic unbelief and the tenuously supported illusion that Cordelia still breathes.

Whether the double plot is, in fact, uneconomic is, of course, relative to interpretative criteria and dimensions, as well as to the type of play it is judged to embody. It is conceivable, for instance, that Bradley's recognition of the work's moral symmetry, its almost equal division into powers of good and evil, might legitimately be extended to structure as to sense. In this drama of duplicity and betrayal the doubleness of man's nature and the irresolution of his mysterious sojourn on earth are mirrored in the two protagonists. Since Shakespearean openings customarily provide clues to the action, it is significant that the initial lines (i i 1–7) deal in dualities: the Albany–Cornwall antithesis, the division of the kingdom, and the observation that 'equalities are so weigh'd that curiosity in neither can make choice of either's moiety'. Similarly, the legitimate Edgar is, to Gloucester, 'no dearer in my account' than the illegitimate Edmund (i i 20–1). Further, while near the beginning the state, the family, as well as the protagonists' hearts are split (Gloucester's 'old heart is crack'd, it's crack'd', ii i 90), at the end, with the family severed and the state still 'gor'd' (v iii 320), Lear's voice would 'crack' the heavens, and both old men die, their hearts cleft in twain. The duality of Hamlet,[33] as reflected, for instance, in his dictional iterations, develops in *Lear* into a structural principle.

In addition, while facilitating an expanding multiplicity, the double plot helps sustain unity and maintain interests by its alternation of diverse characters and events reflecting the focal problems. Hence, in one sense Edgar's succession of quick-change roles may be allied to the general dramatic strategy. Further, through his proxy relationship, as during Lear's madness, Gloucester also assumes a larger expository and choral burden, thereby freeing the main character for more central utterances. From one point of view, therefore, the Gloucester plot may be said to frame the main plot, producing an effect analogous to that obtained by the contrast between prose and verse usual in Shakespeare. Finally, the Gloucester contrast might, in part, 'purge' Lear of some possible theatrical disadvantage of old age and heighten the audience empathy frequently reserved for the *virtù* of a younger hero. For Gloucester's 'We have seen the best of our time' (I ii 117–18) may be, in one sense, an admission somewhat less applicable to Lear.

Indeed, it may be possible to regard the double plot as a developing metaphor, opening up the principal action into two parts that mirror each other. Such a device would be appropriate to a play in which the protagonist expresses a dissociation between his name and his identity (e.g. 'This is not Lear: / Does Lear walk thus?' [I iv 234–5]), so that his person dissolves into a dual personage, a character in search of himself. Paralleled by Edgar's quest for identity, Lear demands his own identity of his daughters, his retainers, his Fool, and himself (I i, iv; II iv), his sane and insane pursuit of his 'name' being, in effect, an image of the dramatic action. In the dissolution of identity which marks the opening, Lear and Edgar lose theirs, Cordelia disappears, and Kent and Edgar assume disguises. While the villains hypocritically ply their new roles, and Albany is 'ignorant' (I iv 282) and confused, Edmund provides the nominalistic rationale which dissolves names, as he displaces their possessors.

From one point of view, indeed, Lear may be said sequentially to dissociate into his children, Goneril and Regan (selfish willfulness) and Cordelia (courageous adamancy), as Gloucester may be seen successively to dissolve into his components, Edmund (lust) and Edgar (pathos). Here, fatherhood, as in Dostoievsky's Karamazov family, involves not only the problem of identity but also that of identity in multiplicity. Thus, through self-alienation and division, characters generate proxies for themselves, as well as analogues of each other. As the play moves, therefore, Lear's problem is seen revolving from different angles, above and below, through the continual presence onstage of proxy characters, as well as of the gods who are in their 'heavens' while all is not right with the world.

Further, if *Hamlet*'s play-within-the-play holds 'the mirror up to nature', Lear's double plot holds the mirror up to the heavens themselves. Just as Cordelia reflects the aspect of steadfast love, Edgar that of unchanging pity, and Kent of virile loyalty, Gloucester generally mirrors, centaur-fashion, Lear's all-too-human side, as the heavens mirror Lear's royal demigod or Promethean side. In addition, while *Hamlet*'s play-within-the-play centripetally reflects its hero in relation to his corrupt courtly audience, *Lear*'s play-within-the-cosmos, with the gods as spectators, more centrifugally throws the image of mankind against the questionable heavens. After a certain point in *Lear*, for example, human actions are invoked to 'show the Heavens more just' (III iv 36).

Lending the central situation sharper reality, Gloucester's physical suffering intensifies Lear's mental anguish, the passion of the blinding (III vii) preceding the height of Lear's mad frenzy (IV vi). In addition to its perspective on pain, Gloucester's role fills out the dimensions of Lear's; the latter's function is identified not only through his own words and actions but also through those of the figures who stand proxy for him. When, for example, Gloucester warns against the 'purpos'd low correction' (II ii 142) in putting Kent in the stocks, both earls act partly as anticipatory Lear symbols. Called 'shame' by Lear (II iv 6) and by Kent (II iv 45), the villains' offense against Kent, the latter observes, is 'Against the grace and person of my master' (II ii 132). Again, as Cornwall and Regan punish both these royal followers, the king's vacated place on the throne descends to Kent's seat in the stocks (II ii iv) and to Gloucester's chair during the old earl's blinding (III vii).

Enriching and underscoring the play's significances, the double plot facilitates its elaborate contrapuntal movements. In I i the king is actively involved in his own duping; while in I ii, II i, and

III iii Gloucester is the more passive victim of a protracted deception. In contrast to Lear's dynamic behavior, the proxy role of the slower-witted Gloucester reveals in less rapid detail how an analogous deception might come about. Similarly, the implicit first-Act debate between Gloucester and Edmund (I ii) is contrapuntal to the Gloucester–Lear antithesis; Edmund's attitude toward Gloucester's credulity in part foreshadows Lear's mounting skepticism of his own previous belief. While the old earl continues to be gulled, Lear in I iv and v is educated in his folly by the Fool.

In the proxy scene of II ii the king is shown abused. In II iv the two protagonists are brought together onstage for comparison, as they are again during the heath scene of III iv and in IV vi. While Gloucester continues, in III iii, to be deceived by Edmund, Lear, in III ii, has already challenged the supernal deceivers, or at least their elemental messengers. Thus Lear is able, earlier than Gloucester (III iv versus IV i), to invoke, through ironically reversed prayers, human examples for heavenly justification. Gloucester's customarily delayed counterpoint reaches his passion of the body (III vii) after Lear has already begun his passion of the mind (III ii 67: 'My wits begin to turn', and III iv, vi). While Lear's eyes have been opened, Gloucester's 'vile jellies' are being extinguished. Indeed, Lear's mad 'trial' of the villains (III vi) ironically introduces the villains' 'trial' (III vii) of Gloucester; madness and 'justice' are juxtaposed. Whereas mental suffering serves to animate Lear, Gloucester's blinding produces a deeper passivity and an implicit presuicidal renunciation of the world of action (IV i 20–1). Gloucester's attempt at self-destruction (IV vi) contrasts, in its futile indignity, with Lear's heroic challenge to the elements (III ii 6), as the latter's fearless jeopardy of life is suggested by Cordelia at IV vii 31–6. In IV vi, by a masterly irony, madman and blind man are brought together and confronted.

Although Gloucester for most of the play lags behind and echoes Lear, the last scenes reverse the order, as the antihero foreshadows the hero's concluding lines. Gloucester's 'suicide' and 'restoration' (IV vi) prepare for Lear's moving 'rebirth' scene

(IV vii). The earl's quiescent acceptance of 'ripeness' (v ii 11) sets the stage for his king's frenzied rejection of Cordelia's most 'unripe' extinction (v iii). And Gloucester's death offstage (described by Edgar, v iii 196–9) anticipates, without distracting from, the intensified pathos of Lear's last earthly moment (v iii 310–11).

While Bradley ascribes confusion to the double plot, it is evident that confusion might only have been compounded by compressing *Lear*'s conceptual elaboration within narrower limits. Indeed, the device may rather be an agent of clarity, assimilating to drama's limited economy the intellectual freight of this cosmic tragedy. For in one respect the double action is related to the fashion in which the play may be said to 'think', the work being, in its own terms, a developed and dialectical argument. Examining the total conspectus of human existence under the heavens and delving also into 'hell', the drama is structurally consonant with Shakespeare's most epic or total play.

Ironically, the structural mode employed depends partly upon the traditional device of analogy in a drama which suggests, through its dissolution of natural law and hierarchy, the incipient breakdown of analogy. In a final sense, however, as the religious poles become assimilated to the dramatic ones, *King Lear* is not 'about' ideas at all but acts out rather its essential tragedy of human experience. Ultimately, then, the double plot is an instrument of complexity, the assurance of a multifaceted ambivalence which, contrary to the salvation hypothesis, probes and tests, without finally resolving, its argument of mysterious human suffering.

SOURCE: *King Lear and the Gods* (1966).

NOTES

1. *Shakespearean Tragedy* (New York, 1955) pp. 205, 210, 211. C. Harley Granville-Barker, *Prefaces to Shakespeare* (1958) I 270, who charges that *Lear* 'suffers somewhat under the burden' of the double plot.

2. *The Dialogues of Plato*, tr. Benjamin Jowett (Oxford, 1953) e.g. I 451 (*Phaedo*, 94d); II 293–4 (*Republic*, 439e); III 143–4 (*Phaedrus*, 237d–238b). Cf '. . . Account of the Allegory of the Poem', in Torquato Tasso, *Jerusalem Delivered*, tr. Edward Fairfax, ed. Henry Morley (1890) pp. 441–2.

3. Erasmus, *The Praise of Folly*, tr. John Wilson (1668: Ann Arbor, 1958).

4. *The Powers of the Crown in Scotland*, tr. Charles F. Arrowood (Austin, Texas, 1949) p. 128.

5. ed. Rudolf Kirk (New Brunswick, N.J., 1951) p. 64.

6. *Of Wisdom*, tr. George Stanhope (1697) I 174.

7. See also Nicolas Coeffeteau, *A Table of Humane Passions* (1621) pp. 5–6, 61–3. See 'La Luxure et la Colère. Chapiteau roman à Vézelay', in Raimond van Marle, *Iconographie de l'art profane* (La Haye, 1931–2) II 73, fig. 85. William Blandie's *The Castle* . . . (1581) fo. 13, finds the amatory and the choleric implanted in us. On the connection of the irascible passions with the heart and the concupiscible with the liver, see Sir Thomas Browne, *Pseudodoxia epidemica* (1646) p. 110. Such writers as Du Vair and Charron lead to Descartes; and since Descartes believed he was the first to demonstrate the untenability of the traditional irascible–concupiscible distinction, it may be supposed that, with few exceptions, the difference was recognized through the Renaissance. See Descartes, *Les Passions de l'âme*, ed. Pierre Mesnard (Paris, 1937) pp. 45–6, 111–19.

8. See Buoni's work for other mind–body parallels; e.g. cf Lear's 'Nature, being oppress'd', which 'commands the mind / To suffer with the body' (II iv 108–9); cf also III iv 11–12 with Buoni's 'Why are griefes of the body communicated unto the minde, and those of the minde unto the body?' (p. 227). Yet Buoni suggests that the 'griefes of the minde' are 'farre greater then those of the Body' (pp. 232–5). On the mind–body relationship, see also Chapman's *Sir Giles Goosecap* (1601–3) v ii 1–50.

9. Cf Lear's description (IV vi 126–9) and Anthony Copley's *A Fig for Fortune* (1596) sig. B. Cf M. P. Tilley, *A Dictionary of the Proverbs in England in the Sixteenth and Seventeenth Centuries* (Ann Arbor, 1950) W520. See Montaigne's citation from Jerome, 'Diaboli virtus in lumbis est', in *Essays*, tr. John Florio, 3 vols (Everyman's Library, 1946) III 86. The distinction is, of course, Platonic. See also Horace, *De arte poetica*, line 4 (tr. H. Rushton Fairclough, Loeb Classical Lib. (1926) p. 450). From the name of Sidney's Arcadian villainess, Cecropia, Shakespeare could have recalled the notion of bodily division, for Cecrops, mythical first king of Athens, had a serpent's form below the waist. On the 'woman-serpent' convention see John M. Steadman, 'Tradition and Innovation in Milton's "Sin": the

problem of literary indebtedness', in *Philological Quarterly*, XXXIX (1960) 93–103. Analogously, Richard Linche's *The Fountaine of Ancient Fiction* (1599) sig. Kii, presents an image of Jupiter, the upper parts naked, suggesting divine light, the lower parts clothed, suggesting darkness and the 'illecebrous blandishments' of the world's delights. Benjamin Rudyerd's *Le Prince d'amour* (1660) p. 33, observes, regarding woman, 'The Equinoctial maketh even the day and the night at the girdle; the upper Hemisphere hath day, and the lower night.' To Chapman, centaurs are a symbol of what man has become. Cf Jonson's Lady Centaure in *Epicoene*; Dekker, *The Seven Deadly Sinnes of London* (1606), in *The Non-Dramatic Works of Thomas Dekker*, ed. Alexander B. Grosart, II (1885) 79.

10. If Coleridge correctly compares the heath scene of III iv to Michelangelo, the protagonists' Brueghelesque decline one Act later may suggest a significant commentary.

11. Pierre Villey-Desmeserets, 'Montaigne et les poètes dramatiques anglais du temps de Shakespeare', in *Revue d'histoire littéraire de la France*, XXIV (1917) 380–1. Cf Ecclesiastes, passim; Tilley S141 ('Much Science much sorrow') and K188. Cf *The Defence of Contraries*, tr. Anthony Munday (1593) pp. 23–32: 'That ignorance is better than knowledge'. See *The Tragedie of Crœsus* (1604), *The Poetical Works of Sir William Alexander*, ed. L. E. Kastner and H. B. Charlton, I (Manchester, 1921) 82, lines 2083–4. See also Webster's *The White Devil*, V vi 259–60, on the unhappiness of confounding 'knowledges'. In addition, compare Lear's name and the current sense of 'lere' as learning (cited in *Oxford English Dictionary* s.v. 'lear', from Spenser, *The Shepheardes Calender* [1579], May, line 262; John Ferne, *The Blazon of Gentrie* [1586] p. 22; Lyly, *Mother Bombie* [1594] II v). Lear, who 'hath ever but slenderly known himself' (I i 293–4), invokes 'marks of . . . knowledge' (I iv 240–1), as he presses further, 'Who is it that can tell me who I am?' (I iv 238). Cf E. R. Curtius's 'Etymology as a Category of Thought', in *European Literature and the Latin Middle Ages*, tr. Willard R. Trask (New York, 1953) pp. 495–500: the tradition of *nomen atque omen*, and the literary practice of symbolic naming in virtually all ages. The heroic eponym, like 'Oedipus' (suggesting both knowledge and pride), functions here as ironical leitmotiv, emphasizing not only self-identity and the means of the work's unfolding but also the irony of the dramatic quest.

12. Cf Pedro Mexía's opposition between grief and joy, *The Treasurie of Auncient and Moderne Times*, tr. Thomas Milles (1613) p. 716; and the table in Nannus Mirabellius, *Polyanthea* (Venice, 1592) p. 76. See also Thomas Nashe, 'A . . . Prognostication', in *Works*, ed. Ronald B. McKerrow, rev. ed. F. P. Wilson, 5 vols (Oxford, 1958) III 390; *Venus and Adonis*, lines 413–14.

13. III 167. Death through joy is also mentioned in *The Problemes of Aristotle* (1597), sig. [F7ᵛ]; John Marston, *Antonios Revenge*, I v, in *Plays*, ed. H. Harvey Wood, 3 vols (Edinburgh, 1934–9) I 81; Buoni, *Problemes*, pp. 242–4; Scipion Dupleix, *The Resolver: or Curiosities of Nature* (1635) pp. 250–2. James Hart in . . . *The Diet of the Diseased* (1633) p. 400, cites Galen in support of the view that 'some might die of too great joy'.

14. ed. H. Warner Allen (New York [1923]) p. 210. See John Davies of Hereford's *Microcosmos* (1603) pp. 45, 75, on the destructive or fatal effect of extremes of joy and grief. The emotions were familiar subjects in the grammar-school study of Cicero's *Tusculanae disputationes*. Gregory of Nyssa's *De hominis opificio* explains joy, grief, and tears as connected with the expansion or contraction of the blood vessels; and Melanchthon considers joy and sorrow to be the explosion and contraction ultimately related to the heart and blood.

15. Cf Webster, *The Devil's Law-Case*, I ii 130–1; Joseph Hall, *Epistles*, I (1608) 143.

16. Tilley L92a. On the *Arcadia* see Muir (at IV iii 18–25) and Henry Wotton cited by George Steevens (New Variorum *Lear*, p. 252). Samuel C. Chew, *The Pilgrimage of Life* (New Haven, 1962) pp. 120–1, relates smiling and grief together to a Renaissance depiction of patience.

17. Robert Armin, who probably played Lear's Fool, speaks in *A Nest of Ninnies* (1608) of one whose manner was 'ever to weepe in kindnesse, and laugh in extreames' (*Fools and Jesters: With a Reprint of Robert Armin's Nest of Ninnies*, Shakespeare Soc. (1842) p. 38). The Fool's song echoes a popular one; see Peter J. Seng, 'An Early Tune for the Fool's Song in *King Lear*', in *Shakespeare Quarterly* IX (1958) 583–5; and Hyder E. Rollins, '*King Lear* and the Ballad of "John Careless"', in *Modern Language Review*, XV (1920) 87–9.

18. Cicero's *De divinatione* distinguishes the two. See bk I, ch. xi; bk II, ch. xxvi.

19. Cf Cassius's earlier view (I iii 46–52). Shakespeare's recollection could have been strengthened by Plutarch's references to Cassius's Epicureanism: before Caesar's murder, again at Sardis, where Cassius reasons with Brutus against the fanciful vision of spirits, and finally before Philippi (*Lives* of Caesar and Brutus). As Cassius later retreats from Epicureanism, so Brutus later seems to debate some notions of Stoicism (v i 101–19). In addition, Macbeth's self-proclaimed endurance (e.g. v iii 9–10) may suggest an analogous dualism in his obdurate scorn of 'English epicures' (line 8).

20. Dale Underwood, *Etherege and the Seventeenth-Century Comedy of Manners* (New Haven, 1957). Stoic virtue and Epicurean pleasure

form antithetical choices in the famous temptation of Hercules; see Erwin Panofsky, *Hercules am Scheidewege* (Leipzig, 1930), and Hallett Smith, *Elizabethan Poetry: a study in conventions, meaning and expression* (Cambridge, Mass., 1952) pp. 290–303.

21. Cambridge, pp. 24–5. In his *De natura deorum*, Cicero singled out the two schools; see Introduction, *De natura deorum. Liber primus*, ed. A. S. Pease (Cambridge, Mass., 1955) pp. 13–14. Cf Cicero's refutation of Epicurean ethics in *De finibus*, bk II; reply in Seneca, *Moral Essays*, tr. John W. Basore, II (Cambridge, Mass., 1935) 121, 123, and Lucian's Epicurean attack on Stoicism. See Ficino on Stoicism and Epicureanism in 'De quatuor sectis philosophorum', in *Supplementum Ficinianum*, ed. Paul O. Kristeller (Florence, 1937) II 7–11; Montaigne repeatedly juxtaposes the two sects; e.g. II 108–9; II 203.

22. More's Utopians share the Epicurean opposition to superstitious fear and dread of death, while they reject Epicurean ethics. The Stoic-Epicurean antithesis is expressed, e.g. in the section headed 'Antonius pro Epicureis & pro natura contra stoicos' in Lorenzo Valla's *De voluptate*, tr. Vincenzo Grillo as *Il piacere* (Naples, 1948) p. 33; and in Erasmus's 'The Epicurean', in *The Colloquies*, tr. N. Bailey (1878) II 326–45, where the serious Spudæus debates with the Epicurean Hedonius.

23. III 272; II 207; III 309; cf III 189.

24. Cf Tilley M172.

25. J.L.S., ed. *Flores Regii . . . Spoken by . . . James* (1627) no. 2.

26. *Works*, ed. James Spedding *et al.* 14 vols (1857–74) VI 510.

27. See Edgar Wind, *Pagan Mysteries in the Renaissance* (New Haven, 1958) p. 69 and n. Cf John Serranus, *A Godlie and Learnea Commentarie upon . . . Ecclesiastes*, tr. John Stockwood (1585) p. 321. Eugene M. Waith, *The Herculean Hero in Marlowe, Chapman, Shakespeare, and Dryden* (1962) pp. 44–5, cites other views favoring righteous anger, including St Thomas Aquinas's *ira per zelum*. Luther's defense of just anger is well known; see Ewald M. Plass, *What Luther Says, an Anthology* (St Louis, Mo., 1959) I 28–9; II 847, 985. See also Frances A. Yates, *The French Academies of the Sixteenth Century* (1947) pp. 116–20, 143.

28. See also Clement of Alexandria, *The Exhortation to the Greeks*, tr. G. W. Butterworth, Loeb Classical Lib. (1919) p. 51, condemning both atheism and 'daemon-worship' as extremes to be guarded against; and Aquinas, *The Summa Theologica*, pt II, qu. XCII, art. 1, on religion as a moral virtue containing a mean opposed both to excess (superstition) and deficiency.

29. *Ecclesiastical Polity*, in *Works*, ed. John Keble, 3 vols (Oxford, 1888) II 23.

30. *Flores Regii*, no. 20.

31. *The Anatomy of Melancholy* (Oxford, 1628) p. 579. See also Howard Schultz, *Milton and Forbidden Knowledge* (New York, 1955) p. 265, for numerous other references. See John Weemes, *A Treatise of the Foure Degenerate Sonnes* (1636) p. 36; Weemes's religion-between-two-thieves analogy recurs, e.g. in Alexander Ross's *Gods House, or the House of Prayer* (1642) p. 9. Cf Sidney's allusion to 'the *Philosophers*, who shaking off superstition, brought in *Atheisme*' (*The Defence of Poesie*, in *Complete Works*, ed. Albert Feuillerat, 4 vols (Cambridge, 1922–6) III 34). Richard Bernard's *Contemplative Pictures* (1610), sig. E3^{r-v}, lists 'carnall Atheistes' along with the 'foolishly superstitious'. See further Hobbes, *English Works*, ed. Sir William Molesworth, 11 vols (1839–45) II 277; IV 293; Tilley D234 ('The Devil divides the world between atheism and superstition').

32. *Works*, VI 415–16.

33. See Harry Levin, *The Question of Hamlet* (New York, 1959).

Northrop Frye

KING LEAR: THE TRAGEDY OF ISOLATION (1967)

At the beginning of *King Lear*, we see the hero preparing to take the fatal step of depriving himself of his own social context. He will exchange the reality for the 'name' of king, and instead of being loved by his subjects for his qualities, he will be loved by his daughters for himself alone. All seems to go well until, with Cordelia's 'nothing', he finds himself staring into the blankness of an empty world. Those who love Lear love him according to their bond, the tie of loyalty which is their own real life. Who is Lear to be loved apart from that? That is, what is the identity of a king who is no longer a king? Lear starts asking questions about his own identity very early, and he gets a variety of answers. 'My lady's father', says Oswald; 'Lear's shadow', says the Fool, a much shrewder person than Oswald. The word 'shadow' recalls Richard II, seeking his identity in a looking-glass. The substance of Lear and of Richard is royalty and loyalty: their shadows, or spectres as Blake would call them, are the subjective Lear and Richard confronting an objective world which is unreal because they are. They are in the position of the Biblical Preacher who was once king in Jerusalem, and who now knows only that all is 'vanity', that is, vapour, mist, shadow. Or, to put the essential paradox more clearly, all things are full of emptiness.

At the beginning of *King Lear* we are introduced to Edmund, making polite murmurs about his duty and services, and immediately after the abdication scene Edmund appears again, saying,

> Thou, Nature, art my goddess: to thy law
> My services are bound.

One of the first points made about Edmund is his contempt for astrology. This contempt has nothing to do with anybody's belief in astrology, but is purely a matter of consistent imagery. The royalty of Lear held his society bound to that greater nature which is symbolized by the stars in their courses, the world of order and reason that is specifically the world of human nature. With the abdication we are now wholly confined to the lower physical nature of the elements, an amoral world where the strong prey on the weak. It is this lower nature, the Dionysian wheel of physical energy and fortune, to which Edmund attaches himself. He is Gloucester's 'natural' son, and on that level of nature he will act naturally.

In this situation Lear is joined by the Fool and Kent, Kent being also a fool, as the Fool himself informs him, for we are now in a world where it is folly to be genuinely loyal. The Fool is a 'natural' in the sense of representing something still unspoiled and innocent in the middle of a fallen nature. The usual symbol of this natural innocence is the child, the two being associated in the proverb 'children and fools tell the truth'. Nothing shows the royal nature of Lear more clearly than his tenderness for his 'boy'; this tenderness becomes increasingly parental, and the great cry at the end, 'And my poor fool is hanged!', represents a blending together in his mind of the two people he loves as a father. Goneril habitually refers to her husband as a fool because he is a 'moral fool', full of childish scruples he ought to outgrow. Goneril, of course, does not distinguish the childish from the childlike, and so does not believe that the Fool really is a fool, as she cannot understand innocence. The jokes of the Fool, like those of the clowns in *Hamlet*, consist largely of puns, conundrums, and parodies of syllogisms, and so establish a comic counterpart to the tragic action in which absurdity is made convincing.

The philosopher first isolates himself and then stabilizes himself: he remains a sane, conscious, normal intelligence, and nature therefore appears to him as an order, though a relatively static order or chain of being, not the controlled force that it is to the successful ruler. In the tragic vision whatever isolates the hero pushes him much further than this, into the nausea of Hamlet or the hell-worlds of Othello and Macbeth. Lear is pushed directly toward the *hysterica passio* he so dreads, and nature therefore appears to him in the objective form of madness, which is storm and tempest. On the heath, a mad shadow confronts a mad shadow-world, for the storm is described in a way that makes it not simply a storm but chaos come again, the cracking of nature's moulds. The turning point of the scene is Lear's prayer, a prayer which addresses no deity, but the dispossessed of the earth. In this prayer Lear finds his human identity again, though in a very different context from kingship, and immediately after it Poor Tom appears.

No one can study *King Lear* without wondering why Edgar puts on this Poor Tom act for Lear's benefit. He has to go into disguise, of course, but none of Cornwall's spies are likely to be listening, and elsewhere on the heath open conspiracy is discussed under the storm's cover. Just as, in a comic context, Petruchio shows Katherina the reflection of her own shrewishness in himself, so Poor Tom is the providence or guardian spirit that shows Lear the end of his journey to find his own nature. What is the nature of man? There are many answers, but Lear is now in an order of nature so disordered that Edmund is called a 'loyal and natural boy'. The Fool, who really is a loyal and natural boy, is all that is left of the 'desperate train' which Regan pretends to be afraid of. The question then takes the form: what is left of a man when we eliminate his social and civilized context and think of him purely as an object in physical nature? The answer given by satire is the Yahoo, the natural man with his natural vices, of which Gulliver's greater cleanliness and intelligence are merely sophistications. The softer and gentler answer given by comedy is Caliban, nature without nurture, the deformed slave who is loyal to the wrong master and resentful of the right one. The answer given by tragedy is

Poor Tom, that eats the swimming frog, the toad, the tadpole, the wall-newt and the water; that in the fury of his heart, when the foul fiend rages, eats cow-dung for sallets; swallows the old rat and the ditch-dog; drinks the green mantle of the standing pool; who is whipped from tithing to tithing, and stock-punished, and imprisoned.

The imagery is deliberately nauseating, and we notice again that nausea is deeply involved in man's contemplation of himself in a physical context. 'Is man no more than this?' asks Lear wonderingly, but he has had his answer. 'Thou art the thing itself,' he says, and starts tearing at his clothes to remove what is left of his relation to human society. Poor Tom, a better mirror of identity than Richard had, is trying to stand between Lear in front of him and the abyss of non-being inhabited by the foul fiends behind him, and provide, so to speak, a solid bottom for Lear's fall into nature. If Lear had been granted the few moments of rest he so needed, Edgar's efforts might have preserved his sanity.

Besides the intricate series of puns on 'natural' in *King Lear*, there is also an emphatic repetition of the words 'all' and 'nothing'. In giving away his crown, Lear gave 'all' to his daughters, and, as the Fool keeps insisting, he is now 'nothing'. Richard II uses the same words:

> Make me, that nothing have, with nothing grieved,
> And thou with all pleased, that hast all achieved!

The word 'nothing' has two meanings: it is a grammatical negative meaning 'not anything', and it is a positive noun meaning 'something called nothing'. Poetry has been exploiting the puns involved in this double meaning ever since Polyphemus in the *Odyssey* screamed that 'nobody' was blinding him. In Shakespeare the word nothing, when it means something called nothing, usually refers to the loss of essence, not to the end of existence. 'Edgar I nothing am,' says Edgar, meaning that he ceases to be Edgar though he goes on living; 'the king is a thing of nothing', says Hamlet, meaning that Claudius is not really the king although he is on the throne; Timon says his friends 'are to me nothing', meaning that friends have vanished from his life although life goes on for both. Timon says later 'nothing brings me all things', referring to his approaching death, but there he is emphasizing a nihilism in it which is symbolized by his suicide. Goneril and Regan, however brusque and insensitive, show a certain hard common sense in their attitude to Lear, and are not revealed as evil until they separate him from what is left of his society. The outcry made about their cruelty in cutting off his 'train' seems excessive at first, but is deeply rooted in the convention of the play. That act shows that they do not merely 'seek his death'; they seek rather his annihilation. To murder Lear, and thereby get the noisy old nuisance out of the way, would show less real malice than wiping out the society he commands and letting him go on living. The latter obliterates the idea or real form of Lear, so to speak: it strikes at a deeper life than his physical one.

SOURCE: *Fools of Time: Studies in Shakespearean Tragedy* (1967).

Jan Kott

KING LEAR, OR ENDGAME (1964)

I

THE world of tragedy and the world of grotesque have a similar structure. Grotesque takes over the themes of tragedy and poses the same fundamental questions. Only its answers are different. This dispute about the tragic and grotesque interpretations of human fate reflects the everlasting conflict of two philosophies and two ways of thinking; of two opposing attitudes defined by the Polish philosopher Leszek Kołakowski as the irreconcilable antagonism between the priest and the clown. Between tragedy and grotesque there is the same conflict for or against such notions as eschatology, belief in the absolute, hope for the ultimate solution of the contradiction between the moral order and every-day practice. Tragedy is the theatre of priests, grotesque is the theatre of clowns.

This conflict between two philosophies and two types of theatre becomes particularly acute in times of great upheavals. When established values have been overthrown, and there is no appeal, to God, Nature, or History, from the tortures inflicted by the cruel world, the clown becomes the central figure in the theatre. He accompanies the exiled trio – the king, the nobleman and his son – on their cruel wanderings through the cold endless night which has fallen on the world; through the 'cold night' which in Shakespeare's *King Lear* 'will turn us all to fools and madmen'.

II

After his eyes have been gouged out, Gloucester wants to throw himself over the cliffs of Dover into the sea. He is led by his own son, who feigns madness. Both have reached the depths of human

suffering; the top of 'the pyramid of suffering', as Juliusz Słowacki has described *King Lear*. But on the stage there are just
two actors, one playing a blind man, the other playing a man who
plays a madman. They walk together.

> *Glou.* When shall I come to th' top of that same hill?
> *Edgar.* You do climb up it now. Look how we labour.
> *Glou.* Methinks the ground is even.
> *Edgar.*   Horrible steep.
>   Hark, do you hear the sea?
> *Glou.*   No, truly.   (IV vi)

It is easy to imagine this scene. The text itself provides stage
directions. Edgar is supporting Gloucester; he lifts his feet high
pretending to walk uphill. Gloucester, too, lifts his feet, as if
expecting the ground to rise, but underneath his foot there is only
air. This entire scene is written for a very definite type of theatre,
namely pantomime.

This pantomime only makes sense if enacted on a flat and level
stage.

Edgar feigns madness, but in doing so he must adopt the right
gestures. In its theatrical expression this is a scene in which a madman leads a blind man and talks him into believing in a non-
existing mountain. In another moment a landscape will be
sketched in. Shakespeare often creates a landscape on an empty
stage. A few words, and the diffused, soft afternoon light at the
Globe changes into night, evening, or morning. But no other
Shakespearean landscape is so exact, precise and clear as this one.
It is like a Breughel painting thick with people, objects and
events. A little human figure hanging halfway down the cliff is
gathering samphire. Fishermen walking on the beach are like
mice. A ship seems a little boat, a boat is floating like a buoy.

It is this abyss of Shakespeare's imagination that Słowacki
makes the hero of his *Kordian* look into:

> Come! Here, on the top stand still. Your head will whirl,
> When you cast your eyes on the abyss below your feet.
> Crows flying there half-way no bigger are than beetles.

And there, too, someone is toiling, gathering weed.
He looks no bigger than a human head.
And there on the beach the fishermen seem like ants . . .

This veristic and perspective landscape created on an empty
stage is not meant to serve as part of the decor, or to replace the
non-existent settings. Słowacki understood perfectly the dramatic
purpose of this scene:

Oh, Shakespeare! Spirit! You have built a mountain
Higher than that created by God.
For you have talked of an abyss to a man blind . . .

The landscape is now just a score for the pantomime. Gloucester and Edgar have reached the top of the cliff. The landscape
is now below them.

Give me your hand. You are now within a foot
Of th' extreme verge. For all beneath the moon
Would I not leap upright.   (IV vi)

In Shakespeare's times the actors probably leant over a balus-
trade above the apron-stage, immediately over the heads of the
'groundlings'. But we are not concerned here with an historical
reconstruction of the Elizabethan stage. It is the presence and importance of the mime that is significant. Shakespeare is stubborn.
Gloucester has already jumped over the precipice. Both actors are
at the foot of a non-existent cliff. The same landscape is now
above them. The mime continues.

Glou. But have I fall'n, or no?
Edgar. From the dread summit of this chalky bourn.
Look up a-height. The shrill-gorg'd lark so far
Cannot be seen or heard. Do but look up.   (IV vi)

The mime creates a scenic area: the top and bottom of the cliff,
the precipice. Shakespeare makes use of all the means of anti-
illusionist theatre in order to create a most realistic and concrete
landscape. A landscape which is only a blind man's illusion.

There is perspective in it, light, men and things, even sounds. From the height of the cliff the sea cannot be heard, but there is mention of its roar. From the foot of the cliff the lark cannot be heard, but there is mention of its song. In this landscape sounds are present by their very absence: the silence is filled with them, just as the empty stage is filled with the mountain.

The scene of the suicidal leap is also a mime. Gloucester kneels in a last prayer and then, in accordance with tradition of the play's English performances, falls over. He is now at the bottom of the cliff. But there was no height; it was an illusion. Gloucester knelt down on an empty stage, fell over and got up. At this point disillusion follows.[1]

The non-existent cliff is not meant just to deceive the blind man. For a short while we, too, believed in this landscape and in the mime. The meaning of this parable is not easy to define. But one thing is clear: this type of parable is not to be thought of outside the theatre, or rather outside a certain kind of theatre. In narrative prose Edgar could, of course, lead the blind Gloucester to the cliffs of Dover, let him jump down from a stone and make him believe that he was jumping from the top of a cliff. But he might just as well lead him a day's journey away from the castle and make him jump from a stone on any heap of sand. In film and in prose there is only the choice between a real stone lying in the sand and an equally real jump from the top of a chalk cliff into the sea. One cannot transpose Gloucester's suicide attempt to the screen, unless one were to film a stage performance. But in the naturalistic, or even stylized theatre, with the precipice painted or projected onto a screen, Shakespeare's parable would be completely obliterated.

The stage must be empty. On it a suicide, or rather its symbol, has been performed. Mime is the performance of symbols. In Ionesco's *Le Tueur sans gages* the Architect, who is at the same time the commissioner of police, shows Berenger round the *Cité Radieuse*. On an empty stage Berenger sniffs at non-existent flowers and taps non-existent walls. The Radiant City exists and does not exist, or rather it has existed always and everywhere. And that is why it is so terrifying. Similarly, the Shakespearean precipice at Dover exists and does not exist. It is the abyss, waiting all the time. The abyss, into which one can jump, is everywhere.

By a few words of dialogue Shakespeare often turned the platform stage, the inner stage, or the gallery into a London street, a forest, a palace, a ship, or a castle battlement. But these were always real places of action. Townspeople gathered outside the Tower, lovers wandered through the forest, Brutus murdered Caesar in the Forum. The white precipice at Dover performs a different function. Gloucester does not jump from the top of the cliff, or from a stone. For once, in *King Lear*, Shakespeare shows the paradox of pure theatre. It is the same theatrical paradox that Ionesco uses in his *Le Tueur sans gages*.

In the naturalistic theatre one can perform a murder scene, or a scene of terror. The shot may be fired from a revolver or a toy pistol. But in the mime there is no difference between a revolver and a toy pistol: in fact neither exists. Death is only a performance, a parable, a symbol.

Gloucester, falling over on flat, even boards, plays a scene from a great morality play. He is no longer a court dignitary whose eyes have been gouged out because he showed mercy to the banished king. The action is no longer confined to Elizabethan or Celtic England. Gloucester is Everyman, and the stage becomes the medieval *Theatrum Mundi*. A Biblical parable is now enacted; the one about the rich man who became a beggar, and the blind man who recovered his inner sight when he lost his eyes. Everyman begins his wanderings through the world. In medieval mystery plays also the stage was empty, but in the background there were four mansions, four gates representing Earth, Purgatory, Heaven and Hell. In *King Lear* the stage is empty throughout: there is nothing, except the cruel earth, where man goes on his journey from the cradle to the grave. The theme of *King Lear* is an enquiry into the meaning of this journey, into the existence or non-existence of Heaven and Hell.

From the middle of Act II to the end of Act IV, Shakespeare takes up a Biblical theme. But this new Book of Job or a new Dantean *Inferno* was written towards the close of the Renaissance. In

Shakespeare's play there is neither Christian Heaven, nor the heaven predicted and believed in by humanists. *King Lear* makes a tragic mockery of all eschatologies: of the heaven promised on earth, and the Heaven promised after death; in fact – of both Christian and secular theodicies; of cosmogony and of the rational view of history; of the gods and the good nature, of man made in 'image and likeness'. In *King Lear* both the medieval and the Renaissance orders of established values disintegrate. All that remains at the end of this gigantic pantomime, is the earth – empty and bleeding. On this earth, through which tempest has passed leaving only stones, the King, the Fool, the Blind Man and the Madman carry on their distracted dialogue.

The blind Gloucester falls over on the empty stage. His suicidal leap is tragic. Gloucester has reached the depths of human misery; so has Edgar, who pretends to be mad Tom in order to save his father. But the pantomime performed by actors on the stage is grotesque, and has something of a circus about it. The blind Gloucester who has climbed a non-existent height and fallen over on flat boards, is a clown. A philosophical buffoonery of the sort found in modern theatre has been performed.

> Whistle from left wing.
> He (the man) does not move.
> He looks at his hands, looks round for scissors, sees them, goes and picks them up, starts to trim his nails, stops, runs his finger along blade of scissors, goes and lays them on small cube, turns aside, opens his collar, frees his neck and fingers it.
> The small cube is pulled up and disappears in flies, carrying away rope and scissors.
> He turns to take scissors, sees what has happened.
> He turns aside, reflects.
> He goes and sits down on big cube.
> The big cube is pulled from under him. He falls. The big cube is pulled up and disappears in flies.
> He remains lying on his side, his face towards auditorium, staring before him. (*Act Without Words*, pp. 59–60)

The *Act Without Words* closes Beckett's *Endgame*, providing as it were its final interpretation. Remaining vestiges of characters, action and situation have been further reduced here. All that remains is one situation acting as a parable of universal human fate. A total situation. Man has been thrown onto the empty stage. He tries to escape into the wings, but is kicked back. From above a tree with some leaves, a jug of water, tailoring scissors, and some cubes are pulled down on ropes. The man tries to hide in the shade of the leaves, but the tree is pulled up. He tries to catch hold of the jug, but it rises into the air. He attempts suicide, but this, too, proves impossible. 'The bough folds down against trunk' (p. 59). The man sits down and thinks. The jug and the tree appear again. The man does not move.

In this ending to *Endgame* the forces external to man – gods, fate, world – are not indifferent, but sneering and malicious. They tempt him all the time. These forces are stronger than he. Man must be defeated and cannot escape from the situation that has been imposed on him. All he can do is to give up; refuse to play blindman's buff. Only by the possibility of refusal can he surmount the external forces.

It is easy to see how close to the Bible this parable is, even in its metaphors: palm, its shadow, water. The force above and beyond man is strongly reminiscent of the Old Testament God. This is also a Book of Job, but without an optimistic ending.

This new Book of Job is shown in buffo, as a circus pantomime. *Act Without Words* is performed by a clown. The philosophical parable may be interpreted as tragedy or grotesque, but its artistic expression is grotesque only. Gloucester's suicide attempt, too, is merely a circus somersault on an empty stage. Gloucester's and Edgar's situation is tragic, but it has been shown in pantomime, the classic expression of buffoonery. In Shakespeare clowns often ape the gestures of kings and heroes, but only in *King Lear* are great tragic scenes shown through clowning.

It is not only the suicide mime that is grotesque. The accompanying dialogue is also cruel and mocking. The blind Gloucester kneels and prays:

> O you mighty gods!
> This world I do renounce, and, in your sights
> Shake patiently my great affliction off.

> If I could bear it longer, and not fall
> To quarrel with your great opposeless wills,
> My snuff and loathed part of nature should
> Burn itself out. If Edgar live, O, bless him!   (IV vi)

Gloucester's suicide has a meaning only if the gods exist. It is a protest against undeserved suffering and the world's injustice. This protest is made in a definite direction. It refers to eschatology. Even if the gods are cruel, they must take this suicide into consideration. It will count in the final reckoning between gods and man. Its sole value lies in its reference to the absolute.

But if the gods, and their moral order in the world, do not exist, Gloucester's suicide does not solve or alter anything. It is only a somersault on an empty stage. It is deceptive and unsuccessful on the factual, as well as on the metaphysical plane. Not only the pantomime, but the whole situation is then grotesque. From the beginning to the end. It is waiting for a Godot who does not come.

Estragon. Why don't we hang ourselves?
Vladimir. With what?
Estragon. You haven't got a bit of rope?
Vladimir. No.
Estragon. Then we can't.
Vladimir. Let's go.
Estragon. Wait, there's my belt.
Vladimir. It's too short.
Estragon. You could hang on to my legs.
Vladimir. And who'd hang on to mine?
Estragon. True.
Vladimir. Show all the same. (*Estragon loosens the cord that holds up his trousers which, much too big for him, fall about his ankles. They look at the cord.*) It might do at a pinch. But is it strong enough?
Estragon. We'll soon see. Here.
         (*They each take an end of the cord and pull. It breaks. They almost fall.*)
Vladimir. Not worth a curse.   (*Waiting for Godot*, II)

Gloucester did fall, and he got up again. He made his suicide

attempt, but he failed to shake the world. Nothing has changed.
Edgar's comment is ironical:

> ... Had he been where he thought,
> By this had thought been past.   (IV vi)

If there are no gods, suicide is impossible. There is only death.
Suicide cannot alter human fate, but only accelerate it. It ceases
to be a protest and becomes the acceptance of world's greatest
cruelty – death. It is a surrender. Gloucester has finally realized:

> ... Henceforth I'll bear
> Affliction till it do cry out itself
> 'Enough, enough,' and die.   (IV vi)

And once again, in the last Act:

> No further, sir. A man may rot even here.   (v ii)

After his grotesque suicide the blind Gloucester talks to the
deranged Lear. Estragon and Vladimir carry on a very similar
conversation, interrupted by the despairing cries of the blind
Pozzo, who has fallen down and cannot get up. Pozzo would find
it easiest to understand Gloucester:

> ... one day I went blind, one day we'll go deaf, one day we were
> born, one day we shall die ... They give birth astride of a grave,
> the light gleams an instant, then it's night once more.
> *(Waiting for Godot, II)*

Shakespeare had said as much, in fewer words:

> ... Men must endure
> Their going hence, even as their coming hither;
> Ripeness is all.   (v ii)

But it was Ionesco who put it most briefly of all, in his
Tueur sans gages: 'We shall all die, this is the only serious
alienation.'

III

The theme of *King Lear* is the decay and fall of the world. The
play opens like the Histories, with the division of the realm and
the king's abdication. It also ends like the Histories, with the proclamation of a new king. Between the prologue and the epilogue
there is a civil war. But unlike the Histories and Tragedies, in
King Lear the world is not healed again. In *King Lear* there is
no young and resolute Fortinbras to ascend the throne of Den-
mark; no cool-headed Octavius to become Augustus Caesar; no
noble Malcolm to 'give to our tables meat, sleep to our nights'.
In the epilogues to the Histories and Tragedies the new monarch
invites those present to his coronation. In *King Lear* there will be
no coronation. There is no one whom Edgar can invite to it.
Everybody has died or been murdered. Gloucester was right
when he said: 'This great world / Shall so wear out to naught.'
Those who have survived – Edgar, Albany and Kent – are, as
Lear has been, just 'ruin'd piece[s] of nature'.

Of the twelve major characters half are just and good; the
other half, unjust and bad. It is a division as consistent and abstract
as in a morality play. But this is a morality play in which everyone will be destroyed: noble characters along with base ones, the
persecutors with the persecuted, the torturers with the tortured.
Vivisection will go on until the stage is empty. The decay and
fall of the world will be shown on two levels, on two different
kinds of stage, as it were. One of these may be called Macbeth's
stage, the other, Job's stage.

Macbeth's stage is the scene of crime. At the beginning there
is a nursery tale of two bad daughters and one good daughter.
The good daughter will die hanged in prison. The bad daughters
will also die, but not until they have become adulterers, and one
of them also a poisoner and murderess of her husband. All bonds,
all laws, whether divine, natural or human, are broken. Social
order, from the kingdom to the family, will crumble into dust.
There are no longer kings and subjects, fathers and children, husbands and wives. There are only huge Renaissance monsters,
devouring one another like beasts of prey. Everything has been

condensed, drawn in broad outlines, characters are hardly marked. The history of the world can do without psychology and without rhetoric. It is just action. These violent sequences are merely an illustration and an example, and perform the function of a black, realistic counterpart to 'Job's stage'.

For it is Job's stage that constitutes the main scene. On it the ironic, clownish morality play on human fate will be performed. But before that happens, all the characters must be uprooted from their social positions and pulled down, to final degradation. They must reach rock-bottom. The downfall is not merely a philosophical parable, as Gloucester's leap over the supposed precipice is. The theme of downfall is carried through by Shakespeare stubbornly, consistently and is repeated at least four times. The fall is at the same time physical and spiritual, bodily and social.

At the beginning there was a king with his court and ministers. Later, there are just four beggars wandering about in a wilderness, exposed to raging winds and rain. The fall may be slow, or sudden. Lear has at first a retinue of a hundred men, then fifty, then only one. Kent is banished by one angry gesture of the king. But the process of degradation is always the same. Everything that distinguishes a man – his titles, social position, even name – is lost. Names are not needed any more. Everyone is just a shadow of himself; just a man.

> *King Lear.* Doth any here know me? This is not Lear.
>   Doth Lear walk thus? speak thus? . . .
>   Who is it that can tell me who I am?
> *Fool.* Lear's shadow.   (I iv)

And once more the same question, and the same answer. The banished Kent returns in disguise to his king.

> *King Lear.* How now? What art thou?
> *Kent.* A man, sir.   (I iv)

A naked man has no name. Before the morality commences, everyone must be naked. Naked like a worm.

Then Job arose, and rent his mantle, and shaved his head, and fell down upon the ground, and worshipped.

And said, Naked came I out of my mother's womb, and naked shall return thither.   (Book of Job, 1: 20–1)

Biblical imagery in this new Book of Job is no mere chance. Edgar says that he will with his 'nakedness outface / The winds and persecutions of the sky' (II iii). This theme returns obstinately, and with an equal consistency:

> I' th' last night's storm I such a fellow saw,
> Which made me think a man a worm.   (IV i)

A downfall means suffering and torment. It may be a physical or spiritual torment, or both. Lear will lose his wits; Kent will be put in the stocks; Gloucester will have his eyes gouged out and will attempt suicide. For a man to become naked, or rather to become nothing but man, it is not enough to deprive him of his name, social position and character. One must also maim and massacre him both morally and physically. Turn him – like King Lear – into a 'ruin'd piece of nature', and only then ask him who he is. For it is the new Renaissance Job who is to judge the events on 'Macbeth's stage'.

A Polish critic, Andrzej Falkiewicz, has observed this process of maiming and mutilating man, not in Shakespeare, but in modern literature and drama.[2] He compares it to the peeling of an onion. One takes off the husk, and then peels the layers of onion one by one. Where does an onion end and what is in its core? The blind man is a man, the madman is a man, the doting old man is a man. Man and nothing but man. A nobody, who suffers, tries to give his suffering a meaning or nobility, who revolts or accepts his suffering, and who must die.

> O gods! Who is't can say 'I am at the worst'?
> I am worse than e'er I was. . . .
> And worse I may be yet. The worst is not
> So long as we can say 'This is the worst.'   (IV i)

Vladimir and Estragon talk to each other in a very similar fashion. They gibber, but in that gibber there are remnants of the same eschatology:

> *Vladimir.* We're in no danger of ever thinking any more.
> *Estragon.* Then what are we complaining about?
> *Vladimir.* Thinking is not the worst.
> *Estragon.* Perhaps not. But at least there's that.
> *Vladimir.* That what?
> *Estragon.* That's the idea, let's ask each other questions.
> *Vladimir.* What do you mean, at least there's that?
> *Estragon.* That much less misery.
> *Vladimir.* True.
> *Estragon.* Well? If we gave thanks for our mercies?
> *Vladimir.* What is terrible is to *have* thought.
>
> (*Waiting for Godot*, II)

Pozzo is proud and pompous when in the first part of *Waiting for Godot* he leads on a rope the starving Lucky. Their relation is still that of master and servant, the exploiter and the exploited. When they appear for the second time Pozzo is blind and Lucky is dumb. They are still joined by the same rope. But now they are just two men.

> 'Tis the time's plague when madmen lead the blind. (IV i)

This is Edgar leading the blind Gloucester to the precipice at Dover. This is just the theme of *Endgame*; Beckett was the first to see it in *King Lear*; he eliminated all action, everything external, and repeated it in its skeleton form.

Clov cannot sit down, the blind Hamm cannot get up, moves only in his wheel-chair, and passes water only by means of a catheter. Nell and Nagg have 'lost their shanks' and are almost breathing their last in dustbins. But Hamm continues to be the master, and his wheel-chair brings to mind a throne. In the London production he was dressed in a faded purple gown and wiped his face with a blood-red handkerchief. He was, like King Lear, a degraded and powerless tyrant, a 'ruin'd piece of nature'. He was a King Lear in the scene in Act IV, where Lear meets the blind Gloucester and after a great frantic monologue gives the order that one of his shoes be taken off, as it pinches him. It is the same pinching shoe that one of the clowns in *Waiting for Godot* will take off at the beginning of the scene.

This is the cruel and mocking 'peeling of an onion', Shakespearean and modern alike. The onion is peeled to the very last, to the suffering 'nothing'. This is the theme of the fall. The concept of man has been reduced and all situations have shrunk to the one ultimate, total and concentrated human fate. To Vladimir's question 'What is in this bag?', the blind Pozzo replies: 'Sand.' Clov in *Endgame* lifts the lid of the dustbin to find out what is happening to Nagg. 'He's crying,' he reports. To this Hamm replies: 'Then he's living.'

He's crying, then he's living. English critics have regarded it as Beckett's reply to the Cartesian formula of man, which was in itself a reduction of the theological formula. But in fact Beckett simply repeats after Shakespeare:

> . . . We came crying hither . . .
> When we are born, we cry that we are come
> To this great stage of fools. (IV vi)

The world is real, and the shoe really pinches. Suffering is also real. But the gesture with which the ruin of a man demands that his pinching shoe be taken off is ridiculous. Just as ridiculous as blind Gloucester's somersault on the flat empty stage.

The Biblical Job, too, is the ruin of a man. But this ruin constantly talks to God. He curses, imprecates, blasphemes. Ultimately he admits that God is right. He has justified his sufferings and ennobled them. He included them in the metaphysical and absolute order. The Book of Job is a theatre of the priests. Whereas in both Shakespearean and Beckettian Endgames the Book of Job is performed by clowns. But here, too, the gods are invoked throughout by all the characters; by Lear, Gloucester, Kent, even Albany:

> *King Lear.* By Jupiter, I swear no!
> *Kent.* By Juno, I swear ay! (II iv)

At first gods have Greek names. Then they are only gods, great and terrifying judges high above, who are supposed to intervene sooner or later. But the gods do not intervene. They are silent. Gradually the tone becomes more and more ironical. The ruin of a man invoking God is ever more ridiculous. The action becomes more and more cruel, but at the same time assumes a more and more clownish character:

> By the kind gods, 'tis most ignobly done
> To pluck me by the beard.   (III vii)

Defeat, suffering, cruelty have a meaning even when gods are cruel. Even then. It is the last theological chance to justify suffering. The Biblical Job knew about it well when he called on God:

If the scourge slay suddenly, he will laugh at the trial of the innocent.   (Book of Job, 9: 23)

From the just God, one can still appeal to the unjust God. Says Gloucester after his eyes have been gouged out:

> As flies to wanton boys are we to th' gods.
> They kill us for their sport.   (IV i)

But as long as gods exist, all can yet be saved:

Hearken unto this, O Job: stand still, and consider the wondrous works of God.   (Book of Job, 37: 14)

And this is a fragment of *Endgame*:

Clov. They said to me, Here's the place, raise your head and look at all that beauty. That order! They said to me, Come now you're not a brute beast, think upon these things and you'll see how all becomes clear. And simple! They said to me, What skilled attention they get, all these dying of their wounds.

Hamm. Enough!

Clov. I say to myself – sometimes, Clov, you must learn to suffer better than that if you want them to weary of

> punishing you. I say to myself – sometimes, Clov, you
> must be their better than if you want them to let you
> go – one day.   (pp. 50–1)

Clov is a clown, but he is more unhappy than Hamm. Clov's
gabble is still eschatological, just as Lucky's in *Waiting for Godot*.
In this dialogue of 'human ruins' Hamm alone has realized the
folly of all suffering. He has one reply to make to eschatology:
'Take it easy ... Peace to our ... arses.' Both couples: Pozzo
who has been made blind, and Lucky who has been made dumb,
on the one hand, Hamm who cannot get up, and Clov who cannot sit down, on the other, have been taken from the Endgame of
King Lear:

> *King Lear*. Read.
> *Glou*. What, with the case of eyes? ...
> *King Lear*. What, art mad? A man may see how the world
> goes with no eyes. Look with thine ears.   (IV vi)

These are Biblical parables. The blind see clearly, madmen tell
the truth. After all, they are all mad. 'There are four of them' –
writes Camus – 'one by profession, one by choice, two by the
suffering they have been through. They are four torn bodies,
four unfathomable faces of the same fate.'[3] The Fool accompanies Lear on the cold night of madness; Edgar takes the blind
Gloucester through a grotesque suicide. Lear's invocations on
the gods are countered by the Fool's scatological jokes; Gloucester's prayers by Edgar's clownish demonology:

> Frateretto calls me, and tells me Nero is an angler in the lake of
> darkness. Pray, innocent, and beware the foul fiend. ... The
> foul fiend bites my back. ... Purr! the cat is gray.   (III vi)

But Edgar's demonology is no more than a parody, a travesty
of contemporary Egyptian dream books and books on witch-
craft; a great and brutal gibe, in fact. He gibes at himself, at Job,
conversing with God. For above 'Job's stage', there is in *King
Lear* only 'Macbeth's stage'. On it people murder, butcher and

torture one another, commit adultery and fornication, divide kingdoms. From the point of view of a Job who has ceased to talk to God, they are clowns. Clowns who do not yet know they are clowns.

> *King Lear.*   ... Come, come, I am a king;
>   My masters, know you that?
> *Gentleman.* You are a royal one, and we obey you.
> *King Lear.* Then there's life in't. Nay, an you get it, you shall
>   get it by running. Sa, sa, sa, sa!   (IV vi)

The zero hour has come. Lear has come to understand it at last. Just as blind Hamm came to understand everything, although he was bound to his wheel-throne. And Pozzo, when he turned blind and fell over his sand-filled bags:

> *Pozzo.* I woke up one fine day as blind as Fortune ...
> *Vladimir.* And when was that?
> *Pozzo.* I don't know ... Don't question me! The blind have
>   no notion of time. The things of time are hidden from
>   them too.   (*Waiting for Godot*, II)

And this is how King Lear ends his final frantic tirade:

> No rescue? What, a prisoner? I am even
> The natural fool of fortune.   (IV vi)

In a moment he will run off the stage. Before that happens he will ask for his pinching shoe to be taken off. He is clown now, so he can afford to do this. On 'Job's stage' four clowns have performed the old medieval *sotie* about the decay and fall of the world. But in both Shakespearean and Beckettian Endgames it is the modern world that fell; the Renaissance world, and ours.

IV

The original clown was Harlequin. There is something in him of an animal, a faun and a devil. That is why he wears a black mask. He rushes about and seems to transform himself into different shapes. The laws of space and time do not seem to apply to him. He changes his guises in a flash and can be in several places at once. He is a demon of movement. In Goldoni's play *The Servant of Two Masters*, as produced by the Piccolo Teatro of Milan, Harlequin, sitting on the brim of a wooden platform, plucked a hair from his head, lengthened or shortened it, pulled it through his ears, or put it on his nose and kept it rigid in the air. Harlequin is a prestidigitator. He is a servant who really does not serve anybody and jockeys everybody away. He sneers at merchants and lovers, at marquesses and soldiers. He makes fun of love and ambition, of power and money. He is wiser than his masters, although he seems only to be more clever. He is independent, because he has realized that the world is simply folly.

Puck from *A Midsummer Night's Dream* is a popular goblin of English folklore, a Robin Goodfellow. But he is also the Harlequin of the Renaissance *commedia dell'arte*. He, too, is a quick-change artist, a prestidigitator and producer of the comedy of errors. He confuses the couples of lovers and causes Titania to caress an ass's head. In fact, he makes them all ridiculous, Titania and Oberon no less than Hermia and Lysander, Helena and Demetrius. He exposes the folly of love. He is accident, fate, chance. Chance happens to be ironical, though it does not know about it itself. Puck plays practical jokes. He does not know what he has done. That is why he can turn somersaults on the stage, just as Harlequin does.

Buffoonery is a philosophy and a profession at the same time. Touchstone and Feste are professional clowns. They wear jesters' attire, and are in service of the prince. They have not ceased to be Harlequins and are not above pantomime. But they do not produce the performance any more; they do not even take part in it, but merely comment on it. That is why they are jeering and bitter. The position of a jester is ambiguous and abounds in internal contradictions, arising from the discrepancy between profession and philosophy. The profession of a jester, like that of an intellectual, consists in providing entertainment. His philosophy demands of him that he tell the truth and abolish myths. The Fool in *King Lear* does not even have a name, he is just a

Fool, pure Fool. But he is the first fool to be aware of the fool's position:

> *Fool.* Prithee, nuncle, keep a schoolmaster that can teach thy
> fool to lie. I would fain learn to lie.
> *King Lear.* An you lie, sirrah, we'll have you whipp'd.
> *Fool.* I marvel what kin thou and thy daughters are. They'll
> have me whipp'd for speaking true; thou'lt have me
> whipp'd for lying; and sometimes I am whipp'd for
> holding my peace. I had rather be any kind o'thing
> than a fool! And yet I would not be thee, nuncle. Thou
> hast pared thy wit o' both sides and left nothing i'th'
> middle.   (I iv)

A fool who has recognized himself for a fool, who has accepted the fact that he is only a jester in the service of the prince, ceases to be a clown. But the clown's philosophy is based on the assumption that everyone is a fool; and the greatest fool is he who does not know he is a fool: the prince himself. That is why the clown has to make fools of others; otherwise he would not be a clown. The clown is subject to alienations because he is a clown, but at the same time he cannot accept the alienation; he rejects it when he becomes aware of it. The clown has the social position of the bastard, as described many times by Sartre. The bastard is a bastard for as long as he accepts his bastard's position and regards it as inevitable. The bastard ceases to be a bastard when he does not consider himself a bastard any more. But at this point the bastard must abolish the division into bastards and legitimate offspring. He then enters into opposition against the foundations of social order, or at least exposes them. Social pressures want to limit the Clown to his part of a clown, to pin the label 'clown' on him. But he does not accept this part. On the contrary: he constantly pins that label on others:

> *King Lear.* Dost thou call me fool, boy?
> *Fool.* All thy other titles thou hast given away; that thou wast
> born with.
> *Kent.* This is not altogether fool, my lord.

Fool. No, faith; lords and great men will not let me. If I had a
     monopoly out, they would have part on't. And ladies
     too, they will not let me have all the fool to myself;
     they'll be snatching.   (I iv)

This is the opening of the 'clowns' play', performed on 'Job's
stage'. In his very first scene, the Fool offers Lear his fool's cap.
For buffoonery is not only a philosophy, it is also a kind of
theatre. To us it is the most contemporary aspect of *King Lear*.
Only it has to be seen and interpreted properly. For this reason
one must reject all the romantic and naturalistic accessories; the
opera and melodrama about the old man who, driven out by his
daughters, wanders about bareheaded in a storm and goes mad
as a result of his misfortunes. But, as in the case of Hamlet, there
is method in this madness. Madness in *King Lear* is a philosophy,
a conscious cross-over to the position of the Clown. Leszek
Kołakowski writes:

The Clown is he who, although moving in high society, is not
part of it, and tells unpleasant things to everybody in it; who dis-
putes everything regarded as evident. He would not be able to
do all this, if he were part of that society himself; then he could
at most be a drawing-room scandalizer. The Clown must stand
aside and observe the good society from outside, in order to discover the non-evidence of evidence, and non-finality of its
finality. At the same time he must move in good society in
order to get to know its sacred cows, and have occasion to tell
the unpleasant things. . . . The philosophy of Clowns is the
philosophy that in every epoch shows up as doubtful what has
been regarded as most certain; it reveals contradictions inherent in
what seems to have been proven by visual experience; it holds up
to ridicule what seems obvious common sense, and discovers
truth in the absurd.[4]

Let us now turn to *King Lear*:

Fool. Give me an egg, nuncle, and I'll give thee two crowns.
King Lear. What two crowns shall they be?
Fool. Why, after I have cut the egg i' th' middle and eat up the

meat, the two crowns of the egg. When thou clovest thy crown
i' th' middle and gav'st away both parts, thou bor'st thine ass
on thy back o'er the dirt.... Now thou art an O without a
figure. I am better than thou art now: I am a fool, thou art
nothing.   (I iv)

After the crown had been torn off his head, Richard II asked
for a mirror. He cast a look, and broke the mirror. He saw in it a
shaking old man. And yet this was his face; the face that had be-
longed to a king. In *King Lear* the degradation occurs gradually,
step by step. Lear divided his kingdom and gave away his power,
but wanted to remain a king. He believed that a king could not
cease to be a king, just as the sun could not cease to shine. He
believed in pure majesty, in the pure idea of kingship. In historical
dramas royal majesty is deprived of its sacred character by a stab
of the dagger, or by the brutal tearing off of the crown from a
living king's head. In *King Lear* it is the Fool who deprives
majesty of its sacredness.

Lear and Gloucester are adherents of eschatology; they desperately believe in the existence of absolutes. They invoke the
gods, believe in justice, appeal to laws of nature. They have
fallen off 'Macbeth's stage', but remain its prisoners. Only the
Fool stands outside 'Macbeth's stage', just as he has stood outside
'Job's stage'. He is looking from the outside and does not follow
any ideology. He rejects all appearances, of law, justice, moral
order. He sees brute force, cruelty and lust. He has no illusions
and does not seek consolation in the existence of natural or supernatural order, which provides for the punishment of evil and
reward of good. Lear, insisting on his fictitious majesty, seems
ridiculous to him. All the more ridiculous because he does not see
how ridiculous he is. But the Fool does not desert his ridiculous,
degraded king, and accompanies him on his way to madness. The
Fool knows that the only true madness is to regard this world as
rational. The feudal order is absurd and can be described only in
terms of the absurd. The world stands upside down:

When usurers tell their gold i' th' field,
And bawds and whores do churches build:

> Then shall the realm of Albion
> Come to great confusion.
> Then comes the time, who lives to see't,
> That going shall be us'd with feet.   (III ii)

Hamlet escaped into madness not only to confuse informers and deceive Claudius. Madness to him was also a philosophy, a criticism of pure reason, a great, ironic clearing of accounts with the world, which has left its orbit. The Fool adopts the language Hamlet used in the scenes in which he feigned madness. There is nothing left in it now of Greek and Roman rhetoric, so popular in the Renaissance; nothing left of the cold and noble Senecan indifference to the inevitable destiny. Lear, Gloucester, Kent, Albany, even Edmund still use rhetoric. The Fool's language is different. It abounds in Biblical travesties and inverted medieval parables. One can find in it splendid baroque surrealist expressions, sudden leaps of imagination, condensations and epitomes, brutal, vulgar and scatological comparisons. His rhymes are like limericks. The Fool uses dialectics, paradox and the absurd kind of humour. His language is that of our modern grotesque. The same grotesque that exposes the absurdity of apparent reality and of the absolute by means of a great and universal *reductio ad absurdum*.

> *King Lear.* O me, my heart, my rising heart! But down!
> *Fool.* Cry to it, nuncle, as the cockney did to the eels when she
>   put 'em i' th' paste alive. She knapp'd 'em o' th' cox-
>   combs with a stick and cried 'Down, wantons, down!'
>   'Twas her brother that, in pure kindness to his horse,
>   buttered his hay.   (II iv)

The Fool appears on the stage when Lear's fall is only beginning. He disappears by the end of Act III. His last words are: 'And I'll go to bed at noon.' He will not be seen or heard again. A clown is not needed any more. King Lear has gone through the school of clown's philosophy. When he meets Gloucester for the last time, he will speak the Fool's language and look at 'Macbeth's stage' the way the Fool has looked at it: 'They told me I was everything. 'Tis a lie – I am not ague-proof' (IV vi).

SOURCE: *Shakespeare our Contemporary* (1964).

NOTES

1. Compare the analysis of this scene in G. Wilson Knight's most original study of the grotesque elements in *King Lear* (treated somewhat differently from in my essay): '*King Lear* and the Comedy of the Grotesque', pp. 118–36 of this volume.

2. A. Falkiewicz, 'Theatrical Experiment of the Fifties', *Dialog*, no. 9, 1959 (in Polish).

3. A. Camus, *Le Mythe de Sisyphe* (Paris, 1942).

4. L. Kołakowski, 'The Priest and the Clown – Reflections on Theological Heritage in Modern Thinking' (in Polish), in *Twórczość*, no. 10 (1959) pp. 82–3.

SELECT BIBLIOGRAPHY

(Books from which extracts are taken are omitted.)

EDITIONS

The Arden Shakespeare, ed. Kenneth Muir (Methuen and Harvard U.P., 1952).

New Shakespeare Series, ed. G. I. Duthie and J. Dover Wilson (Cambridge U.P., 1960).

STUDIES

Wyndham Lewis, *The Lion and the Fox* (Grant Richards and Harper, 1927; Methuen, 1951).
Eccentric and various in approach, but basically concerned with Shakespeare's reaction to the Machiavellian opposition – reconciliation between nobility and cunning, and his attitude to kings and heroes. No lengthy treatment of *Lear*, but will be stimulating to students of that play.

H. Granville-Barker, *Prefaces to Shakespeare* (1927, Princeton, N.J., 1946, 1959; Batsford, 1963) II 1–85.
Studies the modern staging, construction and characterisation of the play; not great criticism, but historically important because of the theatrical emphasis.

J. Middleton Murry, *Shakespeare* (Cape, 1936; Hillary, 1965).
A sensitive but hostile account.

R. B. Heilman, *This Great Stage* (Louisiana State U.P., 1948; University of Washington P., 1963).
The most extensive study of thematic and image patterns in the play.

W. H. Clemen, *The Development of Shakespeare's Imagery* (Methuen and Harvard U.P., 1951).
Chapter 14 has a thorough study of imagery.

Arthur Sewell, *Character and Society in Shakespeare* (Oxford and New York, 1951).

The heroes (Lear and others) represent a striving for ordered vision and society.

William Empson, *The Structure of Complex Words* (Chatto & Windus and New Directions, 1951) ch. 6.

L. C. Knights, *Some Shakespearean Themes* (Chatto & Windus, 1959; Stanford U.P., 1966).

Terence Hawkes, *Shakespeare and the Reason* (Routledge & Kegan Paul, 1964; Humanities, 1965).

Interpretation based on Renaissance differentiation between higher and lower reason.

N. Maclean, 'Episode, Scene, Speech, and Word: The Madness of Lear', in *Critics and Criticisms*, ed. R. S. Crane (University of Chicago Press, 1957).

An example of the Chicago 'neo-Aristotelian' approach, which emphasises the sequential rather than the 'spatial' aspect of the plot.

NOTES ON CONTRIBUTORS

A. C. BRADLEY (1851–1935), Professor of Literature at Liverpool and Glasgow Universities, Professor of Poetry at Oxford; author of *Shakespearean Tragedy* (1904) and *Oxford Lectures on Poetry* (1909).

S. T. COLERIDGE (1772–1834). Coleridge's Shakespeare criticism was done either as marginalia or lectures, which others took down and later transcribed. There are also passages in *Biographia Literaria* (1817).

W. R. ELTON, Professor of English Literature, University of California, Los Angeles.

BARBARA EVERETT, Fellow of Somerville College; author of *W. H. Auden* and of various articles.

NORTHROP FRYE, University Professor of English at Toronto; author of *Fearful Symmetry, a Study of William Blake* (1947), *Anatomy of Criticism* (1957), *A Natural Perspective* (1965) on Shakespeare's Comedy, and *Fools of Time* (1967) on Shakespeare's Tragedy.

TERENCE HAWKES, Lecturer in English, University College, Cardiff; author of *Shakespeare and Reason* (1964).

R. B. HEILMAN, Professor of English Literature, University of Washington; author of *This Great Stage* (1948) and *Magic in the Web* (1956) on *Othello*.

JOHN HOLLOWAY, Professor of English Literature and Fellow of The Queens' College, Cambridge; author of *The Victorian Sage* (1953), *The Charted Mirror* (1960), *The Story of the Night* (1961) and other volumes of criticism and poetry.

SAMUEL JOHNSON (1709–84) first published a prospectus for a new edition of Shakespeare in 1745, but did not begin it till 1756. After a long interruption he resumed work in 1763 and this edition, with the Preface and Notes, appeared in 1765.

G. WILSON KNIGHT, Professor Emeritus, Leeds University, pioneer of Shakespearian 'interpretation'. Among his many books on Shakespeare are *The Wheel of Fire* (1930), *The Imperial Themes* (1931), *Principles of Shakespearian Production* (1936, 1949) and *The Crown of Life* (1947).

JAN KOTT, Professor of Literature, University of Warsaw; dramatist and translator of Sartre and Ionesco; author of *Shakespeare our Contemporary* (1964).

MAYNARD MACK, Professor of English at Yale, editor and Shakespearian critic. *King Lear in Our Time* (1965) is his only book on Shakespeare.

GEORGE ORWELL (pseudonym of Eric Hugh Blair: 1903–50), author of several novels including *Animal Farm* (1945) and *Nineteen Eighty-four* (1949), and many essays on social, political, and literary themes.

A. W. SCHLEGEL (1767–1845), German critic and translator; Professor of Literature at Jena and Bonn, and most famous of Shakespeare's German translators. His lectures on *Dramatic Art and Literature* were published in 1811 and translated into English in 1815.

P. B. SHELLEY (1792–1822). *A Defence of Poetry* was published posthumously in 1840.

C. J. SISSON (1885–1966), Lord Northcliffe Professor of Modern English Literature at University College London; author of *New Readings in Shakespeare* (1951) and *Shakespeare's Tragic Justice* (1962).

NAHUM TATE (1652–1715), Poet Laureate, playwright.

ENID WELSFORD, author of *The Court Masque* (1927) and *The Fool* (1935).

INDEX